EXPERT PROBLEM SOLVING

**SUNY Series,
Educational Leadership**

Daniel L. Duke, Editor

Kenneth Leithwood
and
Rosanne Steinbach

EXPERT PROBLEM SOLVING

Evidence from School and District Leaders

STATE UNIVERSITY OF NEW YORK PRESS

Production by Ruth Fisher
Marketing by Fran Keneston

Published by
State University of New York Press, Albany

For information, address the State University of New York Press,
State University Plaza, Albany, NY 12246

Library of Congress Cataloging-in-Publication Data
Leithwood, Kenneth.
    Expert problem solving: evidence from school and district leaders
/ Kenneth Leithwood and Rosanne Steinbach.
        p.   cm.—(SUNY series, educational leadership)
    "This research was funded by the Social Sciences and Humanities
Research Council of Canada and the Ontario Ministry of Education"—
CIP galley.
    Includes bibliographical references and index.
    ISBN 0-7914-2107-4 (acid-free—ISBN 0-7914-2108-2
    (pbk:acid-free)
    1. Educational leadership—United States.   2. Problem solving.
3. Decision-making.   4. School management and organization—United
States.   I. Steinbach, Rosanne, 1942– .   II. Series: SUNY series
in educational leadership.
LB2806.L385 1995
371.2'00973—dc20   93-42686
                                                                 CIP

10 9 8 7 6 5 4 3 2 1

To our mothers

Beatrice Leithwood
and
Sara Bennett Cohen
and
To the memory of our fathers

T. Kenneth Leithwood
and
William Bennett

CONTENTS

Key Processes

The Relationship Between Thought and Action

From Answers to Questions

LIST OF TABLES

ACKNOWLEDGMENTS

We have the good fortune to be able to count as colleagues, in various aspects of this research, a number of people whose contributions were important to us. Mary Stager played an especially crucial role in the early formulation and conduct of the research. Brad Cousins and Michael Smith contributed significantly to the study described in Chapter 2. Doris Jantzi played a central role in the research related to instructional and transformational leadership reflected in Chapters 10 and 11.

This research was funded by the Social Sciences and Humanities Research Council of Canada and the Ontario Ministry of Education through its block transfer grant to OISE.

Part 1

—◀○▶—

Introduction

Chapter 1

Introduction

This book is an edited compilation of papers which we and our colleagues previously have published, mostly as journal articles, over the past half-dozen years. Based on a systematic program of empirical work generally guided by perspectives and methods from cognitive science, in these articles we piece together much of what we have learned about the nature and development of expert administrative thinking and problem solving. The purposes for the book are to demonstrate the value of adopting a cognitive perspective on administration; to summarize what has been learned to date from one program of research; to identify the implications this might have for practice; and to identify useful areas for subsequent research.

In this introductory chapter we describe the personal genesis of this work as well as a more objective rationale for its focus. We also discuss why we adopted a cognitive science perspective on the theory and methods guiding our research and what that perspective means. We offer this description because we assume that many of our readers will be from the field of educational administration and not, therefore, steeped in background knowledge about cognitive science; the book has been written explicitly with such readers in mind. An overview of the contents of the book concludes the chapter.

Personal Genesis of the Research

In the early 1980s, when serious study of school leadership began to flourish in North America, we were in the midst of our own efforts to better understand why some principals seemed so good at what they did. It was an exciting and productive time for us, one outcome of which was a book which described four different patterns of principals' practices, each of which seemed to make quite different contributions to school improvement (Leithwood and Montgomery, 1986). Indeed, our evidence suggested that these patterns formed a hierarchy, with each level representing a more inclusive and effective form of school leadership than the one before it.

The more effective forms of school leadership practices which we described in our work had many similarities with the outcomes of others' efforts during the same period (e.g., Blumberg and Greenfield, 1980; Morris et al., 1984). Furthermore, descriptions of "instructional leadership" emerging from effective schools research (e.g., Mortimore et al., 1988; Dwyer et al. 1983) and more recent studies of the impact of instructional leadership (e.g., Hallinger, Bickman, and Davis, in press; Heck, Larsen, and Marcoulides, 1990) conspire to create confidence in the robustness of the conclusions we and others drew about the nature of effective school leadership practices.

But there was something about this work that was dissatisfying. Our sense of dissatisfaction was never more acute than when we looked at "Jack." In the course of multiple opportunities to talk with Jack and observe him at work in his school we had concluded that he was the Wayne Gretsky of principals. No one we studied did so much with so little apparent effort. Jack was active in many district initiatives but was still a pervasive presence in his school; he worked closely and regularly with teachers on instructional improvement, knew the kids in his large elementary school very well, and had exceptionally well-developed relationships with parents and many other members of the school community. While we frankly marveled at his repertoire of behavior, we had to admit almost no idea of its source.

Other questions arose from this admission which challenged the basic premises of our work at that time. Whereas Jack's repertoire of behavior had features broadly similar to those displayed by other effective principals in our studies, much of Jack's impact seemed to depend on his sensitivity to the people and contexts in which he worked and on his ability to flexibly adapt his repertoire to suit the circumstances. What good would be served to describe generally effective behaviors if we could not also describe how principals decided on their use? We began to realize that perhaps even more important than what Jack did was how he thought; this was most certainly the case given our goal of helping other principals or prospective principals increase their own contribution to their schools. And so, in 1986, we began the fairly extensive series of studies on expert administrative thinking and problem solving reflected in this book.

Why a Cognitive Science Perspective was Adopted

Cognitive science perspectives offer important and unique insights about the nature of expert administrative practice, how it develops, and what can be done to assist in that development. As yet, however, only a modest fraction of these insights actually have been realized due to neglect of cognitive perspectives by all but a handful of active educational administration researchers and educators. In this section, we offer some reasons why we thought more research in educational administration from a cognitive science perspective would be productive.

Understanding of human thought and problem-solving processes has increased at an unprecedented rate over the past 20 years, even though, as Toulmin (1972) noted, it has been an enduring preoccupation for 25 centuries. This is largely due to the efforts of psychologists, linguists, philosophers, neuroscientists, and students of artificial intelligence who have formed a loose, interdisciplinary alliance called "cognitive science" (Simon and Kaplan, 1990). Principal among the items on cognitive scientists' agenda has been unlocking the mysteries of how the mind works—from the chemical and neurological microlevel (or what Johnson, 1992, refers to as the "wetworks" of brain functioning) to the level of the highly theoretical, symbolic architecture explaining complex mental processes (e.g., Newell, Rosenbloom, and Laird, 1990). Clearly this is research in its purest, most basic form and it provides the cornerstone of what we refer to as a cognitive science perspective.

Proceeding apace, however, have been a wide variety of projects which together constitute the applied portion of cognitive science's agenda. Three such projects, of special relevance to educational administration, illustrate how productive has been this portion of the work of cognitive science. Carried forward by educational psychologists, the furthest advanced of these projects has been the study of learning in school-related areas and the development of implications for both curriculum and instruction: Bereiter and Scardamalia's (e.g., 1982) work on written composition and Schoenfeld's (1985) work on mathematical problem solving are prime examples of the yield from this research. Indeed, as Murphy (1991) has noted, at the core of most current school restructuring initiatives underway in North America, as well as in many other parts of the world, is the general "constructivist" model of learning and teaching developed within this project. Leinhardt (1992) recently has provided a quite accessible thumbnail sketch of this model. In the case of this first project, then, cognitive perspectives have stimulated widespread initiatives aimed at fundamentally reshaping the technical core of educational administrators' schools.

A second well-developed project within the applied portion of the cognitive science agenda is the study of teacher thinking. Given a jump-start in 1976 with the establishment of the Institute for Research on Teaching at Michigan State University, this project can boast of a rich theoretical infrastructure and a substantial body of empirical evidence (Shulman, 1986; Clark and Peterson, 1986; Lampert and Clark, 1990). From the outset, the goal of this project was reforming teacher education; this is a field of professional preparation arguably surpassed in the disdain with which it was held only by school administrator preparation (Duke, 1992; Hallinger, 1992). Evidence that encouraging progress has been made toward that goal can be observed, for example, in reconceptualizations of how teachers plan their instruction (Clark and Yinger, 1978); new appreciation of how teaching expertise is dependent on pattern recognition abilities; the understandings of stages through which teaching expertise develops (Berliner, 1988); and the creation of much more school-based programs of teacher development (Fullan, Bennett, and Rolheiser-Bennett, 1990) in recognition of the situated nature of cognitions needed for practical problem solving (Brown, Collins, and Duguid, 1989; Rogoff, 1984). Cognitive perspectives, in this second project, have redefined ways of thinking about the role of those with whom educational administrators work most directly and what is meant by the development of expertise in that role. Furthermore, since teaching, like administration, is centrally about "people management," some of what has been learned may provide clues about expert administrative practice.

Strategic decision making, the preoccupation that has historically defined much of the field of management studies, has been extended considerably in the past 20 years by research using cognitive perspectives: in this case, inquiry about the cognitions of individual executive decision makers. The aim of this third applied cognitive science project has been to better understand executive behavior—how senior executives turn thought into effective action and what attitudes and abilities make such executives effective. As Schwenk (1988) observes in his review of cognitive perspectives on decision making: "interest in strategic cognitions is growing because of increased awareness of their role in strategic issues diagnosis and problem formulation" (p. 53)—uncontestably "bottom-line" skills.

Examples of important and unique insights from this research include: evidence that expert senior managers use common, predictable categories for sorting and interpreting problems in their work environments (e.g., technical vs. operational), and that different mental processes are used in response to each category (e.g., Cowan, 1990, 1991); recognition of a limited, identifiable set of values used by executives in their problem solving, and a compelling theory to explain the relationship between executives' values, thoughts, and actions (Hambrick and Brandon, 1988); discovery of the specific biases and cognitive errors most common among executives in their strategic decision making (Hogarth, 1980; Schwenk, 1988); and greater appreciation of the ways in which tacit knowledge is used in managerial problem solving and the forms such knowledge take (Wagner and Sternberg, 1986). Results such as these, emerging from research using cognitive perspectives, are of considerable value to government, business, and industry in the selection, development, and appraisal of executives. Comparable evidence about the thinking of educational administrators may perform the same valuable function for school systems.

As the sample of important and unique insights available from these three applied cognitive science projects suggest, a cognitive science perspective is especially useful in addressing two classes of questions fundamental to educational administration. The first set of questions is about desired, effective, or expert administrative practice. Cognitive perspectives remind us that what administrators do depends on what they think—their overt behaviors are the result of covert thought processes. Like teaching, furthermore, expert administration is a complex and contingent act requiring sensitivity to a broad and ultimately unpredictable host of contextual elements; our study of Jack gave us first-hand appreciation of this. At best, prior efforts to accommodate the need for such sensitivity have given rise to descriptions of a limited number of behavior variations which are more or less matched to a restrained number of variations in situations and tasks—situational leadership theories. At worst (and more recently), similar efforts have prescribed, as effective, a single set of behaviors. Termed "instructional leadership," these behaviors implicitly assume nonvariation in administrative contexts, having been identified largely (although by no means exclusively) through research on inner-city, low SES, small elementary schools—the focus of attention for much of the effective schools movement. Such behavior-based theories are of limited practical value, however, because the reductionism they entail so poorly reflects the complexity of administrators' real worlds.

In contrast, cognitive perspectives redefine expertise or effectiveness in terms of problem-solving processes rather than behaviors. From this perspective, although behavior may be contingent, expert administrative problem-solving processes may be quite constant; that is, the same kinds of expert thought processes applied to different school circumstances may produce appropriate variation in administrative behavior. Improving the sophistication of administrative problem-solving processes is also emancipating. One need not be chained to a prescribed set of practices, however large one's repertoire of practices might be.

A second set of questions especially useful to examine from a cognitive science perspective concerns the development of administrative expertise. As VanLehn (1990) explains:

> the ultimate explanation for the form and content of the human expert's knowledge is the learning processes that they went through in obtaining it. Thus the best theory of expert problem solving is a theory of learning. (p. 529)

Cognitive perspectives on learning stress the central role of learners' existing knowledge structures and emphasize the development of personal meaning through social interaction. These perspectives also give rise to implications for instruction considerably different than the forms of instruction traditionally used in the preparation of educational administrators. Such forms are generally encompassed in the meaning of "problem-based" learning (e.g., Boud, 1985; Bridges, 1992), and offer the promise of helping to reform administrator preparation programs.

The Meaning of a "Cognitive Science" Perspective

In most subsequent chapters we describe those specific aspects of cognitive science theory that we considered relevant to the study described in that chapter. Here we offer a brief, general background to these more specific accounts, again on the assumption that many of our readers may be moving into relatively unfamiliar territory. In particular, we take up three questions: What is a problem? What does expertise mean? and How does it develop?

A problem. Cognitive approaches conceptualize educational leaders as problem finders and problem solvers with varying levels of expertise. The starting point for clarifying cognitive science perspectives, then, is the idea of a problem itself. Standard information processing frameworks for viewing problems include a current state, a goal state, and operators or solution paths for transforming the current state into the goal state (Baird, 1983; Fredericksen, 1984). These are the components of Newell and Simon's (1972) "problem space." Typically, a problem is said to exist whenever there is a gap between where the solver is (current state) and where she or he wants to be (goal state), and the means for closing the gap is ambiguous (e.g., Gagné, 1985; Hayes, 1981).

This definition of a problem, however, does not accommodate very well several critical distinctions in the literature. One distinction is between routine and ill-structured problems. When a leader encounters a situation or a challenge (for example, setting school goals) which is highly familiar because of past experiences, the response is usually rapid and largely automatic. In such cases the current state, the goal state, and the operators are all known. Other leaders faced with the same challenge, but without the familiarity resulting from past experience, may lack clarity about one, two, or all three elements in the problem space.

It seems confusing to claim that setting school goals is a problem in the second case but not in the first, simply because of variation in leaders' relevant knowledge. And so the distinction between routine and ill-structured problems has arisen, spawning considerable research about differences in processes used to solve each type. In fact, the distinction between experts and nonexperts in knowledge-rich domains (e.g., chemistry), is largely the distinction between those who have acquired sufficient knowledge to respond successfully to challenges considered part of the domain and those lacking such knowledge. For purposes of clarity, it may be more useful to define a problem in terms of its objective elements, without reference to the amount of knowledge possessed by the solver regarding those elements. Problems, then, are synonymous with tasks—something to be done, such as setting school goals. Future research aimed at better understanding the task structure of school leadership may prove as useful as have been, for example, Doyle's (1983) efforts to understand the task structure of classrooms. Nevertheless, this is a conclusion we have come to in hindsight and was not a position we adopted in framing our own research. The studies included in this book all adopted a subjective view of problem structure.

The meaning of expertise. Most cognitive science treatments of "expertise" leave the meaning of the concept largely implicit; they jump immediately to such matters as processes associated with expertise, how such processes are developed, and what accounts for them. For example, in a chapter entitled "Expertise in Problem Solving," Chi, Glaser, and Rees (1982) suggest only that "expertise is, by definition, the possession of a large body of knowledge and procedural skill" (p. 8). Posner's (1988) chapter, entitled "What It Is to Be an Expert," dispenses with the concept in an introductory paragraph by referring to exceptional or gifted people, "An adult or child who composes exceptional music, runs extremely fast, or receives particularly high scores on academic or achievement tests" (p. xxix). Kennedy's (1987) work, however, does push along our understanding of what expertise means. She points out that there are at least four different conceptions of expertise, no single one of which appears satisfactory: "Technical Skill," "Application of Theory or General Principles," "Deliberate Action," and "Critical Analysis." The Technical Skill view focuses attention on the repertoire of techniques experts draw on to solve the predictable problems which they confront in their practices. According to this view, expertise is a function of the size of the professional's repertoire, the degree of skill developed in exercising elements of that repertoire, and (to a lesser extent) how choices are made about when to apply those elements. Referred to by Schön (1983) as the "technical rationality" model of the professions, expertise is developed through the processes of becoming aware of the skill, seeing it demonstrated, practicing the skill, receiving feedback, and eventually coaching. A technical skills view encompasses a significant portion of what expert school administrators do in response to such predictable and/or routine problems as timetable building, budgeting, teacher evaluation, and student discipline. Responses to these problems by experts are relatively automatic, directed as they are by well-organized and frequently used cognitive schema. Growth in expertise in this area of administrative practice involves the acquisition and refinement of such schema, thereby freeing cognitive resources for the more truly novel or puzzling problems to be addressed.

Kennedy refers to another view of professional expertise as the Application of Theory or General Principles. Professional practice, from this view, is based on a broad foundation of basic, disciplinary knowledge. The foundation generates powerful frameworks for understanding specific problems and rules-of-thumb or principles that can be used in response to many specific cases. After foundational knowledge has been acquired, development occurs as the novice is assisted in practicing the application of principles to particular cases. Examples of school administrators demonstrating this aspect of professional expertise can be found with problems requiring the application of educational law (i.e., Does case A fall within the "jurisdiction" of law X?) or district policies and regulations.

The Deliberate Action view:

> assumes that expertise evolves and develops with experience, but that experience can only contribute to expertise if practitioners are capable of learning from it. (Kennedy, 1987, p. 148)

Deliberate Action is how Schön's professionals survive "in the swamp." It is Argyris' (1982) "double loop learning," a form of learning which takes place when professionals are able to transcend their assumptions and ways of thinking and question not only their actions but their interpretations of problems stimulating those actions. In its most straightforward form, expert school administrators demonstrate the reflective capacities associated with Deliberate Action when, for example, they put aside time to think about what they have done and why, when they keep a journal and review it occasionally, or when they sense, themselves, a professional development need and take action to meet that need.

Critical Analysis, a fourth and final view of professional expertise offered by Kennedy, concerns itself with problem-solving processes thought to be of considerable value in many specific situations faced by professionals. Expertise develops in this area of practice as professionals become more adept at interpreting the situations they face in more fundamental ways, set a broader array of goals for problem solving, use their values more explicitly, develop more elaborate, information-rich solution processes, and the like. This view of professional practice is especially applicable to nonroutine problems faced by administrators. These are problems for which administrators have little relevant knowledge or prior experience. Although little empirical research has been accumulated about school administration from this perspective, it is the primary orientation to expertise adopted by the studies in this text.

These four alternatives differ in the number of components in the problem space they explicitly acknowledge (e.g., Technical Skills focuses explicitly on operators, giving little or no attention to how current and goal states are defined) and the amount of attention they devote to thought processes alone or both thought and action. The alternatives also vary in their ability to explain the solving of ill-structured (vs. routine) problems.

A further limitation of these alternative views of expertise, even when considered together, is that they do little to distinguish between the terms *expert* and *effective*, at least in the minds of those who are not card-carrying cognitive scientists. Is there a difference between an "effective leader" and an "expert leader"? Common-sense uses of the language suggest an answer to this question based on a distinction between action or behavior and the mental processes giving rise to such action. For example, a typical dictionary definition (Webster's, 1971) of the term *effective* is: "to bring about, accomplish . . . produce" and "producing a decided, decisive, or desired outcome." A leader who is effective, in these terms, acts in such a way as to accomplish an outcome that someone values. This is essentially the sense in which the term is used in the literature on effective leaders and effective schools and seems to be the meaning Posner (1988) attributes to expertise. It is also part of Kennedy's Deliberate Action view of expertise.

In contrast, typical dictionary definitions (Webster's, 1971) of an *expert* are more similar to the concept offered by Chi, Glaser, and Rees (1982) noted earlier: "one who has acquired special skill or knowledge of a particular subject." Technical skill, application of principles, and critical analysis views of expertise all conform to this definition. So, we might conclude that expertise refers to one's potential for effective action; indeed we will often infer expertise, or lack of it, by observing actions and their consequences. But this is an inference and may be in error, since circumstances will sometimes conspire to produce either undesirable or desirable ends incorrectly thought to be caused by the leaders' actions. This is the "attributional bias" associated with leaders, about which so much has been written (e.g., Yukl, 1989).

To this point, then, expertise seems best thought of as the possession of complex skills and knowledge (after Chi, Glaser, and Rees, 1982) rather than actions or behaviors associated with desirable consequences. But a further refinement appears necessary. Experts are often forgiven for not accomplishing desirable consequences; patients die, defendants end up behind bars, and student achievement scores fall rather than rise. What is unforgivable is for the expert to engage in actions, no matter how skillfully, intended to accomplish other than generally endorsed goals. It is also unforgivable for the expert to demonstrate low levels of skill or knowledge with respect to current states and operators. In addition to simply possessing complex skills and knowledge, expertise includes their use in an effort to accomplish desired goals. It does not include, however, actually accomplishing the desired goals always or even most of the time.

This is a fine point, but one of some consequence. While the expertise of those in most occupations is judged by their accomplishment of desired goals, it is the person's accumulated *record* of accomplishment rather than the person's *individual* accomplishments that is of note. Also, across occupations, the standards for an acceptable record vary enormously: nothing less than 100 percent in the case of airline personnel (acting as a system) but as low as 20 percent in the case of some baseball batters. The central determinant of these standards appears to be how much control the person has over the outcome, not the consequences of failure to reach the outcome. Therefore, baseball batters, teachers, and many types of medical practitioners are judged by relatively low standards of goal accomplishment because pitchers, families, and God are considered to be worthy challengers to their control.

Based on this discussion, then, expertise is defined as (a) the possession of complex knowledge and skill; (b) its reliable application in actions intended to accomplish generally endorsed goal states; and (c) a record of goal accomplishment, as a consequence of those actions, which meets standards appropriate to the occupation or field of practice, as judged by clients and other experts in the field. Leaders are effective when they accomplish a desired goal state, so experts will sometimes be effective, but not always, and nonexperts will sometimes be effective, but not as often as experts. This definition of expertise provides considerable warrant for research studies, some of ours included, to initially select for study administrators with a reputation among their colleagues for being good at what they do.

How expertise develops. The primary focus of the work in this book concerns the nature of administrative expertise. Only in Chapter 12 do we explicitly address the development of expertise and this chapter is limited to the effects of formal instruction. Nevertheless, because this is such an important matter, we offer a brief and necessarily incomplete illustration here of how it has been approached in cognitive science. Anderson's (1983) Act* (adaptive control of thought) theory, among the best known, describes three stages in the development of cognitive skill (arguably a part but not all of the expert's repertoire)—the declarative, the associative, and the autonomous stages. However, these stages serve to simplify understanding of what is essentially a continuous process of growth; they are benchmarks in that process. Progression from the declarative to the autonomous stage consists of acquiring additional domain-specific propositional (or declarative) and procedural knowledge; it also involves transforming an increasing proportion of propositional knowledge (facts, ideas, theories) into procedural form (eg. steps to take to solve a problem). As this occurs, propositional knowledge ceases to be inert and becomes a more useful source of guidance in problem solving. Progress also occurs through an increase in the amount of integration and connectedness of the knowledge base. This results in more efficient reorganizations of knowledge including its being chunked together in ways which allow it to be processed more efficiently by working memory; this also increases one's ability to recognize patterns of events or cause-effect relationships—a hallmark of expertise. Finally, expertise develops through greater "conditionalizing" of one's knowledge. That is, the expert becomes clearer about the circumstances under which certain actions are appropriate, transforming more general procedural knowledge into a complex series of "if-then" combinations of conditions and actions which are sometimes referred to as "domain-specific strategies." Such strategies are much more powerful problem-solving tools than are general heuristics.

What can be done in an instructional context to foster such changes in expertise? Cognitive approaches identify six categories of instructional conditions in response to this question. The first category of conditions is concerned with the initial development and subsequent refinement of procedural schema to guide problem solving. Underlying these conditions are theories about how information is selectively encoded, integrated, and compared with existing schema (Sternberg and Caruso, 1985), the role of practice and feedback in schema refinement, and the need for careful sequencing of the complexity of instructional demands on the student (Burton, Brown, and Fischer, 1984).

A second set of instructional conditions, identified by cognitive approaches, acknowledges the important role that social interaction plays in learning. The specific conditions in this category arise from theories about the social construction of knowledge (Berger and Luckmann, 1966) and Vygotsky's (1978) concept of a "zone of proximal development," a concept explained further in Chapters 3 and 12.

Evidence concerning the importance of learning in circumstances the same as, or approximating, those circumstances in which knowledge is to be used gives rise to a set of two further conditions.

Labeled "situated cognition," theoretical work explaining the importance of both authentic instructional settings and tasks as a means of avoiding the acquisition of "inert knowledge" can be found in Brown, Collins, and Duguid (1989), for example.

A fifth set of conditions arises from work on the transfer of training. Perkins and Salomon (1988) outline conditions for both "low road" and "high road" transfer; the former is relevant to the extension of increasingly automatic responses to a similar array of routine problems; the latter is best suited to fostering highly flexible and deliberate uses of knowledge in response to ill-structured problems.

Finally, cognitive perspectives attach importance to processes of reflection and metacognition in the development of expertise.

Methods Used for the Research

Each subsequent chapter describes the methods used in the study or studies it reports. Nevertheless, all of these chapters draw on a small family of data collection procedures which result in "think-aloud protocols." Such protocols consist of tape-recorded discussion by principals in our studies (subsequently transcribed). In some studies the stimulation for this discussion was a brief case problem which the principals were asked to solve on the spot, thinking out loud about what they would do and why, prompted as needed by an interviewer. In other studies, principals were asked to identify a problem in which they were or recently had been engaged. Usually this was a school improvement problem and principals were asked to reconstruct to the interviewer their thinking about the problem as they had worked on it.

Finally, "stimulated recall" methods were used in several of these studies and seemed to be better for generating more valid data about principals' problem solving than were other available methods. This conclusion can be explained in the context of the substantial debate about the validity of verbal reports as evidence of cognitive processes (e.g., Nisbett and Wilson, 1977; Ericsson and Simon, 1984). Based on a simple model of information processing, Ericsson and Simon (1984), for example, hypothesize that recently acquired (or needed) information is kept in short-term memory and, hence, is directly accessible for producing verbal reports. Information stored in long-term memory, however, must be retrieved before it can be reported; the retrieval process can threaten the validity of verbal reports because it can be incomplete and subject to many different types of distortion by the retriever. In the case of some of the research methods we used (e.g., retrospective interviews), questions were asked which could not be answered without retrieving contents of long-term memory or which demanded inferences on the part of the respondent rather than retrieval. Researchers used stimulated recall methods to help respondents to avoid relying on the contents of their long-term memories and to compensate for limitations on short-term memory. They did this by playing back the tape recording of the interaction that took place during the actual problem-solving task and using that tape as the basis for discussion and data collection. Having the playback and discussion immediately after the original interaction also helps avoid memory distortion. The method does not prevent respondents from relying on inferences, however.

For the range of questions addressed in our research program, we needed to use all three methods. Often we used them in parallel and we were always interested in whether our results varied as a function of the methods which we used.

Overview of the Book

The remainder of the book consists of twelve chapters, eleven of them descriptions of individual research studies or syntheses of several such studies. The final chapter offers some observations on what we think we have learned and what that might mean for subsequent research.

In Chapter 2 we describe a study aimed at better understanding the nature of problems principals encountered. The study consisted of a series of monthly interviews conducted with elementary and secondary school principals between September and April of a single school year. Evidence provided by these interviews was used to determine the types of problems encountered by principals and what proportion of these problems were nonroutine. Also addressed by this evidence was the distribution of principals' problems over the course of the year and differences between elementary and secondary school principals in the problems they encountered. Other studies reported in this book were exclusively about administrators' problem-solving processes. Only occasionally did we identify the contents of problems being solved and then, for the most part, only by way of indicating circumstances under which we collected our data. But, the specific content of problems faced by administrators and their relative difficulty is by no means an incidental matter. Problem content is a key determinant of the knowledge domains in which administrators must become sophisticated if they are to act expertly in their organizations. Problem structure or difficulty has a crucial bearing on how important it might be to engage prospective and existing administrators in education designed to improve their problem-solving capacities beyond the levels acquired normally through typical administrative experience. The general purpose of the study in Chapter 2, then, is to paint a picture of the principals' world from a problem-solving perspective.

In Chapters 3 through 6 we report studies of administrators' problem solving carried out within the same grounded model of problem solving initially uncovered in the first of these chapters. In these chapters we examine the problem solving of administrators, both alone and in groups, and include studies concerning both principals and superintendents. The study described in Chapter 3 aimed to identify the central elements in school principals' problem-solving processes and the differences between experts and their more typical colleagues. Responses of elementary principals were used to identify the basic components of the problem-solving model that was used as a framework for the studies reported in the next three chapters.

In Chapter 4 we describe processes used by superintendents to solve problems by themselves. Both conceptually and methodologically, the study parallels our inquiry with principals reported in Chapter 3 but without an expert-novice research design. Results describe processes used by superintendents in relation to each of the components in our problem-solving model. Comparisons also are made between superintendents and principals and between superintendents and senior executives in nonschool organizations.

Much of the problem solving engaged in by educational administrators occurs in a social context, that is, with other people. In Chapter 5, we report the results of a study that compared the group problem-solving processes of expert and typical elementary school principals. Experts' group problem-solving processes, we argue to begin with, seem likely to give rise to forms of leadership practice typically thought of as "transformational." Although this chapter touches on the links between leadership thinking and practice, we address this link much more directly in Chapters 10 and 11.

Building directly on the results reported in Chapter 5, in the next chapter we describe how comparable are the group problem-solving processes used by expert superintendents and expert principals. We did not find what we expected! More precisely, some aspects of superintendents' problem solving were clearly similar to the results for principals reported in Chapter 5. But, we found evidence also of superintendents striving to accomplish several purposes not evident in our earlier data. The Framework section of this chapter provides the most detailed theoretical account of our multicomponent model of problem solving available in the book.

The next three chapters are included in a section called Key Processes. These are processes that seem to us, on the basis of our prior evidence, to offer particularly powerful insights concerning the differences between expert and nonexpert administrators. These processes include problem interpretation, the nature and use of values, and processes associated with cognitive flexibility.

The study reported in Chapter 7 aimed to better understand administrators' problem interpretation processes in both their cognitive and organizational contexts. By cognitive context we mean those factors, including those in the external environment, that administrators actually think about as they frame their problems. Administrators' general approaches to problem solving were also considered part of cognitive context. By organizational context we mean primarily the size of the organization in which administrators find themselves. We undertook this study with principals of secondary schools. Results are compared with evidence from two other identical studies, one with superintendents and one with principals of elementary schools.

In Chapters 4, 5, and 6 we demonstrate the pervasive role of values in administrators' problem-solving processes. Moreover, in these chapters we begin to clarify the types of values most frequently influencing such problem solving. Equally important, however, but not addressed in those chapters, are questions about how conflicts among competing values are resolved and what influences the development of administrators' values. Results of three additional studies are summarized in Chapter 8 to help answer these questions.

Underlying expert human problem solving, many claim (e.g., Schwenk, 1988) is the disposition or ability to think flexibly about problems. The study described in Chapter 9 was intended to determine whether principals' problem solving demonstrates some of the same attributes of cognitive flexibility and inflexibility found in the problem solving of those working in other domains and, should it be evident, to illustrate the nature of such flexibility in the context of school administration.

In both Chapters 10 and 11 we explore the relationship between how administrators think and solve problems and the patterns of overt action in which they engage. How do practices used by principals to foster school improvement differ? Do differences in the nature of the thinking or problem solving of principals offer an explanation for variations in principals' practices? What is the nature of these differences? To answer these questions, data reported in Chapter 10 were collected from principals and teachers in schools implementing British Columbia's new Primary Program. A conception of instructional leadership was used to guide the study.

Recent school restructuring initiatives have stimulated questions about appropriate forms of leadership practices to foster such restructuring. Efforts to address these questions argue for subsuming "instructional leadership" practices within more broadly focused forms of practice termed "transformational." In Chapter 11, we argue that such leadership is necessary but not sufficient—that expert thinking is also required to accomplish school restructuring goals. Evidence collected from secondary school principals and teachers is used to support this argument.

Chapter 12 is the only chapter in which we address the development of expertise. In most other chapters we describe aspects of school administrator expertise. Whereas the nature of such expertise is of some theoretical interest in its own right, the most practical justification for it is instructional; that is, to serve as one resource for systematically improving administrative expertise. Answers to three key questions seem necessary, however, before such instruction can proceed with confidence: Can problem-solving expertise be improved through systematic instruction? Will an instructional focus on general problem-solving processes enhance administrators' expertise? and, if so, What are the most promising forms of instruction? To answer these questions, a four-day experimental program was designed and implemented with school administrators and changes in their problem-solving expertise were compared with changes in a control group with similar characteristics.

In the final chapter of the book we briefly summarize what has been learned from the program of research reflected in earlier chapters. We also nominate items to be included on an agenda for further research concerning educational administration viewed from cognitive perspectives.

Reading the Book

Readers should be alert to several features of the book before proceeding. First, we have already indicated the intent of making sense of our work to those not heavily steeped in the cognitive sciences, and so we have used technical language sparingly. Second, whereas we have edited out of the chapters excessive redundancy, they were, originally, independent journal articles. That feature, along with a desire for chapters that could stand on their own, as much as possible, means that some redundancy remains; we hope we have found a helpful balance but, inevitably, that will not be the case for all readers. Finally, the chapters represent a selection of our completed work, not a comprehensive set. We are continuing with the work, so we view what is here with the sort of tentativeness that we hope our readers will appreciate.

Chapter 2

The School Administrators' World from a Problem-Solving Perspective

A series of monthly interviews were conducted with 52 elementary and secondary school principals between September and April of a single school year. Evidence provided by these interviews was used to determine the types of problems encountered by principals and what proportion of these problems were nonroutine. Also addressed by this evidence was the distribution of principals' problems over the course of the year and the differences between elementary and secondary principals in the problems they encountered.

The first of this two-part study was originally published as K. Leithwood, B. Cousins, and G. Smith. 1990. Principals' problem solving. *The Canadian School Executive,* January 9–12; March 18–22. Reprinted with permission. In the first part of the study, data were collected from a total of 21 principals; the second part provided data from an additional 31.

Other studies reported in this book are exclusively about administrators' problem-solving processes. Only occasionally do we identify the content of problems being solved and then, for the most part, only by way of indicating circumstances under which we collected our data. But the specific content of problems faced by administrators and their relative difficulty is by no means an incidental matter. Problem content is a key determinant of the knowledge domains in which administrators must become sophisticated if they are to act expertly in their organizations. Furthermore, problem structure or difficulty has a crucial bearing on how important it might be to engage prospective and existing administrators in education designed to improve their problem-solving capacities beyond the levels acquired through typical administrative experience. The general purpose of this study, then, was to paint a picture of the principals' world from a problem-solving perspective.

The study explored four specific questions about the nature of principals' problems. The first of these questions was: What types of problems do principals encounter in their schools? Previous research most relevant to this question has identified categories of "tasks" (or roles) such as curriculum, budget, supervision, and the like (e.g., Franklin, Nickens, and Appleby, 1981; Gousha, 1986). Results of this research are usually restricted to broad categories of activities closely aligned to conventional conceptions of administrative duties. Such research often reports the proportion of time that principals perceive they actually devote to each category of tasks as compared with the proportion of time they wish they could devote. Whereas these results provide a broadly gauged sense of what occupies principals' time, little is revealed about the specific nature of the tasks and what it is about these tasks that demands principals' mental energy.

The second question for this study was: What proportion of problems are viewed by principals as routine versus nonroutine and are some types of problems more nonroutine than others? This question was considered important because of evidence in many problem domains which suggests significant differences in how people think about "structured" or routine problems as compared with "ill-structured" or nonroutine problems (Greeno, 1976; Simon, 1973); these terms denote the amount of relevant knowledge and skill principals possess when encountering a problem and, as a consequence, the degree of certainty they have concerning a successful solution. Routine problems stimulate well-developed but automatic responses that place few demands on conscious thought processes. In contrast, non-routine problems demand, for example, conscious attention and reflection, often bring fundamental values into play, and create a significant role for information-collection skills. In sum, they require more thought. A high proportion of nonroutine problems faced by principals would suggest a working environment much more cognitively demanding than would be suggested by a low proportion of such problems. Development of administrative problem-solving capacities would be much more likely to influence administrative effectiveness in a cognitively demanding environment than in one that was less demanding.

A third question asked in the study concerned the distribution of problems encountered by principals over the school year. Much has been written about the number of decisions made by principals, the hectic pace of their work (e.g., Martin and Willower, 1981), and the stress created by that pace as well as uncertainties surrounding the role (e.g., Kotkamp and Travlos, 1986). Were results to suggest an uneven distribution of problems throughout the year, principals might be assisted in redistributing the workload or developing supplementary problem-solving mechanisms to assist during the most problem-intense periods. At present, we are not aware of existing information concerning this question.

Finally, the study inquired about possible differences between elementary and secondary principals in the problems which they encountered. This question has obvious utility in designing principal preparation programs, as well as contributing to a more general appreciation of the two roles. The larger size and more complex organizational structure typical of secondary schools has led to speculation about differences in secondary and elementary principals' roles, but differences identified in the small number of relevant empirical studies are of questionable significance and generalizability (e.g., Johnson, 1983; Gersten, Carnine, and Green, 1982; Leithwood, 1986).

Method

Twenty-seven elementary school principals and 25 secondary school principals and vice principals provided data for the study. Each of these administrators was interviewed approximately monthly during the period of September to April of a single school year. Interviews lasting from 30 minutes to more than an hour were conducted by graduate students enrolled in a principal preparation program. Most of these students were teachers in the schools of the principals they were interviewing. The choice of principal was the student's and was usually based on ease of access to a willing interviewee. A common interview format was used, and rough notes were taken during the interview and subsequently extended and typed into a report. Principals were guaranteed anonymity at the stage of reporting the results of the interviews.

Training in interview techniques was conducted prior to the initial interviews and these techniques were monitored on a monthly basis thereafter, in the context of a graduate course taken by the students, and under the supervision of the instructor. Each interviewer followed the same interview format. Essentially, this involved asking the principal to review problems encountered over the past two weeks using his/her planning calendar or appointment book as an aid to memory; all problems were recorded. Principals were then asked to identify those problems they considered to be "muddy" or nonroutine. Further questions focused on what made such problems nonroutine and how they had attempted to solve them.

A preliminary classification of principals' problems was developed in collaboration with the graduate students and subsequently refined by the researchers. Using this refined classification system, all interview reports were content analyzed.

Results and Discussion

In Tables 2.1 and 2.2 we summarize results of the content analysis. These results are described as responses to each of the four research questions.

What Types of Problems Do Principals Encounter in Their Schools?

Analysis of all problem types encountered by principals over the entire period of the study resulted in the identification of 16 categories of such problems; these are listed in the left-hand column of Table 2.1. Four problem categories were reported much more frequently than the rest:

1. Teachers (247 Problems)

1. Assignment of Teaching Duties

2. Conflicts among Teachers

3. Conflicts between Teachers/ Students/Administration
4. Curriculum Review, Development, Implementation
5. Dereliction of Duty (reporting, deadlines, supervision)
6. Dress Code
7. Extra Curricular
8. Judgment of Teacher-Proposed Ideas
9. Level of Competency
10. New Teachers
11. Personal Problems
12. Professional Development
13. Staff/Department Meetings
14. Teacher Coverage
15. Teacher Evaluation
16. Teacher Exchange

2. **School Routines (138 Problems)**

1. Assemblies
2. Attendance
3. Budget
4. Commencement Planning
5. Dances
6. Drills and Routine For Students
7. Feeder School Visit
8. Field Trips
9. Fire Drills
10. Fund Raisers
11. Graduation Awards
12. Home Room Visits
13. IPRC and Spec. Ed. Meetings
14. PA Announcements Meeting
15. Retimetabling of Classes
16. Registering Students
17. Report Cards
18. Sept. Report
19. Student Council Meetings
20. Teacher Routines/Plans
21. Timetabling
22. University Night

3. **Students (113 Problems)**

1. Abuse
2. Adult Students
3. Attendance
4. Cafeteria
5. Commendation
6. Complaints
7. Discipline
8. Evaluation
9. Injuries
10. Placement
11. Special Requests
12. Student Council
13. Student Problems
14. Vandalism

4. **Parents (105 Problems)**

1. Communication
2. Complaints
3. Parent Councils/Groups
4. Parent's Night
5. Parental Involvement in the School or Lack Thereof

As the specific problem labels within each of the four categories indicate, fully two-thirds of principals' problems (603) revolve around

Table 2.1 Frequency of Occurrence of Different Types of Problems Reported by Elementary and Secondary School Principals

CATEGORIES OF PROBLEMS	ROUTINE			NONROUTINE			GRAND TOTAL (%)
	ELEM.	SEC.	TOTAL ROUTINE (%)	ELEM.	SEC.	TOTAL NONROUTINE (%)	
1. Community at large	8	6	14 (2)	1	2	3 (2)	17 (2)
2. Ministry of Education	2	3	5 (1)	—	1	1 (1)	6 (1)
3. Nonteaching Staff	13	10	23 (3)	—	1	1 (1)	24 (3)
4. Other Principals	28	25	53 (7)	—	—	—	53 (6)
5. Outside Agencies	5	4	9 (1)	—	—	—	9 (1)
6. Parents	67	18	85 (11)	13	7	20 (13)	105 (12)
7. Plant	8	1	9 (1)	3	5	8 (5)	17 (2)
8. Principal	14	1	15 (2)	—	1	1 (1)	16 (2)
9. School Routines	93	42	135 (18)	—	3	3 (2)	138 (15)
10. Senior Administration	36	30	66 (9)	2	4	6 (4)	72 (8)
11. Special Events	26	14	40 (5)	2	1	3 (2)	43 (5)
12. Students	26	27	53 (7)	38	22	60 (39)	113 (13)
13. System Partners	11	3	14 (2)	—	—	—	14 (2)
14. Teachers	102	104	206 (27)	18	23	41 (27)	247 (27)
15. Trustees	—	1	1 (.1)	—	—	—	1 (.1)
16. Vice Principals/ Department Heads	6	21	27 (4)	—	5	5 (3)	32 (4)
TOTAL	445	310	755	77	75	152	907

the internal workings of the school, its staff, and clients. These are problems over which the principal has a fairly high degree of control. The remaining problems arise from aspects of the internal workings of the school which appear to require very infrequent attention by the principal (e.g., nonteaching staff, plant, special events). Problems arising from sources external to the school require relatively infrequent attention by principals, as well. Senior administrators are the most frequently cited ($N = 72$) of these sources; they place accountability demands on principals, visit their schools, provide approval or nonapproval of principals' initiatives, request attendance by principals at board meetings for a variety of purposes, and insist on adherence to system procedures. Trustees, the Ministry of Education, and outside agencies of several types (e.g., social service groups, community health groups) appear to impinge very little on principals' problem space.

Boyd and Crowson's (1981) review of research concluded that principals typically have an "insider" focus and spend the bulk of their time on organizational maintenance tasks and pupil control tasks. Our evidence concerning the types of problems encountered by principals is consistent with only a part of this conclusion. Three of the four most frequently encountered categories of problems were found inside the school: teachers, school routines, and students. The fourth, parents, could also be viewed as an "inside" problem category. If parents are so considered, "outside" problems encountered by principals amounted to only about 19 percent of the total.

It is not difficult to understand the need for school principals (indeed middle managers in other organizations, as well) to have an "insider focus." This is why they were hired, one may argue. But is the focus of their work actually just maintenance and control? This question is best answered by examining specific subcategories of problems. Such problems do not suggest a necessary preoccupation with maintenance and pupil control. For example, the sub-category of teacher problems entitled "assignment of teaching duties" contained 15 cited problems (not shown in text). Several of these problems clearly were of a maintenance nature (e.g., plan for lunchroom supervision, finding supply teachers), but most could be plausibly linked to the school's instructional program (e.g., setting goals with teachers, reorganizing the seventh-grade class, arranging more planning time for teachers). Over the total of 247 specific teacher problems, at least a majority had the potential for a direct impact on instruction.

Further, "student" problems were by no means limited to the control of students. The majority had some direct link to the likeli-

hood of student growth: for example, incidences of child abuse, coun-
seling adult students on diploma requirements, "behavioral" students running away from school. A minority of this category of
problems did involve control: discipline, attendance, and the maintenance of order were examples.

What Proportion of Principals' Problems are Routine Versus NonRoutine?

Three of the four categories in which principals encountered most
problems overall also showed the highest incidence of nonroutine
problems—60 in the student category, 41 in the teachers category,
and 20 in the parents category (Table 2.1). Whereas problems related to school routines were frequently encountered by principals,
their responses appeared to be well rehearsed, requiring little conscious attention. Only three nonroutine problems were reported in
this category.

In Table 2.2 we report ratios of nonroutine to routine problems
in each of the 16 categories. These ratios are a much better estimate
of just how "thorny" were the problems in each category for principals: at least this is the case where the data provided a sufficient
sample of problems for such estimates to be meaningful. With a ratio of 1.13, student problems were clearly the most nonroutine in the
minds of principals. Problems related to the school plant were the
next most nonroutine but very few such problems were reported.
Categories of problems including the community at large, the Ministry of Education, parents, teachers, and vice principals/department
heads were similar in their ratio of nonroutine to routine problems
(range .16 to .23). There was about a five to one ratio of routine to
nonroutine problems encountered in these five categories, as well as
all 16 categories combined.

Descriptions of the day-to-day activity of principals has por-
trayed their jobs as hectic, fast paced, and characterized by brief encounters and spontaneous face-to-face interactions (Willower and
Kmetz, 1982; Martin and Willower 1981; Wolcott, 1978; Morris et al.,
1984). Such characterizations of what principals do often leave the
impression that their problems, while numerous, are largely routine.
In contrast, our data suggest that experienced principals perceive a
much higher proportion of their problems to be nonroutine (about
one in five and considerably higher in the case of student problems).
Principals do not see themselves simply applying a well-rehearsed
repertoire of solutions over and over again to the same problems, a

Table 2.2   Ratio of Nonroutine to Routine Problems Encountered by Principals

Categories of Problems	RATIO OF NONROUTINE TO ROUTINE PROBLEMS		
	Elementary	Secondary	Combined
1. Community at Large	.13	.33	.21
2. Ministry of Education	.00	.33	.20
3. Nonteaching Staff	.00	.10	.04
4. Other Principals	.00	.00	.00
5. Outside Agencies	.00	.00	.00
6. Parents	.19	.39	.23
7. Plant	.38	5.00	.89
8. Principal	.00	1.00	.06
9. School Routines	2.00	.07	.02
10. Senior Administration	.06	.13	.09
11. Special Events	.08	.07	.06
12. Students	1.46	.81	1.13
13. System Partners	.00	.00	.00
14. Teachers	.18	.22	.20
15. Trustees	.00	.00	.00
16. Vice Principals/Dept. Heads	.00	.24	.16
OVERALL RATIO	.17	.24	.20

technical view of their role. Rather, adaptation of old solutions to new contexts and circumstances, as well as fresh thinking about largely novel problems, seem to better describe the demands faced by principals.

This characterization is consistent with Schön's (1983) depiction of expert practice in other professional fields. It is also consistent with what we know about the number of reforms, new expectations, and shifting environments schools now face. Furthermore, the willingness and ability of principals to see novelty in problems which have a familiar cast appears to be an important feature of expert administrative problem solving. For example, in comparing a sample of typical and expert principals, Leithwood and Stager (Chapter 3) found that typical principals were much more likely to become hostages to their existing knowledge and experience; they were unable, as a result, to recognize new features of a problem that required special attention if the problem was to be adequately resolved. Expert principals were quick to see and to act on such features.

Earlier studies have suggested that principals perceive senior administrators not only as a significant source of problems but as an impediment to, rather than a resource for, their school improvement efforts. Crowson and Morris (1985) found that from one-third to one-half of Chicago principals' school-site activity was governed by what they called "hierarchical controls." Principals in Leithwood and Montgomery's (1984) study reported that the major hurdles they faced in improving their schools were: hierarchical structures which made change difficult; excessively rigid and time-consuming policies and procedures; provision of inadequate resources; and the conservative stance of central administrators toward school-initiated change. Similarly, Duke's (1988) inquiry about why principals quit their jobs suggested five sources of job dissatisfaction, three of which were associated with the work of senior administrators.

Data from the present study appear to reinforce the claim that principals view the work of senior administrators as less than helpful. Senior administrators were viewed by principals as the greatest source of problems outside the school (about 13 percent of the total). Yet, only six of 66 problems identified were considered to be nonroutine by principals and even these included a number with a clear maintenance focus. Problems one might have expected principals to view as nonroutine, such as development of a professional growth plan, were not. This suggests that at least some procedures characteristically relied on by senior administrators as change strategies may turn out to be relatively benign as they are implemented. These data also provide support for the move toward greater school-based management advocated in the school restructuring movement (e.g., Murphy, 1991).

Is There Any Pattern to the Distribution of Problems Over the School Year?

Our data permitted this question to be addressed for the September to April period of the school year only. Further, these data do not include 85 problems identified which were not dated by the interviewers; hence the total sample for this part of the analysis is 822 problems (not 907, as with other parts of the analysis). In addition, the relatively high incidences of problem identification in November and February, as will be discussed, may be explained in part by the fact that in both these months some interviewers in the sample conducted unusually extensive interviews. Equally, the relatively low incidence of problems in April might reflect the interviewers' or the principals' fatigue with the process.

With these limitations in mind, the data reveal a distinct pattern to the year. Looking at the interview records, September and October show a predominance of routine events associated with school opening—registration, communications with the home, parent evenings, board and staff meetings. While nonroutine problems may arise here (especially in categories like Parents), most are routine. Students tend to be on their best behavior in the early months of school, and teachers are refreshed and proactive. However, by November, a much greater frequency of problems surfaces. In the schools included in the study, November marked the first major cycle of reporting to parents, and the arrival of Commencement ceremonies, school-wide events, and trips that had been planned since early Fall. Also, students prone to disruptions may have reached their courage (or boredom) level at about this time of year. For these and other reasons, November was a very busy month for principals. A noticeable drop in number of problems in December may reflect reduced demands and improved attitudes associated with the holiday season. Reduced problems were also apparent in January, possibly for similar reasons. February was both a common semester turnaround and a regular reporting cycle; this may explain the rise in problems identified here. Data for March and April may have reflected a lessening of problems toward the end of any school year, when major issues have either been settled or abandoned. Alternatively, this period might represent the "lull before the storm" as principals head into May and June with a host of end-of-year and planning problems confronting them. Without data for May and June, it is difficult to determine which explanation seems more plausible.

Do Elementary and Secondary Principals Encounter Different Problems?

Tables 2.1 and 2.2, as well as evidence of when problems occurred, provide data relevant to possible differences in problems encountered by elementary and secondary principals. Since the total sample of 52 principals interviewed included two more elementary than secondary principals, the frequency of occurrence of each category of routine and nonroutine problems was adjusted accordingly (adjusted results not shown in tables).

In terms of categories of problems experienced (Table 2.1), there appeared to be few differences between elementary and secondary principals with respect to nonroutine problems. Student problems were the sole exception to this result; elementary principals encountered over 50 percent more such problems. Substantial differences were evident with respect to four categories of routine problems—in each case, elementary principals faced a greater number: approximately three times as many Parent problems, eight times more Plant problems, fourteen times more problems associated with Other Principals, and twice as many School Routine problems.

Elementary and secondary principals also differed in regard to the proportion of nonroutine to routine problems with which they were faced (Table 2.2). For elementary principals, the overall ratio was about one to six (.17) and for secondary principals, about one to four (.24). In other words, secondary in contrast with elementary principals perceived about 40 percent more of their problems to be nonroutine. The greatest of these differences appeared in the category "Plant," but smaller differences were evident in most categories. Only the Student and (marginally) Special Events categories presented a larger proportion of nonroutine problems to elementary as compared with secondary principals. The general pattern of increased frequency of problems in November and February was similar for both elementary and secondary principals with respect to both routine and nonroutine problems.

The modest amounts of evidence reported in earlier research concerning differences between elementary and secondary school administrators suggests that, in comparison with elementary principals, secondary principals:

- have more complex communication problems;
- are more distant from classroom instruction;
- have less influence on school directions;
- spend more time on paperwork;
- are able to delegate more decision making;
- encounter more severe student problems; and
- are much less directly involved with parents.

Data from this study are relevant to three of these reported differences. Secondary principals did appear to be much less directly involved with parents; they cited only about one-third as many of these types of problems as were cited by elementary principals. Given the usual staff of vice principals and counselors (at least in large secondary schools) these results are easy to understand. With data showing school routine problems cited twice as frequently by secondary as compared with elementary principals it would appear (not surprisingly) that evidence is available for greater delegation of decision making by secondary principals. Not supported by the present evidence, however, is the claim that secondary principals' student problems are more severe. On the contrary, elementary principals not only reported 50 percent more problems in this category, but also viewed a much higher proportion as nonroutine.

Conclusion

This study has begun to describe the principal's world from a problem-solving perspective. While the evidence on which the study is based has important limitations, it has provided a tentative appreciation of the problems faced by principals, the demand such problems place on principals' thinking, and the pattern of problem appearance over the year. The study also helped clarify several differences in the work contexts of elementary and secondary principals reported in earlier research.

Four related but broader issues are also raised by the study. First, we interpret the evidence about the nature of principals' problems to suggest that the "naturally" occurring problems encountered by principals provide them with ample opportunities for exercising educational leadership. But this leadership is not often the type that comes to mind when the term "instructional leadership" is used; this term implies direct and pervasive interactions with teachers about their teaching strategies. Our data suggest that, more typically, principals influence instruction by establishing the conditions within which such instruction occurs. In our view, this is important work which was largely overlooked in many of the efforts over the past decade or so to better understand what principals do. Nor is the influence of such work on classroom practice likely to be fully recognized or appreciated by teachers who are more likely to view such conditions as givens or starting points for their own decision making.

There is no need to restructure the principal's role, as some have suggested, or to assume that unless principals are constantly in classrooms observing instruction they have little effect on the quality of education in their schools. Principals, it seems, are confronted with literally hundreds of small spontaneously occurring leadership opportunities (problems to be solved). The trick to curriculum and instructional leadership is to have these opportunities accumulate in a consistent and desired direction. Many principals are unable to develop such consistency, most likely, we believe, because they do not have a set of goals and values, and a vision for their staffs and schools clearly formulated, at least in their own minds. In Chapters 10 and 11 we pursue this matter in more detail.

Second, a large enough proportion of principals' problems are nonroutine to suggest that education effective in improving administrative problem-solving capacities would have a marked effect on principals' effectiveness. This is an important area for study and one we pursue further in Chapter 12.

Third, our results also argue strongly for the development of a better understanding of the nature and impact of what senior administrators do. In particular, until we are better able to advise senior administrators on how they can carry out their responsibilities in a way that facilitates school improvement, principals' efforts are likely to be seriously frustrated. The extensive focus on effective schools has often created the impression that the larger organizational context in which schools function is irrelevant to their decisions. Evidence from this study suggests, however, that there is an urgent need to better understand how senior administrators can best facilitate principals' problem solving.

Finally, the secondary school administrative context that emerges from this study is one which is marginally less fast-paced, with increased opportunities and a greater need to focus one's energies on a larger proportion of nonroutine problems. At the same time, the role seems likely to demand more systematic and sustained attention to the development of staff such as department heads who mediate principals' relations with teachers and students.

Part 2

—◄o►—

Toward a Comprehensive Model of
Expert Processes

Chapter 3

Principals' Individual
Problem-Solving Processes

To identify the central elements in school principals' problem-solving processes and the differences between "experts" and their more typical colleagues, 22 elementary principals were interviewed. We analyzed their responses to brief hypothetical case problems. Differences between expert and typical principals were most evident in response to "messy" or ill-structured problems. This study identified the basic components of the problem-solving model that was used subsequently to frame the studies reported in Chapters 4, 5, and 6.

This chapter was originally published as K. Leithwood and M. Stager. 1989. Expertise in principals' problem solving. *Educational Administration Quarterly* 25(2), 126–161, copyright © 1989 by the University Council for Educational Administration. Reprinted by permission of Corwin Press, Inc.

When practitioners respond to the indeterminate zones of practice by holding a reflective conversation with the materials of their situations, they remake a part of their practice world and thereby reveal the usual tacit processes of worldmaking that underlie all their practice. (Schön, 1987, p. 6)

Schön's assertion concerns that part of school administration that is the primary focus of our research: "indeterminate zones of practice" or, more simply, "unstructured problems." His assertion also assumes a constructivist epistemological perspective on such problem solving; the framework for our research is the psychological expression of such constructivism, that is, information-processing theory.[1] With this focus and perspective, our study set out to (a) discover the central elements of school administrators' problem-solving processes, describe the nature and function of each of these elements, and explore the relationship among elements; and (b) determine the extent and nature of differences in problem-solving processes between highly "expert" school administrators and their more typical colleagues.

This study was part of a long-term research program aimed at exploring the nature, determinants, and consequences of school administrators' practices (e.g., Leithwood and Montgomery, 1982a, 1982b, 1984, 1986; Leithwood and Stager, 1986; Trider and Leithwood, 1988). Through this research, we have come to view the school administrator's problem-solving processes as crucial to an understanding of why principals act as they do and why some principals are more effective than others.

In an effort to justify our assertion that the core of administration is problem solving we have compared this focus with those of "technical action" and "decision making" (Leithwood and Stager, 1986). The technical action focus on school administration has been reflected more recently in descriptions of typical and effective principal behaviors (e.g., Blumberg and Greenfield, 1980; Dwyer et al., 1984; Hall et al., 1984; Martin and Willower, 1981) and the "effective schools" movement, more broadly. Results of this research, when focused on effectiveness, provide examples of solutions to administrative problems that have appeared to work well in particular contexts. However, the results reveal little or nothing about how actions were selected or created, and treat the administrator's mind as a "black box."

The decision-making focus on school administration dates back at least to Simon's seminal work in 1945 (see Simon, 1957). This focus was part of a more comprehensive effort to undergird administrators' practice with social science knowledge (the New Movement[2] in educational administration) and was based on positivistic assumptions. In principle, the focus seems promising and well intentioned. For example, although Greenfield (1986) was well known as an articulate critic of science in administration, he was prepared to recommend that "we might well return to one of Simon's original starting points and seek to understand the logic and psychology of human choice" (p. 45). He did not criticize this orientation to administrative inquiry but rather the ways in which it has been employed—in particular, the narrow focus on only rational aspects of decision making, with the failure to recognize that values pervade the educational issues about which administrators must make decisions, and with the reification of the organization in place of understanding the phenomenology of the individual administrator.

Our research interest in administrators' problem-solving processes[3] includes inquiry into nonrational aspects of these processes, "the study of decisions, will and intention in all their depth, perplexity and subjective uncertainty" (Greenfield, 1986, p. 75), although it was not a major focus of the present study. However, we remain interested in the rational aspects of problem solving as well. Although it may be that this has been the exclusive focus of inquiry concerning decision making for the past 30 years, we still know little about it; 30 years is a short time for a research undertaking of this sort under the best of conditions, and relatively few empirical studies of such decision making have actually been completed during that time.

Finally, conventional definitions of decision making narrow the generic task of the administrator unnecessarily. From this view, decision making is a relatively simple category of problem solving, involving the choice of a solution from known alternatives, by applying readily available critieria.[4] Decision making looks inside the "black box" but detects only the simple structures and functions associated with rational processes. School administrators use this type of decision making in response to the many well-structured problems for which they are responsible. However, school administrators also face "messy" situations in which they first must spend considerable effort identifying the problem and the values at stake in the solution. When they have achieved such clarification, they may still be uncertain about the goals to be accomplished, an adequate solution process, and the constraints or obstacles to solutions that they are likely to encounter. By studying how expert school administrators handle these unstructured problems (or indeterminate zones of practice), we expected to learn about what Schön refers to as the "artistry" of school administration.

Framework

Our study of problem solving began with previous research guided by information-processing theory. Of particular relevance were findings concerning the structure of problems and the expertise of those solving problems.

Until recently, information-processing-oriented research concentrated on the type or characteristics of the problem itself (particularly its structure) and studied problems that were well structured (i.e., clearly presented, with all the information needed at hand, and with an appropriate algorithm guaranteeing a correct solution; Frederiksen, 1984) and/or "knowledge lean" (i.e., involving novel situations, where specialized knowledge and skill were not required; Glaser, 1984; Simon, 1973, 1975). However, research in the field has taken several new directions. First, there has been increasing awareness that the solution process used has more to do with the solver's knowledge of a particular problem than with problem type or characteristics per se (Frederiksen, 1984). Second, because of the importance of knowledge, studies of problem solving increasingly have been conducted within specific knowledge domains rather than in knowledge-lean ones. Baird (1983) and Glaser (1984) have provided substantial evidence of the appropriateness of this direction for research. Finally, there is evidence of more interest in ill-structured problems (i.e., those with indefinite goals and/or incomplete materials provided; Greeno, 1976), along with an awareness of the limitations of generalizing results from research using well-structured problems to processes involved in solving ill-structured problems.

This treatment of problem structure and solver's knowledge, demonstrating the importance of domain-specific knowledge in accounting for problem-solving processes, led us to see the need for a detailed study of problem solving by principals. Little in the existing literature can be safely generalized to the principal's role. Indeed, we were able to find only two empirical studies (Hayes-Roth and Hayes-Roth, 1979; Voss et al., 1983) that provide accounts of ill-structured problems, problems concerned with everyday life, and/or those that Scriven (1980) termed "evaluation problems." One of these studies (Voss et al., 1983) considered problem solving in the domain of the social sciences; this study's application of the general information-processing model to ill-structured problems and its approach to the characterization of social science problems (considering more than "structure") has influenced the direction of our research significantly.

Studies of problem solving which compare novices and experts, and reviews of these studies, have identified seven differences between them. Experts, as compared with novices:

(1) are better able to regulate their own problem-solving processes. This metacognitive control appears to be what Schön (1983) refers to as "reflecting-in-action" and "reflecting-on-action" (Berliner, 1986);

(2) possess more problem-relevant information (Berliner, 1986; Norris, 1985) and have it stored in memory in a better-organized, more richly linked manner, thereby increasing its accessibility and extending its application (Bereiter and Scardamalia, 1986);

(3) represent problems using more abstract categories (as opposed to more superficial features of the problem) and with reference to more basic principles (Berliner, 1986; Chi, Feltovich, and Glaser, 1981; Voss et al., 1983); they also have better and faster pattern-recognition skills (Bereiter and Scardamalia, 1986; Berliner, 1986);

(4) identify and possess more complex goals for problem solving and goals related to action plans (Bereiter and Scardamalia, 1986;[5] Berliner, 1986);

(5) spend more time at the beginning planning their initial overall strategies, are more flexible, opportunistic planners during problem solving, and are able to use a greater variety of approaches to a solution (Berliner, 1986; Norris, 1985);

(6) have automated many recurring sequences of problem-solving activity (Norris, 1985); and

(7) are more sensitive to the task demands and social contexts within which problems are to be solved (Berliner, 1986).

For the most part, these seven differences have been observed in relation to either well-structured problems or (much less frequently) to ill-structured problems in knowledge-rich domains. Results of information-processing-oriented studies, then, shed very little light on the area of the school administrator's job that is most difficult to deal with. We know even less about the sources of expertise for this aspect of the job. Although they were useful as background, we did not believe that the available conceptualizations of the problem-solving process could be justified a priori as frameworks for inquiry about principals' problem solving. An initial purpose of our study, then, was to develop a grounded (Glaser and Strauss, 1967) framework within which to describe principal problem solving.

Method

Sample

A total of 22 elementary school principals (21 men, one woman) from three boards of education took part in the study. We received permission at the central board level to contact potential participants for the study; only one of those contacted was unable to take part.

We designated six of the 22 principals as "experts." We did not feel that any single method for arriving at this designation was sufficiently robust to be relied on exclusively. As a result, principals considered effective in this study had to pass through two screens, each with its own compensating strengths and limitations. First, we asked two central administrators from each board to indicate independently which of all principals in their boards they would recommend as highly effective: Only principals nominated by both administrators passed this screen. The strengths of this method are that (a) it is based on extensive data, (b) it requires agreement by two people who may have different experiences with the principal, (c) it is thoroughly grounded in the actual work of the principal, in a wide variety of contexts, and (d) it allows for the application of alternative criteria as the basis for defining effectiveness. Weaknesses inherent in this method include (a) the informal, clinical nature of the data base, (b) the unknown reliability of those judging the principal's expertness, and (c) the unknown criteria influencing the judge's decisions.

As a second screen, we interviewed all principals passing the first screen with an extensive instrument keyed to a four-stage conception of growth in principal effectiveness called *The Principal Profile* (Leithwood and Montgomery, 1986). These interviews were conducted by researchers familiar with the *Profile* but uninvolved in other aspects of the study.[6] The strengths of this method are that (a) the criteria on which judgment was made are explicit, (b) the criteria were based on a synthesis of all relevant empirical research reported in English up to 1985, (c) the interview instrument used to collect the data had been developed and refined during approximately 200 interviews conducted prior to this study, and (d) formal steps were taken to ensure high levels of reliability among interviewers. The weaknesses of this method include those typically associated with self-report data: There may be a discrepancy between what principals say they do and what they actually do.

As Table 3.1 indicates, the two methods used in designating principals "effective" compensated for one another's weaknesses reasonably well. Those principals who not only were judged as highly effective by both administrators from their boards but also obtained very high scores (3+ or 4) on the Profile interview were designated as "experts." Six principals met both of those criteria. The remaining 16 principals were considered as "nonexperts" in reporting results.

The six experts had an average of 15 years of experience as school administrators; the remaining 16 principals had an average of 17 years of experience. Experts' schools had an average of 506 students; four of these schools had vice principals. The remaining principals' schools had an average of 350 students; five of them had vice principals. The size of this sample, its restriction to principals in only three districts, and their gender (primarily male) are important limitations on the generalizability of results.

Data Collection Procedures

In the first interview of the study itself, we asked the principals to perform a problem-sorting task, to reflect on their own problem solving and the factors influencing it, and to indicate how they selected

Table 3.1   Strengths and Limitations of the Two Methods of Determining Principals' Effectiveness

Sources of Variation	Reputation-Based Judgment	Principal Profile-Based Judgment
(1) Amount of data on which judgment was based	extensive	modest
(2) Period over which data were collected	long	short
(3) Explicitness of criteria	implicit	explicit
(4) Validity of criteria	unknown	highly valid
(5) Reliability of data collection procedures	informal	formal

which of the many problems they faced deserved priority. Results of this interview are discussed in Chapter 7.

In a second interview, designed to study differences in problem solving associated with variations in problem structure, we asked principals to rank six brief problems (see Table 3.2) according to how clear, at the outset, the course of action to be taken was; to present, in as much detail as possible, their solutions to the clearest and least-clear problems; and to describe, from their own experience, problems with similar degrees of clarity to each of these. We based this chapter on the solutions to the two problems, of the six presented, that each principal saw as least and most clear. Half of the principals, randomly selected, responded to the clearest problem first, and the other half responded to the least clear. We used the terms *clear* and *unclear* in the interview because we felt that they were the closet synonyms in ordinary discourse to the terms *structured* and *unstructured;* however, we will use the two latter terms to report results.

Data Analysis Procedures

To analyze the 44 problem solutions, we paid particular attention to approaches to protocol analysis suggested by C. Bereiter (personal communication) and to qualitative analysis outlined by Miles and Huberman (1984). After transcripts had been prepared, two researchers (one of whom had collected the data and one of whom had not been involved in the study until that point) worked together for several months developing a system for analyzing the protocols in these 44 problems. This work involved, briefly, (a) developing, in consultation with the senior author, a set of grounded categories (described in the results section) to which almost all statements contained in the protocols could be assigned, (b) refining definitions and assignments to these categories until a satisfactory level of agreement was reached, (c) developing, again in consultation with the senior author, a set of subcategories to which statements in each category could be assigned and a method for arraying this information, and (d) refining this method until agreement was again reached. Once we all agreed on the detailed technique for analysis, the researchers (initially two, but chiefly one) applied this technique to the 44 solutions. We (the authors) then summarized the data, and compared the groups as designated experts and nonexperts. Not until the final stage of comparisons were data analysts aware of the predetermined level of expertise of the principals whose responses were being analyzed.

Table 3.2 Problems Presented to Principals

Resource staff	Your board provides consultative services to support personnel such as subject coordinators, program consultants, social workers, and psycho-educational consultants. However, as there are increasing demands made upon teachers (relating, for example, to computer use or special education), there is more and more demand for the services of these persons. You want your school to make the most efficient use of the resource staff allocation.
Principal entry	You have been assigned to a new position. The present principal, who is very highly regarded by staff, community, and students, is being moved to a larger school after only two years in his present assignment. The school community (staff and parents) are very displeased that a new principal has been assigned. They feel that the board has not considered their wishes. How would you enter this situation?
School consolidation	All year, you have been a member of a committee concerned with an emotion-charged issue, that of consolidating six schools in your area into five. In April, the committee makes the decision that a neighboring school will be the one to close and that approximately one-third of its students should be attending your school next year. How would you prepare for fall?
Primary language program	Your school's population is now 50 percent Chinese. It is found that most of the Chinese students entering kindergarten and grade 1 have little or no English. You don't know if the primary language program being offered is meeting the needs of all students as well as it might.
Rumor in the community	Next year, your school will begin to have a French Language immersion program. Your trustee phones to say that there is apparently a rumor abroad in the community that the regular English program will be phased out. This is not true, but a widespread rumor will be disruptive.
Setting school objectives	Your new school is one in which staff have never been involved in the setting of school objectives and are not apparently very interested in doing so. You have come to believe that it is a very important thing for staff to set school objectives and to evaluate them at the end of the year.

We will present results from our analysis of the 22 principals' responses to the six problems presented to them in four parts. First, we describe components of the problem-solving processes that emerged from our preliminary data analysis. Second, we present a quantitative comparison of responses to the problems that principals considered least structured and most structured. Next, we examine the nature of the problems themselves and what the principals' responses revealed about problem solving. Finally, we describe the results of a qualitative analysis of expert and nonexpert principals' responses to the problems.

Problem-Solving Components

"Grounded" components of problem solving were evident in principals' responses to the six problems presented to them. Following are these components, along with an abbreviated definition of each.[7]

- *Interpretation:* a principal's understanding of the specific nature of the problem, often when multiple potential problems could be identified

- *Goals:* the relatively immediate purposes that the principal was attempting to achieve in response to his or her interpretation of the problem

- *Principles:* the relatively long-term purposes, operating principles, fundamental laws, doctrines, and assumptions guiding the principal's thinking

- *Constraints:* "immovable" barriers, obstacles, or factors severely narrowing the range of possible solutions the principal believed to be available

- *Solution Processes:* what the principal did to solve a problem (in light of his or her interpretation of the problem, principles, and goals to be achieved, and constraints to be accommodated)

Quantitative Differences between Expert and Nonexpert Principals' Responses to Least-Structured and Most-Structured Problems

In Table 3.3 we display results of an overall "quantitative" comparison of the protocol statements of expert and nonexpert principals. In contrasting least- and most-structured patterns for this quanti-

Table 3.3 Average Percentages of Statements Assigned to Problem-Solving Components for Experts, Nonexperts, and Total Sample

PROBLEM TYPE	LEAST STRUCTURED			MOST STRUCTURED		
PROBLEM-SOLVING COMPONENT	EXP. (n = 6)	NONEXP. (n = 16)	TOTAL (n = 22)	EXP. (n = 6)	NONEXP. (n = 16)	TOTAL (n = 22)
Interpretation	27	38	35	28	25	26
Goals	15	9	11	7	7	7
Principles	4	2	3	3	4	4
Constraints	—	5	4	—	1	1
Solution Processes	52	34	39	53	50	51
Unclassified	3	12	10	9	13	12
*Total number of statements**	*66*	*69*	*68*	*48*	*46*	*47*

*Figures in this row are based on frequencies; all other numbers in the table are based on percentages.

tative analysis, we treated the six principal experts and the 16 nonexperts separately. For each group, the percentage of statements assigned to each of the five components (or to an "unclassified" category) of the analysis was averaged separately for those problems that group members regarded as least structured (i.e., regardless of which exact problem each group member classified as least structured) and for those that the group members regarded as most-structured problems.

Insights available from a frequency analysis of this type are, in general, relatively limited. In this case, however, the results foreshadowed some of the most important findings that emerged from the more detailed, qualitative analysis reported subsequently.

When we combined the responses of expert and nonexpert principals, several different patterns for least-structured and most structured problems were evident. First, although there were no differences between expert and nonexpert groups in the total number of statements generated, this total was much greater for the least-structured (68 on average for all 22 principals) than for the most-structured (47 on average) problems. This may reflect the greater complexity of the least-structured problems and the corresponding greater complexity of their solutions. Second, there were considerably more interpretation statements and considerably fewer solution process statements for problems regarded as least structured. However, this pattern was almost entirely due to the nonexperts' responses. Expert principals responded to least-structured problems in much the same way that they and nonexpert principals responded to more-structured problems, whereas nonexpert principals displayed an unusually high percentage of interpretation statements and an unusually low percentage of solution process statements when they faced a less-structured problem.

Differences in the remaining problem-solving components, not obvious when we compared the least- and most-structured problems for the total group of principals, did emerge when we compared experts and nonexperts in detail. These differences, once more, were more marked for the least-structured problems. This pattern of differences suggested in Table 3.3, and revealed more clearly in the qualitative analyses that follow, indicated that experts, when compared with nonexperts:

- focused fewer of their efforts on problem interpretation; they appeared to clarify the problem for themselves more easily;

- expended more effort on determining the goals to be achieved through problem solving;

- identified marginally more principles, at least in the least-structured problems, to use in problem solving;

- did not identify any constraints to problem solving;

- provided much more detail about their actual solutions; and

- made fewer unclassifiable or irrelevant statements.

The Problems

In Table 3.4 we indicate the number of experts and nonexperts who classified each of the six problems as "most structured" or "least structured" when they were asked to rank these problems. Substantial consensus concerning the nature of the problems is evident among the whole group of principals. Using a criterion of 75 percent agreement among those principals who dealt with a particular problem, we identified principal entry, school consolidation, and primary

Table 3.4   Classification of Problems as Most- or Least-Structured by Expert and Nonexpert Principals

PROBLEM	NO. OF PRINCIPALS SELECTING PROBLEM	MOST-STRUCTURED	LEAST-STRUCTURED
(1) Resource staff	5	1 expert 2 nonexperts	1 expert 1 nonexpert
(2) Principal entry	8	1 nonexpert	3 experts 4 nonexperts
(3) School consolidation	6	1 nonexpert	1 expert 4 nonexperts
(4) Primary language program	8	2 nonexperts	1 expert 5 nonexperts
(5) Rumor in the community	10	3 experts 5 nonexperts	2 nonexperts
(6) Setting school objectives	7	2 experts 5 nonexperts	

language program problems as least structured. Rumor in the community and setting school objectives were most structured. (Although only 60 percent of the five principals who dealt with the resource staff problem considered it as "most structured," it was included with the two most-structured problems in subsequent analyses.)

It was useful that several different problems were included in our data collection procedures because each contributed additional, and sometimes unique, insights to our understanding of the problem-solving process. In general, responses to the three least-structured problems indicated many differences between experts and nonexperts; the principal entry problem did so especially well. The school consolidation problem clearly illustrated the particular concern of experts with both understanding and having others understand the nature of the problem. Even though the primary language program problem was not seen as too difficult, responses to it by nonexperts revealed something of their difficulties in "getting a handle" on the problem.

The three most-structured problems, rather than highlighting differences between experts and nonexperts, furthered our understanding of some of the processes that underlie problem solving by principals. The setting school objectives problem allowed us to observe, for the first time, patterns of similarity as well as differences between these two groups. Responses to the resource staff problem showed us that even experts may narrow or confine their interpretation of a problem in light of their particular working environment and/or personal history. Finally, the problem of rumor in the community helped to clarify the relationship among perceived problem difficulty, principals' views of the obstacles to their solutions, and their prior negative experiences (or their total lack of relevant experience). Without including even this relatively modest range of problems in the study, we probably would have overlooked important features of the problem-solving process. This indicates a need for further inquiry, using additional problems.

Qualitative Differences between Expert and Nonexpert Principals' Responses to Least-Structured and Most-Structured Problems

In this section, we report differences between expert and nonexpert problem solvers for each of the five components of problem solving and for a final category dealing with "other" sources of variation between expert and nonexpert problem solvers. In Table 3.5 we summarize these results for unstructured problems.

The quantitative analysis reported earlier indicated clearly that differences between expert and nonexpert problem solvers depended on another variable, problem structure. For this reason, differences between experts and nonexperts were considered separately for the problems identified here as least and most structured.

Interpretation

Statements classified as "interpretation" indicated how principals were attempting to make sense of a problem and included their views of the mess and efforts to sort out problematic parts of a situation. We focused on four elements of such interpretation: the basis on which problems were awarded priority, the perceived difficulty and/or complexity of problems, the ways that principals attempted to understand problems, and principals' use of anecdotes to interpret problems or to explain their understanding of problems.

Most-structured problems. Principals gave a high priority to this category of problems only when they appeared to require a long time to solve (e.g., rumor in the community). Most principals considered these problems relatively easy to solve. Although two experts

Table 3.5 Solving Unstructured Problems: Differences between Expert and Typical Principals

COMPONENT	EXPERT	TYPICAL
Problem Interpretation		
(a) Basis for priority	consequences for school and academic growth of large numbers of students	more concerned about consequences for themselves
(b) Perceived difficulty	difficult problems are manageable if one used careful thinking	difficult problems are frightening and stressful
(c) Ways to understand	collect information	makes assumptions in lieu of collecting information
	provides clear, comprehensive interpretation of problems	irrelevant issues tend to cloud interpretation
(d) Use of anecdotes	directly relevant to problem	recounts difficult experiences rather than highly successful ones
Goals for Problem Solving	concerned with implications for students and program quality	more often mentions staff-oriented goals
	concerned with providing parents with knowledge	concerned with making sure that parents are happy
	more concerned with knowledge	more concerned with feelings
Principles	Considers slightly more principles	not mentioned
	used as basis for determining long-term goals	not mentioned
Constraints	indicates few, if any, constraints	indicates more constraints
	finds ways to deal with constraints	sees constraints as obstacles
Solution Processes	uses detailed prior planning	gives little attention to planning
	uses consultation extensively to get specific information	consults less frequently with fewer specific purposes

Table 3.5   *continued*

COMPONENT	EXPERT	TYPICAL
	identifies detailed steps in solution process	
	stresses importance of information collection	
	plans for follow-up	
Affect	calm, confident	fearful

did note (in setting school objectives) that the solutions were sometimes complex, they indicated that they knew *how* to solve the problem. Past experience was the main tool for understanding these problems: they were like problems the principals had solved many times before. When principals told anecdotes intended to help explain their approach to or solution of the problem, the anecdotes tended to be directly relevant and to illustrate successful experiences in solving similar problems. Nonexperts, however, occasionally recounted unsuccessful experiences. In sum, the most-structured problems did not stimulate many interpretative responses; principals usually had ready-made solutions. There did tend to be certain differences in the *nature* of the interpretations; for example, in the setting school objectives problem, experts felt the problem required a solution that taught staff how to set objectives, and nonexperts tended to interpret the problem in a manner that led to a more autocratic solution.

Least-structured problems.   When principals gave this category of problems a high priority, experts' reasons tended to include consequences for the school and for the academic growth of large numbers of students (e.g., in primary language program and principal entry), whereas nonexperts were more concerned about consequences for themselves (e.g., in principal entry).

Most principals considered the least-structured problems to be complex and difficult to solve. Experts, however, appeared to believe that the problems were manageable with careful thinking. As one principal said, in response to the principal entry problem:

That is a difficult one because you have a really rough row to hoe personally. The person who was in before you was highly regarded and was very, very competent, and people are upset that he's gone . . . and so you would really have to think through your strategies very carefully.

A second expert, who had encountered a similar experience, said, "It was one I gave a lot of thought to when I found out that I'd been assigned, [because] it was tough for me going into this."

In contrast, many nonexperts found least-structured problems frightening and stressful and did not suggest that careful thinking was the way to deal with them. For the same problem, a nonexpert said:

You can get yourself in a lot of difficulty . . . you can alienate yourself from the staff very quickly if they perceive you are just coming in and they don't like you as well as the fellow that just left, and they make no bones about it, and that puts you in a very difficult position. . . . I guess I have been in the position so I know what it feels like. . . . I don't know if there is a right or wrong way to solve it. I can tell you how I would go about it. Probably what I would do first of all is make as few changes in the running of the school as I could. You don't stand up and make a great statement . . . because you are going to put yourself in an awful position.

Perceptions of difficulty tended to depend on whether respondents identified major constraints to problem solving. For example, in response to a question as to why the school consolidation problem was difficult, one nonexpert pointed out:

This is a very emotional issue . . . it takes up a great deal of superintendent time, trustee time . . . a good amount of phone calls on the nasty side to people in directors' positions. . . . The little issues within the large one can explode into something.

Principals attempted to understand the least-structured problems in three ways: by relying on past experience (as with the most-structured problems); by collecting new information; and/or by making assumptions. In this study, the only assumptions made by experts concerned the hypothetical nature of the problems presented to them; the experts were very explicit about their assumptions. On the other hand, nonexperts tended to make assumptions rather than collect information and were somewhat less explicit about their assumptions. For example, the analysis of one nonexpert response to the principal entry problem revealed six such assumptions, though they were not identified explicitly as such, made by the principal: the previous principal was "doing a good job"; the established procedures in the school "were good"; changing procedures would lead to confrontations with staff; there were cliques to be dealt with "ruthlessly"; there would be a core of staff opposed to the principal's initiatives; and there were "people who control the school." As the example also indicates, many assumptions of nonexperts were concerned with constraints or obstacles to problem solving.

These assumptions, along with an observed tendency to consider a number of tangential or irrelevant issues, led to considerable floundering on the principal's part in interpreting the least-structured problems. For example, one nonexpert, in considering the principal entry problem, reported that he would spend a great deal of time and energy trying to find out why the previous principal had been moved; to him it was an issue of substantial importance whether his predecessor had been moved to another school or promoted to a superintendency, and he mentioned the matter repeatedly. Principals frequently used anecdotes to explain and illustrate their approaches to problems. In contrast to nonexperts, experts' anecdotes tended to be directly relevant to the problems at hand. Nonexperts were more likely to recount difficult experiences than highly successful ones. The third quotation in this section came from the protocol of a principal who went on to describe a particular situation in which he had great difficulty entering a new school.

In short, experts differed from nonexperts in their ability to arrive at a clear, comprehensive interpretation of a problem, one that would enable them to get to the actual solution of the problem. Experts did not appear to become involved in irrelevant issues and did not become dysfunctionally preoccupied with the feelings of others associated with the problem.

Goals

Our analysis of the goals that principals attempt to achieve during problem solving focused on the nature and number of such goals. We classified statements as goal-related when they referred to what the solver was trying to accomplish in the specific problem, that is, the relatively immediate ends to be served by their problem solving.

Most-structured problems.   Goal-related responses of principals to the three most-structured problems showed little variation. For the rumor in the community problem, goals were exceptionally straightforward, with most principals concerned only with eliminating the rumor. For resource staff and setting school objectives problems, most of the goals identified by both experts and nonexperts were related to staff (e.g., achieving staff understanding or focusing staff on school priorities). In the latter problem, the expert problem solvers demonstrated a particular concern with the process itself. Among the staff-related goals, one mentioned "to build staff trust and confidence in the collective process," and another mentioned wanting "a group of people on [the] staff to take responsibility for monitoring and putting together the goal package."

Least-structured problems.   Principals indicated, through their responses to the three least-structured problems, that they were attempting to accomplish five types of goals. These goals concerned staff, students and programs, parents and the community, perceptions of others about the principal's expertise, and finding an appropriate balance among goals.

Most principals had staff-oriented goals for problem solving. Nonexperts mentioned this type of goal more often than other types. There were certain differences between experts and nonexperts in the particular staff-related goals that they expressed. For instance, nonexperts were rather directly concerned with staff feelings; in dealing with the principal entry problem, one principal's goal was to have "good feelings about what you are doing . . . and everybody happy with that." An expert, dealing with the same problem, believed that a more important goal was to have the staff understand his philosophy of education: "I spent two or three hours . . . sharing [with staff] what I believed to be important about education so that they would gain an insight into my philosophy."

All principals identified goals related to students and programs in response to the primary language problem; they wanted to improve the quality of student programs. With the problems that had less obvious impact on students, however, an important difference between expert and nonexpert principals was apparent: only the experts outlined how they would include the student and program category of goals in their problem solving. In the school consolidation problem, an expert identified implications for the grouping of new students in terms of program, whereas the closest a nonexpert came to a student-oriented goal was "selling the school" (i.e., to prospective students). In the principal entry problem, one expert was particularly emphatic about the program and student goals that should be addressed in solving the problem:

> The whole fine reputation of the school . . . and the confidence in the school and the programs that are in place are at stake . . . so you are dealing with the continuation of the program with the kids . . . and so you want that to be continued.

In this problem, also, goals of two experts included a concern with achieving a balance between their own and others' ideas concerning the nature of programs.

Most principals had goals for problem solving that were related to parents or the larger school community. In this category, experts were concerned with providing parents with knowledge to better understand the problem and its eventual solutions. Examples of such goals from the school consolidation problem were statements such as: "parents get to know where their kids are going to be," "provide a vehicle for parents of new students to ask questions," and "have parents' questions answered." Nonexperts, on the other hand, wanted parents to be happy and comfortable with the solutions, as indicated in such statements as "to make people feel better about the new school" and "make them feel comfortable."

Two other goals were mentioned much less frequently, and for the most part in connection with the principal entry problem. One of these was to be knowledgeable about educational matters and the school, and to be seen by the staff and community in this light: "I would [want people to get the] impression very, very quickly that I knew what the situation was, that I'd done my homework, and that I knew the community and the program. I'd endeavor to be really well informed."

The second goal was to achieve an appropriate balance, in this case between continuity (of the most desirable features of the present school) and change (of those features that could be improved); experts were very concerned about developing personal initiatives that would contribute to their new school, but they wanted to do so in an appropriate manner.

In summary, principals' goal-related thinking suggested that experts pursued a broader range of goals and were more concerned than nonexperts with knowledge (their own and others) as distinct from feelings. They were also better able to see the implications, for students and for program quality, of problems not obviously or directly concerned with students or programs and were in general more concerned about giving suitable attention to all legitimate goals.

Principles

Like goals, "principles" are what the problem solver wants to accomplish but are, however, long term and may include statements about fundamental laws, doctrines, and assumptions. This category also includes "operating principles," that is, usual practices such as involving others in decision making. Our data suggested variations in the number of principles actively considered during problem solving, the functions such principles served, and the nature of the principles.

Most-structured problems. We found little evidence of principles in either expert or nonexpert responses to the most-structured problems, with one exception: the setting school objectives problem did stimulate a considerable number of statements that could be classified in this way. Many of these responses reflected the principal's belief in the value of the objective-setting process per se and the consequent importance of finding a good solution to the problem. Other principles elicited by this problem had more to do with precisely how the principal might solve the presented problem (i.e., how to introduce the objective-setting process). The function of these principles seemed similar to that for least-structured problems. But fewer uncertainties about these problems appeared to reduce the value of explicit thinking about principles in successful problem solving.

Least-structured problems. Experts actively considered slightly more principles than did nonexperts. Furthermore, the nature of the principles considered by the experts seemed somewhat more defensible. For example, in the principal entry problem, most experts saw themselves as responsible for a successful entry and transition period. One principal, in recounting how he had actually approached this problem, noted that in his first communication with parents:

> I pledged my allegiance more or less that I would do my very best for their children, and that I planned to work hard with the staff as a team to really make [the school] continue with the fine educational program.

Most nonexperts ignored the issue of responsibility and two actively rejected it. One, who would call on the superintendent for large amounts of assistance in this situation, said:

> Recommendations for principal transfers are made at a level above us, and I'm not sure that I'm completely responsible

> or accountable for that damn decision nor should I own it my-
> self. . . . It's not really mine . . . and I've been, you know, foisted
> in a situation.

Experts' principles sometimes were evident in the priorities they attached to the problems themselves; this occurred in setting school objectives, as described here, and in the primary language program
problem, where experts saw the problem as extraordinarily important because it involved the academic program for a considerable
number of students.

Principles served several closely related functions in problem
solving. First, they helped interpret the problem and provided tools
for finding solutions that were not contained within the problems
themselves. This is nicely illustrated by one expert's response to the
principal entry problem, which he saw as having potential for both
continuity and improvement:

> No matter how good a school is, there are always areas that
> need some improvement, [and so, while] accentuating the pos-
> itive, at the same time be very proactive on the things that you
> think need to be done.

As another example, an expert solving the school consolidation problem noted that "problems don't just get dropped, there is a background I'd have to know about"; this appeared to account for the
principal's marked information-collection activities in solving the
problem.

Second, principles sometimes served as long-term goals and
provided a context within which choices could be made concerning
alternative solutions to the presented problems. For example, in response to the principal entry problem, one expert suggested "if the
kids are turned off, they will start to look for things to criticize." This
principle helped him decide what should get his attention. In this
way, principles appeared to be providing a kind of structure to help
solve the problems not otherwise structured.

Finally, principles in some cases underlay the actual solution
steps that principals would use. For instance, in the principal entry
problem, one expert who had not dealt with this problem before noted
that in his experience "there are people in the school community that
always seem to get hold of information, good and bad, and really communicate it throughout the community"; accordingly, in discussing
this novel situation, he indicated that he would be careful to locate
and impress such influential communicators.

In sum, "principles," although not numerous in our classification scheme, constitute an important feature of administrators' problem solving, particularly that of experts, and one worthy of further investigation (several subsequent chapters provide more evidence related to this component—see especially Chapter 8).

Constraints

We classified statements which identified immovable barriers, obstacles, or factors markedly restricting the range of possible solutions as "constraints"; that is, when a principal indicated that he was unable to go forward with a problem because of some factor, we used this term.

As with principles, the number of responses coded as constraints was rather small, however, the observed variation in their function was extremely important. There appeared to be little difference in the nature and operation of constraints for the most-structured and least-structured problems, but there were marked differences between experts and nonexperts with both types of problems. As was noted in the quantitative analysis, experts did not indicate any constraints, whereas many nonexperts did, particularly with the least-structured problems. Factors that nonexperts indicated as constraints or obstacles were viewed by experts simply as matters to take into account during problem solving; potential constraints were addressed through the solutions that they generated. Rather than viewing public opposition to school consolidation as a constraint, for example, one expert simply noted, as part of the solution process, that

> I'd provide a vehicle for parents of new students to ask questions . . . perhaps through letters and return slips of paper. . . . They have to have the opportunity to get to know where their kids are going to go. . . . I would have open-house public meetings, invite families and perhaps students to come see the building, and [hold] a meet-the-teacher night with some kind of general assembly.

In contrast, a nonexpert dealing with the same question mentioned a number of constraints, which are representative of those mentioned by others; a lack of knowledge or information ("so there's all sorts of questions that are coming up that will need answers before I can really sit down and prepare"); opposition from others ("I'm going to be dumped on with a lot of this stuff," "people in the other school are probably going to fight it and be very anti this move"); and a potential lack of resources ("it may be too much of a drain on the resources of the school, and we may not be able to handle all they think we can").

Solution Processes

To this category we assigned statements about everything that the principals would do to solve a problem. These data provided insights about principals' planning and ordering of solution activities, their use of resources and support from others, their efforts to communicate with others to collect information through consultation and in other ways, and to follow up or evaluate the consequences of their solution activities.

Most-structured problems. Neither experts nor nonexperts spent much effort planning solutions to most-structured problems. Two experts, however, gave considerable attention to the sequence of steps they would follow in the rumor in the community and setting school objectives problems. Efforts to consult and meet with staff, parents, students, or others about solving a problem were less pronounced with this class of problems than with the less-structured ones. When consultation did occur, it was only for the rumor in the community problem, and was done mainly by experts. In these cases, consultation, usually with the superintendent prior to a public meeting, apparently was a matter of "bouncing" possible solutions off him or her to evaluate the proposed solution and avoid unanticipated consequences. In general, principals collected less information in solving these problems than in the least-structured ones.

Least-structured problems. Responses of experts indicated marked efforts at thinking through the solution process in considerable detail and planning how the process would be carried out. In response to the principal entry problem, one expert stated:

> But the actual steps . . . I guess is what wasn't really clear to me exactly what I would do. . . . I would have to sit down and I'd have to think it through and plan it out and look at the individual steps and where I could go with each one.

Nonexperts showed very little evidence of attention to planning. Most principals met in some way with staff, parents, and/or students, depending on the nature of the problem. All but a few nonexperts stressed the importance they attached to the details of the solution process in the context of such meetings. Again, in response to the principal entry problem, one expert noted, for example:

> In my first communication with parents, I would talk about a lot of the good things that the former principal had started and what my plans are. I would want to state my particular goals over the next school year.

Experts and nonexperts differed substantially, however, in their orientation to such meetings. Experts provided evidence of high levels of consultation in working out a solution process. One of the most marked features of the principal entry problem was that two of the three experts who solved it described explicitly (and the third expert alluded to) very extensive consultation about their new school with the best possible informant, the outgoing principal; none of the nonexperts did this. Experts also stressed a broad array of features of the problem to be examined through such consultation. One expert, for example, in solving the school consolidation problem, mentioned numbers of students at each grade level, nature of students, community support, projected enrollments, school organization, staffing ratio, student groupings, budget preparations, and plans for textbooks and supplies. In general, the consultations of the experts in the least-structured problems had to do with information collection. Nonexperts consulted less frequently than did experts; when they did, some may have done so because they were confused as to how to proceed. For instance, two nonexperts sought the support of the superintendent before they even attempted to deal with the problem, rather than going to him or her for a specific purpose after they had begun to formulate a solution.

All but one principal attached some importance to information collection as a solution activity in the least-structured problems. Experts awarded this activity greater importance and spent more effort on it than did nonexperts. Nonexperts never followed up the consequences of solution activities. Although it was not a marked aspect (as was, for example, information collection) of the problem solving of experts, three of the six experts did include some sort of monitoring or follow-up process.

In sum, experts and nonexperts differed markedly in their responses to least-structured problems. Experts spent more effort planning for the solution process and identified more detailed steps to be included in the process than did nonexperts. Experts also consulted others more about the solution and attempted to elicit widespread support for it. They stressed the value of careful information collection. Some of these differences appeared, but in a more muted form, in the solutions to the most-structured problems, in which principals' response may have been better rehearsed.

Other Sources of Variation

To this point, we have reported, independently, evidence concerning five components of the problem-solving process (interpretation, goals, principles, constraints, and solution processes). Experts and nonexperts differ in their responses to each of these components; these differences were especially marked in the case of the three least-structured problems (principal entry, school consolidation, and primary language program). The data suggest two additional variations between experts and nonexperts: the degree of interrelatedness among the problem-solving components and the importance of the principal's affect in problem solving.

By "degree of interrelatedness," we mean coherence or internal consistency. Given a particular interpretation of a problem, to what extent do the goals the principal strives to achieve, the principles considered relevant, the constraints identified, and the solution processes used appear to be consistent? Judging such consistency was more complicated than any analysis reported in the results to this point; it involved a high level of interpretation on the part of the researchers. We illustrate the nature of our interpretation with examples from two principals' protocols; the first we judged to present a highly coherent process, and the second a relatively incoherent one.

When presented with the primary language program problem, one of the experts:

- (in interpretation) indicated that the problem might take a fair while to solve, for it involved curriculum renewal, which was a slow process; stated that this involved the formal language program; stated that since at present the principal has ESL resources, this might influence the solution outlined; indicated that if such resources were lacking, the principal would solve the problem differently.

- (in goals) stated intentions to adapt the formal program, to meet the needs of the Chinese students, and to have parents informed.

- (in principles) indicated that the parents need to know the difficulties their children are having.

- had no constraints (note that this principal regarded the problem as "least structured").

- (in solution processes) would look at existing curriculum with ESL teacher to see what it was about the program that was not meeting the needs of students; would meet with the consultant to see how they could adapt the program to meet those needs; would seek ESL support if it was currently unavailable; would set up a communication system with the parents, with an interpreter; would also have a translator for newsletters going home.

In contrast, one of the nonexperts:

- (in interpretation) stated that the problem has to do with communications; stated that to him the problem was very clear; said that there may or may not be a problem; indicated the problem would be easier to solve if there were a board directive; stated his hope that everyone is on board; indicated that there was something (never indicated what) hidden in the problem.

- (in goals) stated his desire for a consensus judgment and his intention to teach parents "the reason for language resources."

- (in principles) indicated his belief that most of what we do is a function of communications.

- had no constraints (note that this principal regarded the problem as "most structured").

- (in solution processes) would have experts in to look at and judge the program; would sit down with the parent involved; would sit down "with somebody, probably the teacher," to talk about the program; would attempt to have teachers "get their feelings out"; would express his own concerns if he has them; might communicate with others who have concerns.

Experts' responses to the least-structured problems showed greater coherence or interrelatedness across all components than did the nonexperts' responses. The sources of such coherence often appeared to be the principles evoked by the experts to guide their problem solving. When nonexperts provided responses showing coherence, this coherence was often more limited, for instance, to that between interpretation of the problem and constraints identified. In addition, because nonexperts frequently interpreted the problems more narrowly, the coherence that did exist was also across a more limited array of variables.

Finally, principals approached and solved problems in many different ways. Experts were invariably calm and relatively confident in their own abilities. Nonexperts, especially when responding to least-structured problems, were sometimes fearful, often not confident, and occasionally somewhat belligerent and/or arrogant.

Responses of an expert and then a nonexpert describing setting school objectives, a problem that both regarded as easy, illustrate several of these differences.

From the expert:

> This did not present a difficulty for me at all, because, first of all, I believe in having staff give their input in terms of providing directions for the school. So I had no difficulty with that, and I've done that as a principal from day one. I don't feel, just because I'm the principal, that I set the entire goals of where the school is going. There are certainly many, many directions that come from staff, and always have, in my experience. And, as a teacher, I wanted input. And so that was just a simple solution for me, not even a problem.

And in contrast:

> Setting school objectives, that's a process that's built in, it's a process that I've done for a number of years. I can show you the outcomes, and I can show how. . . . You know, it's there, it's a book, I could give it to you, it's done. . . . If I were coming to a new school, I believe as the principal, you say, "here's what I stand for. Here are my expectations." And you say all the stuff up front at the opening staff meeting. Anybody who waffles and says, "I'm going to spend six months looking around" is either lying or stupid.

Conclusions

To identify the main elements of principals' problem-solving processes and to determine the nature and extent of differences in such processes between highly expert and more typical principals were the two purposes for the study. In pursuing these purposes, we assumed no specific, a priori framework or problem-solving model because of the limited amount of research about the types of problems and problem contexts faced by school administrators. Nevertheless, the work was informed, in a general way, by information-processing theory and differences in the problem-solving processes of novices and experts that have emerged from research using that perspective.

We collected data through structured interviews in which 16 "typical" and six "expert" principals first ranked a series of presented problems for their clarity (or degree of structure) and then provided detailed information about how they would solve the most and least clear of the problems. We transcribed the data, developed grounded categories, and developed descriptions for responses by each principal to each problem. Only at that point did we identify responses with the typical and effective principals and make comparisons.

Results identified relatively few differences between effective and typical principals' responses to problems they judged to be clear or well structured. This may have been a result of the relatively high levels of expertise possessed by our "typical" principals, as compared with subjects in studies contrasting experts with novices. Most "typical" principals were carrying out their job in a more effective than average fashion according to the evidence used to designate them initially. As a consequence, all principals in our sample displayed skilled, automated responses to well-structured problems and appeared to possess well-organized accessible knowledge about such problems; both are characteristics associated with expertise in other fields (Norris, 1985; Berliner, 1986; Bereiter and Scardamalia, 1986).

Substantial differences were evident, however, in typical and highly effective principals' responses to unclear or ill-structured problems (see Table 3.5 for a summary of these differences).

There are similarities between our study of principals and descriptions derived from studies of novices and experts in other fields (summarized in our introduction to this chapter). These similarities include, for example, the higher degree of metacognitive control exercised over problem solving (Berliner, 1986), especially evident in what effective principals said about their solution processes. School administrators, like experts in other fields, used more basic principles to define the specific nature of a problem (Chi, Feltovitch, and Glaser, 1981; Voss et al., 1983); furthermore, their ability to quickly and accurately detect similar and different features (from past situations) of a problem situation during problem interpretation indicates the better and faster pattern-recognition skills generally attributed to experts (Bereiter and Scardamalia, 1986; Berliner, 1986). It also indicates the expert's greater sensitivity to the task demands and social contexts within which problems are to be solved (Berliner, 1986). School administrators appear to be comparable to experts in other fields in the number and complexity of their goals for problem solving. Like other experts in other fields, principals also devote more time to planning overall strategy, as was clear in our data concerning solution processes (Norris, 1985; Berliner, 1986). In sum, our data suggest that in response to ill-structured problems, highly effective principals use processes similar to those used by experts in other fields. We collected no obviously disconfirming data.

The main implications of the study concern theory and further research. We accomplished our goals of identifying components of problem solving and attributes of effectiveness within each component. Further research is needed to confirm these components and attributes and to determine how well they generalize to other contexts (e.g., superintendents; see Chapter 4). More detailed comparisons with results of research on expertise in other fields would also sharpen distinctions unique to principal functioning, if such distinctions exist.

Furthermore, although the components "mood" and "principles" or values appeared to be important, our data did not achieve much clarity about the specific nature and role of these components. Yet they are the "nonrational" elements of problem solving so severely neglected in previous research on administrator decision making, and warrant much further study. In Chapter 8, in particular, we pick up the challenge concerning principles and values; in Chapter 9 we have more to say about mood.

Chapter 4

Superintendents' Individual Problem-Solving Processes

In this chapter we describe processes used by eight superintendents to solve problems by themselves. Both conceptually and methodologically, the study parallels our study of principals reported in Chapter 3 but without an expert-novice research design. Results identify processes used by superintendents in relation to the same five aspects of their problem solving: how problems are interpreted; goals to be met through problem solving; the nature and role of values in problem solving; perceived constraints; and the nature of superintendents' solution processes. Comparisons are made between superintendents and principals and between superintendents and senior executives

A version of this paper was published previously as K. Leithwood, and R. Steinbach. 1991. Components of chief education officers' problem-solving processes. In K. Leithwood, and D. Musella (eds.), *Understanding school system administration* (pp. 127–153). London: Falmer Press. Reproduced with permission.

*in nonschool organizations. Superintendents' individual prob-
lem solving appeared to be more like the problem solving of other
senior executives than that of principals. A number of explanations are offered for these similarities.*

administration is the profession of leadership, the art of intelligent coping with an arbitrary fate. It is a minor matter; but
our prospects for human control over events are built on collec-
tions of minor matters. (March, 1974, p. 17)

Both Bridges (1982) and Crowson (1987) have pointed to the
lack of knowledge about the effects superintendents have on their
school systems and about the nature of their practices. Nevertheless,
there are signs of growing attention to this vacuum; this is evident,
for example, in the work of Coleman and LaRocque (1987), Rosenholtz (1989), Peterson, Murphy, and Halliday (1987), and Louis
(1987). Given the considerable payoff from efforts over the past
decade to better appreciate the nature, causes, and consequences of
what principals do (for a review, see Leithwood, Begley, and Cousins,
1990), turning attention to the superintendent's role seems timely
and potentially productive in continuing efforts to foster educational
improvement through administrative practices.

It also seems timely and productive to ask what has been
learned in the study of school principals that might enhance subsequent study of superintendents. As related to principals' practices,
we believe one relevant "observation" is that descriptions of overt behavior have proven to be of little practical or theoretical value. Studies of the overt behavior of effective principals, for example, were
frequently intended to provide models of exemplary practices which
others might emulate. Such studies, often conducted within one type
of school (urban, elementary, students with low SES), failed to acknowledge the contingent nature of administrative practice, however. Specific overt behaviors attributed to principals in one school
or one type of school were more or less effective depending on a host
of at least partly unique conditions related to the school's history,
parental expectations, school district characteristics, staff compe-
tencies, and the like. Descriptions of categories of overt behaviors
common among principals across schools were sufficiently abstract
as to be largely meaningless guides to action.

Of much more value than research resulting in descriptions of
overt behavior have been studies aimed at understanding the roots

of such behavior. Through such work, we have come to appreciate the importance of the covert mental processes that are part of principals' solutions to whatever administrative problems they encounter wherever they happen to be working. Such processes demonstrate, for example, an important role for the principals' vision of what their school could be (e.g., Stevens, 1987), their own professional goals (Leithwood and Montgomery, 1986), the quality of their reasoning processes (e.g., Leithwood and Stager, 1989), and the values they use as standards for evaluating both the actions they take and the ends they are trying to accomplish (e.g., Begley, 1987; Campbell, 1988).

In an attempt to benefit from these experiences with research on principals, we sought to better understand the nature of what superintendents do through an examination of their problem-solving processes. Our initial study (Leithwood, 1988) of such processes focused on how superintendents classify, manage, and give priority to their problems, as well as on factors which influence these processes. The purpose of the present study was to describe, more comprehensively, superintendents' problem solving from the early stages of noticing the existence of a problem through the steps taken to solve it.

Framework

The study was guided by a general orientation to research on problem solving and the specific outcomes of applying that orientation to the study of school administration.

General Orientation

The adoption of a problem-solving perspective on educational administration, although rare, is not new. Hemphill (1958) saw value in such a perspective thirty years ago. At that time, however, theories of problem solving were extremely primitive, avoided direct attention to basic cognitive processes involved in problem solving, and were grounded in very little empirical evidence. All of these limitations are evident in Hemphill's formulation, which appears to have stimulated little subsequent research. Theories of problem solving are no longer so limited, however, largely due to advances in cognitive science over the past decade. Consequently, an information processing conception of problem solving was adopted as a general orientation for this study and its predecessor (Leithwood, 1988). In the previous chapter we described, in a general way, what it means to adopt, as we have, an information-processing-oriented research on problem solving. In that chapter, we also provided a rationale for focusing our attention on the study of ill-structured problems in knowledge-lean domains. In addition to type of problem and its relationship to solver's knowledge, the context in which administrators' problems were solved (i.e., whether alone or not) is an important determinant of the process involved. Clark and Peterson (1986), in a review of teachers' thought processes, indicate that there appeared to be an important distinction between the kind of thinking that teachers do during classroom interaction and that done before and after such interaction. Presumably, there is an analogous distinction to be made for administrators. Shulman and Carey (1984) reviewed evidence concerning the number of people involved in problem solving and provided a theoretical argument for the importance of this dimension based on Simon's (1957) conception of bounded rationality; the limits on an individual's problem-solving ability, imposed by the boundaries of his/her information processing capabilities, can potentially be extended through group problem-solving processes.

The amount of empirical research on administrative problem solving, in an educational context, is extremely modest. Results of our previous research with principals were used as a framework for this study. These results provided not only tentative directions for inquiry into superintendents' problem-solving processes; direct comparisons of processes used by principals and superintendents also seemed likely to help understand the nature and extent of influence on administrative problem solving of role and organizational context. This study of superintendents used the same five-component model (interpretation, goals, principles, constraints, and solution processes) as the basis for data coding but with two refinements. One modest refinement was to reconceptualize constraints to problem solvers as obstacles to be overcome in problem solving—not necessarily insurmountable. Viewed this way, the ability to anticipate difficulties seems likely to be an attribute of an effective problem solver.

A second, more fundamental refinement of the original problem-solving model for this study was to narrow the conception of "principles" to values. After Rokeach and Hofstede (cited in Hambrick and Brandon, 1988), a value was defined as "a broad and relatively enduring preference for some state of affairs" (p. 5). Based on recent research with principals (Begley and Leithwood, 1989; Campbell, 1988) and a review of values literature, a classification of values potentially relevant to administrators was used as the basis for analyzing data related to values in the present study. This classification system includes four major categories of values and some 16 specific values within these categories.

Building on this prior research with principals, this study addressed five specific questions:

- How do superintendents interpret the problems which they encounter?

- What type and how many goals do superintendents pursue in their problem solving?

- What is the nature and role of values in superintendents' problem solving?

- What constraints to problem solving are perceived by superintendents and how are they dealt with?

- What are the main features of superintendents' solution processes?

Method

Sample

Eight superintendents were selected for the study to ensure variation in length of time as superintendents (from two to 13 years, average = six years), size of school systems administered (from 10,000 students to one of the largest in Canada), and gender (two were women); these three variables were viewed as potential influences on problem solving although the sample was too small to permit an analysis of the relationship between these variables and superintendents' problem solving. Biographical information collected at the beginning of a previous interview indicated that five superintendents had prior in-school experience at the elementary level, two at the secondary level, and one at both levels. All but one superintendent had entered the role from the assistant superintendent's position; one had entered from an assistant deputy minister's position in the Ministry of Education. Three superintendents had worked in faculties of education at an earlier point in their careers and at least two had been superintendents in other school systems prior to their current posts.

Data Collection Procedures

Data were collected through two interviews, each lasting from 45 minutes to about three hours. In the first interview, superintendents were asked to perform a problem-sorting task; to reflect on their own problem solving and the factors influencing it; and to indicate how they selected which problems, of the many they faced, deserved priority. Results of this interview and related data are reported in Chapter 7.

In the second interview, superintendents were asked to rank a set of six brief problems (see Table 4.1) in terms of the clarity, at the outset, of each possible course of action; to present, in as much detail as possible, their thinking regarding solutions to the clearest and least-clear problems; and to describe from their own experience problems similar in degree of clarity to each of these. The solutions to the two problems, from the set of six presented, chosen by each superintendent as least and most clear constituted the data on which this chapter is based (as with the principals, the terms "clear" and "unclear" were judged to be the closest synonyms in ordinary discourse to the terms "structured" and "unstructured" and hence were used in the interview). Each interview was tape recorded and verbatim transcripts were made.

Data Analysis Procedures

A coding system, originally developed for research with principals, was adapted and applied to the transcripts, initially by one analyst. Statements which could not be coded with confidence by the initial researcher were given to a second and a consensus was reached on their coding. Subsequently, the reliability of this coding was tested by having two independent analysts code a sample of 25 statements. There was 92 percent agreement between these two researchers.

Table 4.1   Problems Presented to Superintendents

Violence in the Schools	Evidence mounts daily of a dramatic increase in violence in the high schools in your board. There are reports, from principals and police, of incidents involving youth gangs who have attacked or threatened students in at least half the high schools in the system. These gangs, it is reported, belong primarily to one ethnic group.
Problem Principal	One of the principals in your board has been charged by the police with possession of marijuana for the purpose of trafficking. When his case comes up, the judge discharges him for lack of evidence. What should you do in this situation?

Table 4.1   Problems Presented to Superintendents

New Policy	Although you have personally been aware of the need for a policy regarding race relations for some time, your board as a whole has not felt the need to have one. However, in response to a Ministry initiative, the board does vote to have you develop and implement such a policy. How would you proceed with this task?
Trustee Disagreement	As a new [superintendent], you discover that there appears to be considerable disagreement among the members of your board concerning the board's budget. A number of trustees appear to want you to take action on trimming the budget, because both educational taxes and teachers' salaries are relatively high in the board. However, a smaller but significant group of trustees do not want change. They are strongly committed to the existing policies and practices of the board, even though they are costly. What would you do in this situation?
Staff Morality	You have been aware that there has been some concern from some trustees regarding the morals and behavior of some board employees. However, you are unprepared when, late at night, they suddenly move, second, and pass the motion that the [superintendent] be requested to develop a code of behavior for all board staff. At least some of the trustees support the motion of developing some sort of checklist, so that employees would lose demerit points for various infractions. What could you do?
Walkouts	Negotiations in your school district have been going slowly and morale has deteriorated. The union has been increasingly militant, threatening work stoppages and resorting to various kinds of harassment. Teachers have called in sick and withheld the usual kinds of cooperation found in school. Suddenly things take a turn for the worse; two principals call to say that all their teachers have walked out in midmorning. At these two schools, the union representative gave the principal a half hour's warning of the walkout. What would you do?

Results and Discussion

Results of analyzing protocol data from the eight superintendents are described in five sections corresponding to the specific research questions.

How Superintendents Interpret Problems

Statements classified as "interpretation" were those which indicated how superintendents were attempting to clarify the nature of the problem. Specifically defined as interpretation were statements concerning (a) the reasons for awarding priority to a problem; (b) the reasons why a problem was considered difficult or easy, complex or simple; and (c) ways of understanding the problem. Anecdotes used by superintendents to explain their understanding of problems (d) were also coded as interpretation.

Superintendents demonstrated a reasonably high level of consistency in the choices of problems which they considered most and least difficult and complex. As the most-structured problems, four superintendents chose the New Policy on race relations, three chose Trustee Disagreement, and one chose the Problem Principal. As the least-clear problems, four superintendents chose Walkouts, three chose Violence in the Schools and one superintendent chose Staff Morality. No problem identified as most clear was identified as least clear by anyone and vice versa (this is in contrast with results from our studies of principals [see Chapter 3] in which there was no such uniformity in the labeling of problems).

In reference to the most-structured problems, none of the superintendents provided data about the conditions that would make such a problem a high priority. For least-structured problems, the need for immediate action (two superintendents) and the need to prevent the problem from getting any worse (one superintendent) were identified as conditions that would increase the priority of such a problem.

In Table 4.2 we identify the criteria on which the superintendents' definition of problem structure (difficulty, complexity) was based. Structured (easy, simple, clear) problems, were, in superintendents' terms, "straightforward"; this seemed to mean that the superintendent was familiar with at least some aspect of the problem already—the general topic, or the background of the problem. In response to the Trustee Disagreement problem, one superintendent noted:

Table 4.2   Bases on Which Superintendents Determined Problem Difficulty and Complexity (Structure)

NUMBER OF SUPT'S	BASIS FOR DEFINING "STRUCTURED" PROBLEMS	NUMBER OF SUPT'S	BASIS FOR DEFINING "UNSTRUCTURED" PROBLEMS
8	• frequent occurrence, familar topic	6	• unfamiliar, lots of unknowns, complexity of decision
1	• "factual" problem	2	• lack of background information
1	• superintendents' responsibility is clear	3	• no immediate solution is likely
2	• not a crisis or emergency	1	• involves people's feelings
5	• "mechanism" or procedure "in place"	1	• philosophically "uncomfortable"
		3	• number of people/ groups involved
		2	• affects parents and other nonstaff
		2	• dire or unpredictable consequences
		1	• problem encountered at advanced stage

this is a familiar kind of scenario. And it often comes up in boards where you've got an old guard component and some newer trustees who are gung-ho and want to move and the old guard is sort of reflecting what they think is the community standard and don't like these renegades . . . spending all their money.

Clarity was also a function of a problem involving primarily matters of "fact" as opposed to feelings (e.g., "I never have any more difficulty than with the human problems") and the superintendent's level of responsibility for solving the problem. Problems which did not require immediate solution and for which a routine solution procedure was in place also were seen as structured.

Problems were defined as unstructured (difficult, complex, unclear) when important aspects of the problem reduced the superintendents' perceived ability to control the problem-solving process. Such a perception was partly a function of lack of information of various sorts. For example, in response to the Staff Morality problem, a superintendent noted: "the thing that's completely unclear here is what is being defined as staff morality. Are we talking about after-hours activity, are we talking about one teacher. . . . ?" Lack of control was also a function of high levels of complexity in decisions that might be required as part of the problem solving, large numbers of people involved (especially nonstaff), and low probability of finding a solution, perhaps because the problem had become greatly exacerbated prior to the superintendent encountering it. In response to the Walkout problem, for example, one superintendent commented: "you're facing a fait accomplis now. And they are out of school and the decison has to be made." Problems also were viewed as unstructured when people's feelings were a central part of the problem; when the likely outcome of the problem was unpredictable or "dire," or when the problem involved values and beliefs in conflict with those of the superintendent ("philosophically uncomfortable").

Superintendents used two strategies to understand the problem better, whether they viewed the problem as structured or unstructured. The most frequently used strategy was to relate the problem to similar experiences encountered in the past; this strategy was used by six of the eight superintendents in response to clear problems and two superintendents in response to unclear problems. One superintendent said, for example:

> The walkout [problem] is a very difficult one because it's very complex and the problem I have answering it is one that I have actually lived through. It didn't have to do with negotiations but it had to do with the reported closure of a school and in this case the staff walked out of their classes.

Three superintendents also decomposed or unpacked problems (e.g., " you have to approach this problem from two standpoints") or rephrased problems in their own terms in order to better understand them. For unclear problems, in addition to the two strategies already mentioned, one superintendent examined immediate effects. In response to the walkout problem, that superintendent pointed out:

> the public has a keen interest in this, so, right away, when you are talking about what principals and teachers do you directly affect the students and the parents, . . . there will not be enough telephone lines just to satisfy the communication

process . . . and I'm not even touching what the solution is. I'm just talking to you about the immediate effect.

One superintendent also identified alternative possible causes and made sure that all the necessary facts were available (e.g., "you have to find the information first"). Another superintendent also considered carefully who "owned" the problem.

One superintendent sought to better understand the clearest problem by searching for an existing problem-solving procedure.

Superintendents' use of anecdotes was extremely limited in relation to the interpretation of either structured or unstructured problems; three superintendents used analogies or comparisons with relevant existing policies as a way of clarifying clear problems. No use was made of anecdotes in relation to unclear problems.

In Chapter 7 we examine problem interpretation processes in more detail. Here we note several similarities and differences between superintendents and principals (as already reported in Chapter 3). First, like superintendents, time lines and the number of people affected by a problem influenced its priority for principals. But the people concerned, in the case of principals, tended to be students and others in the school, whereas superintendents did not explictly mention students but did focus on trustees. Second, both superintendents and principals judged problems as difficult when many people were involved in the solution, no immediate solution was evident, and the problem had significant emotional content. Principals, like superintendents, also identified value conflicts as an element in their perception of problem difficulty. Expert principals, as well, saw problems as difficult when they required careful thought and planning. Superintendents did not show much evidence of requiring such thought and planning; indeed their problem-solving processes overall seemed less sensitive to problem clarity than did the processes used by principals.

Finally, like expert and typical principals, superintendents attempted to better understand the nature of problems by drawing on past, relevant experiences and by ensuring all necessary information was available. Superintendents identified a number of additional procedures, however: rephrasing the problem, searching for existing procedures, examining probable immediate effects, and identifying alternative causes. Whereas expert principals made frequent use of relevant anecdotes (or analogies) to understand the problem, this tactic appeared not to be used by superintendents.

In sum, available evidence suggests that superintendents possess a relatively extensive array of strategies for interpreting their problems. Many of these strategies are similar to those used by expert principals but the number of strategies used by superintendents appears to be somewhat greater. In this respect, superintendents appeared similar to Isenberg's (1987) general managers who devoted more of their mental resources to initially defining and framing their problems than did a less-experienced control group. In addition, superintendents' interpretation strategies, as compared with expert principals, were applied in a more automatic fashion and were more closely attuned to the larger school system and political climate which constitutes their work environment.

Nature and Number of Goals For Problem Solving

Statements classified as goals were those which indicated the relatively immediate ends to be served by the superintendents' problem solving, either the overall problem solution or some significant stage in the solution process. Of interest were both the nature and number of superintendents' goals.

Evident in the nature of superintendents' goals was the distinction between those primarily concerned with aspects of the problem-solving process and those concerned with the outcome (process vs. product goals). Process goals were usually of two types. One type was aimed at ensuring that members of the organization played appropriate roles in the problem-solving process. In response to the Violence in the Schools problem, for example, one superintendent's goal was: "[to mobilize principals] to look clearly at the problem and decide upon their own methods of dealing with it." The Trustee Disagreement problem was viewed by several superintendents as an opportunity for educating trustees in their role: "make sure the trustees all recognize that at any particular time they are not all going to think alike"; "set up a series of in-services for the trustees." This concern for playing appropriate roles in problem solving might be seen as part of a more fundamental, secondary goal of superintendents—to control the problem-solving process. As one superintendent said when confronted with the New Policy problem, "[don't leave it open ended] so we're managing it to some extent and we have fewer suprises." This control theme is evident, as well, in such other comments as:

- "the very best thing is the communication. You have to have very central control of every aspect of your operation" (Walkouts);

- "Let the politicians fight amongst themselves, once all the work has been done" (Trustee Disagreement);

- "make sure both the minority and majority [of trustees] understood that the process is sound" (Trustee Disagreement).

Problems directly involving trustees elicited more expression of control-oriented goals than did other sorts of problems.

Product goals also appeared to be of two sorts. One sort, usually implicit in the superintendents' statements, was to solve the problem as requested, for example, to comply with the trustees' request in the case of the New Policy problem. A second type of product goal, explicit in superintendents' remarks, was to ensure that certain key subgoals, critical to a successful overall solution, were achieved. For example:

- "I think that we have to give a lot of concentration to finding out the diffused frustrations that exist at that level" (Violence in the Schools);

- "I would have to deal with the immediate [situation] of the school and the children" (Walkouts);

- "Have those reports or items on a special list—in order of priority, or in any order, to help the trustees rank order" (Trustee Disagreement).

Twenty-four goal statements were generated by the eight superintendents in response to the total set of six hypothetical problems. This amounts to about four goals per problem with a range of two to five. Although there were many subgoals not counted, it seems clear that superintendents did not generate very many explicit goals and they never used the term *goal* or a reasonable facsimile in talking about their problem solving.

Problem clarity or structure did not appear to make any difference in the number of goals generated. Each set of three least-clear and three most-clear problems elicited 12 goal statements.

Number of goals elicited from superintendents did vary when the nature of the goals (process vs. product) was considered in relation to problem structure or clarity. The set of three least-clear problems generated twice as many process as product goals (eight vs. four). In contrast, the set of three most-clear problems produced twice as many product as process goals (eight vs. four). This suggests that superintendents responded to lack of problem clarity by attending to what they considered to be crucial aspects of the problem-solving process in order to ensure a satisfactory resolution. Problem clarity meant the superintendent could envision a satisfactory outcome, perhaps, as well as the process for arriving at it.

Isenberg (1987) claims that, by definition, unstructured problems are likely to have multiple goals; such goals may be conflicting with inherent trade-offs. Data from our study of expert principals (Chapter 3) suggested that they responded to such multiplicity and conflict by focusing on people and groups. Expert principals' goals acknowledged the various stakeholders in the problem and espoused a relatively large number of product goals balanced among these stakeholders, with special attention to students.

Data from the present study imply that, in this goal-setting component of their problem solving, superintendents' responses to unclear problems were more like the responses of other senior managers than those of expert principals. They set relatively fewer goals and these goals were dominated by a concern for process. Such practice is consistent with Isenberg's (1987) finding that senior managers appeared to think and act in close tandem. For them "the process of thinking through a problem involved attempting to solve it, and only through its solution could anything approximating true understanding emerge" (p. 180).

Nature and Role of Values in Problem Solving

Statements classified as values reflected, as we noted above, a broad and relatively enduring preference for some state of affairs. Our system for coding such statements was keyed to the four categories of values mentioned earlier: basic human values, general moral values, professional values, and social and political values. Data analysis aimed to clarify both the nature and function of superintendents' values in problem solving.

In Table 4.3 we report the frequency of occurrence in the protocols of statements coded according to the four categories of values (described more fully in Chapter 8). As a means of clarifying the nature of values considered by superintendents in their problem solving we considered first the broad categories and then the specific values within each category. Finally, we examined the overall ranking of specific values.

More than 50 percent of all value statements (41 of 81) were coded as Professional Values and about one-quarter (21 of 81) were coded as Social and Political Values. General Moral Values and Basic Human Values accounted for the remaining value statements (14 percent and 10 percent respectively). Superintendents showed rela-

Table 4.3   The Frequency of Different Types of Value Statements Made by Superintendents in Response to Most and Least Clear Problems

CATEGORIES OF VALUES	FREQUENCY MOST CLEAR	LEAST CLEAR	TOTAL	RANK
1. Basic Human Values				
1.1 Freedom	1	0	1	7
1.2 Happiness	0	0	0	8
1.3 Knowledge	0	4	4	4
1.4 Respect for Others	2	1	3	5
1.5 Survival	0	0	0	8
2. General Moral Values				
2.1 Carefulness	2	0	2	6
2.2 Fairness (or justice)	5	4	9	2
2.3 Courage	0	0	0	8
3. Professional Values				
3.1 General responsibility as educator	1	1	2	6
3.2 Specific role responsibility	16	15	31	1
3.3 Consequences for Immediate Clients (students, parents, staff)	2	6	8	3
3.4 Consequences for others (community, society-at-large)	0	0	0	8
4. Social and Political Values				
4.1 Participation	4	4	8	3
4.2 Sharing	0	2	2	6
4.3 Loyalty, Solidarity, and Commitment	2	6	8	3
4.4 Helping others	2	1	3	5
TOTAL	**37**	**44**	**81**	

tively extensive use of some specific values within each category and little or no use of others. Within the category Basic Human Values, Knowledge and Respect for Others received modest use; there was virtually no evidence of use of Freedom, Happiness, or Survival. Fairness was the only frequently (9) used General Moral Value, although Carefulness was mentioned twice. The category Professional Values was dominated by superintendents' sense of their own Specific Role Responsibilities (mentioned 31 times). Consequences for Immediate Clients was mentioned 8 times. Use was made of all the specific values associated with Social and Political Values; Participation and Loyalty, Solidarity, and Commitment were most frequently used, however (mentioned eight times each).

The right-hand column of Table 4.3 ranks specific values without reference to their broader classification. Ranked highest, the superintendents' sense of their Specific Role Responsibility was mentioned at least three times more frequently than any other specific value. The form this value took is evident in these statements:

- "I wouldn't even be involved with it. I have two superintendents that are the resources to that committee" (New Policy);

- "and I was sitting there as what we call a principle resource person" (Trustee Disagreement);

- "[I would probably be] involved initially but [would be] making a determination of some kind of role that I would play as you get more information" (Violence in the Schools).

A cluster of specific values from three different value categories were ranked second and third and appeared about equally as frequently. These include:

- Fairness (e.g., "once a decision . . . is made, that we recognize that the process was fair and that somebody didn't get their own way");

- Consequences for Immediate Clients (e.g., "if these were generally known [i.e., Violence in Schools] . . . and parents were afraid to send their children to school because of this, then the [superintendent] would make a statement to the press");

- Participation (e.g., "I would have that meeting right away . . . and try to work with [the principals] and the [assistant superintendents] on what we feel can be done");

- Loyalty, Solidarity, and Commitment (e.g., "the nature of the talk [with staff] would be positive and constructive and as forward looking as possible . . . and try to get people back together again").

Responses by superintendents demonstrated the generally acknowledged role of values as broad guidelines for action and as standards against which the goodness of a solution or solution process is judged. Our data, however, provided only modest support for the more frequent use of values in response to unstructured or least-clear problems: 37 value statements in response to most-clear problems and 44 value statements in response to least-clear problems.

Finally, there were no statements made that could not be accommodated within the a priori categories of values.

As compared with principals (Begley, 1987; Campbell, 1988), superintendents in the present study demonstrated a similar, strong commitment to most of the specific values in the category Social and Political Values. Superintendents differed from principals, however, in a number of ways: they showed a more uniform use of values whether problems were defined as most or least clear; they identified consequences less frequently as a value guiding their problem solving; and they used as a value much more frequently their own understanding of their specific role responsibilities.

While the framework used in this study appeared to capture superintendents' values satisfactorily, it has several significant differences in comparison with an alternative framework developed by Hambrick and Brandon (1988) to guide the study of executive behavior. The Hambrick and Brandon framework consists of six broad categories of values, four of which also appear in our framework. Their fifth category, "materialism" (to value wealth and pleasing possessions), does not appear in our framework because our earlier data from principals found no evidence of this value. The present study of superintendents provides no support for its inclusion, either. More support can be found for the Hambrick and Brandon category "power" (to value control of situations and people). Control was a strong theme in the superintendent data, which we coded as Goals. However, its pervasiveness probably warrants reconceptualizing the theme as an expression of a value and expanding our values framework accordingly.

Perception of and Responses to Constraints

Statements classified as "constraints" indicated the superintendents' awareness or anticipation of an obstacle that might be encountered in working out a solution. Data were summarized to indicate the number and nature of constraints identified by superintendents as well as the superintendents' general orientation to constraints.

The eight superintendents identified a relatively small number of constraints: 11 in response to the most-clear problems (Trustee Disagreement, New Policy) and nine in response to the least-clear problems (Violence in the Schools, Walkouts). For the most-clear problems, three superintendents did not cite any constraints, one identified one, two cited two, and two cited three constraints. In the case of the least-clear problems, seven superintendent's identified one constraint. Two constraints were identified by one superintendent.

Five different types of constraints were included in superintendents' responses to the most-clear problems. One such constraint, not viewed as serious, was limitations on the superintendent's authority. For example, one superintendent, in response to the Trustee Disagreement problem, outlined a long-term solution involving educating the trustees in board priority-setting prior to entering into budget decisions. He concluded, however, by noting:

> I don't know that there is much more that the [superintendent] can do. If you have provided all the information, you've made every reasonable effort to educate them in terms of what needs to be done and their responsibility as a trustee, I think you have to live with the results.

Other types of constraints included lack of information about the background to the problem and possible opposition from other people or groups. An example of the latter type of constraint is evident in one superintendent's response to the New Policy problem:

> a typical kind of complication is that some . . . representative of some group, real or otherwise, is likely to phone in or write and say: "Listen, I've heard that you're developing this policy. I'm an expert on it and I'd like to be involved." And that person may indeed by very effective in helping or may be a real problem because they've got a single issue that they want to promote and could really complicate the development of the policy.

A final constraint identified (by three superintendents) in response to most-clear problems was organizational policies and practices and the limitations they created in how flexibly one could approach a problem.

In response to least-clear problems, superintendents identified two of the five constraints already discussed—lack of information (three superintendents) and opposition from other people or groups (two superintendents). Other types of constraints included the personalities of specific people involved in problem solving and lack of existing guidelines to help manage the problem (e.g., "the parameters of the problem would have to be far more clearly set out before I even begin to tackle the problem" [Staff Morality]).

Constraints identified by superintendents ranged in nature from those they considered relatively minor (e.g., limitations on their own authority) to those that were potentially quite disruptive (e.g., opposition of others). Nevertheless, virtually all superintendents viewed constraints as an inevitable part of problem solving—things to anticipate but not to prevent one from getting on with the job. Therefore, for each constraint, they also generated an approach for dealing with it. In response to the Walkout problem, for example, one superintendent readily generated contingency plans in case the teachers refused to go back to their classes (as he had directed the principal to request), in case they wanted to meet with him during school hours, in case they wanted more information about negotiations, and the like.

Because constraints were conceptualized differently in the present study than in our previous studies of principals, it is possible to compare superintendents' responses with those of principals in only a limited way. Both expert principals and superintendents similarly viewed constraints as subproblems to be solved, not insurmountable hurdles. We are unaware of data about constraints from other types of senior managers which would permit a comparison with the superintendent data.

Main Features of Superintendents' Solution Processes

Statements about the relatively specific actions or sequences of actions superintendents would take once the problem was interpreted were labeled "solution processes." By way of example, one superintendent's response to the unclear Violence in the Schools problem included eight actions:

- Check the facts with several sources including the principals;
- Discuss the problem with police and other social agencies;
- Check for relevant information in the media;
- Arrange a meeting with police, social agencies, and responsible members of ethnic groups;
- Elicit the support of these groups in finding a solution;
- Try to develop a common understanding of the problem;

- Determine the school's role in solving the problem;

- Search out key players to take an active role in solving the problem.

The mean number of actions identified by all superintendents in response to the set of three unclear problems was 8.5.

In response to a clear problem, Trustee Disagreement, another superintendent outlined five actions:

- Provide trustees with information about the meaning of a high-quality education;

- Discuss with trustees the setting of budget priorities based on educational goals;

- Provide information to assist trustees in setting priorities;

- Educate trustees regarding their responsibilities;

- Accept the results of whatever decisions are made by trustees after these actions.

Superintendents identified, on average, 6.9 actions in response to the set of three clear problems.

In Table 4.4 we summarize the number of superintendents who responded in particular ways to five additional aspects of solution processes. These data indicate a strong propensity for forward planning in response to either clear or unclear problems with some circular, nonlinear or iterative planning activity among three superintendents. Only one superintendent divided a problem into subproblems. The sources of their solution processes depended a good deal on problem clarity. In the case of clear problems, there was usually an existing procedure that could be used, at least in adapted form (seven superintendents). Least-clear problems demanded more invention for at least three superintendents.

Least-clear problems also led to either extensive or modest information collection by the majority of superintendents (six) and extensive consultation with others as part of the solution process (six). Irrespective of problem clarity, however, there was little evidence of planning for follow-up, that is, monitoring the solution and evaluating its success.

Superintendents' solution processes were similar, in a number of ways, to those of expert principals (see Chapter 3). Both groups attempted to consult all those with a stake in the problem and saw information collection as an important action. Although more visible among expert principals, neither group gave much attention to mon-

Table 4.4   Elements of Superintendents' Solution Processes

ELEMENTS		MOST-CLEAR PROBLEMS	LEAST-CLEAR PROBLEMS
1.	**Direction of solution process planning***		
1.1	forward planning	8	7
1.2	backward planning	—	—
1.3	iterative	3	3
1.4	decomposes problem	—	1
2.	**Source of solution process plan**		
2.1	existing institutionalized procedures	4	1
2.2	adaptation of procedures	3	1
2.3	novel process	—	3
2.4	can't tell	1	3
3.	**Evidence of attention to information collection as part of solution process**		
3.1	extensive	1	3
3.2	modest	3	3
3.3	none	4	2
4.	**Consultation with others as part of solution process**		
4.1	extensive	2	6
4.2	modest	5	1
4.3	none	1	1
5.	**Evidence of planning for follow-up**		
5.1	yes	2	1
5.2	no	6	7

* For this element some superintendents' solution processes fall into two categories.

itoring and following up the consequences of their solutions. For the most part, expert principals generated a larger number of more-detailed actions as part of their solution processes than did superintendents; they appeared to plan more extensively.

In the context of studying the thinking of senior managers, Isenberg (1987) depicts the solution processes for unclear administrative problems as involving multiple paths toward solutions which are not initially identifiable. Further, attempted solutions often changed the originally perceived causes of the problem and feedback about success or progress was slow and often ambiguous. In the face of such problems, Isenberg claims that senior managers typically reject a hierarchical model of action planning, a model others have labeled "backward planning." This model begins with general goals and systematically refines the related subgoals until specific actions have been identified; actions are then implemented. Such backward planning was not strongly evident in our data from either expert principals or superintendents. However, the more detailed action steps and greater number of goals suggest that principals were more inclined in that direction than were superintendents.

The solution processes of superintendents, like other senior managers in Isenberg's (1987) study, more closely approximated an opportunistic model. This model assumes that:

> the plan develops incrementally, there is jumping around within the planning space, several unrelated specific sequences are planned without linking them together, . . . priorities may be ignored at any one point, and each new decision produces a new situation. (p. 190)

Opportunistic planning requires an active, flexible memory, the ability to make new connections among previously unrelated phenomena, and a positive attitude toward exploiting possibilities, some of them surprising. Such planning also requires the ability to simulate action-result sequences during implementation because they cannot all be planned in advance. This pattern seems similar to the one advocated by Hayes (1981) as a way to solve ill-defined problems. "[It may be necessary] to jump into the problem before we fully understand it. Very often the real nature of a problem is hidden from us until we actually try to solve it" (p. 22).

Acknowledging that, from time to time, some senior managers do engage in planning more like the hierarchical model, Isenberg (1987) describes a third model that seems to take advantage of the strengths of the other two (clear direction, flexible action), while avoiding their weaknesses. Labeled "strategic opportunism," this model combines a clear understanding of one's general or long-term purposes and how a person takes advantage of opportunities that arise to achieve these goals. Senior managers show signs of using this model, claims Isenberg, as they move back and forth between relatively abstract strategies, goals, and policies and quite specific thinking about specific people and organizational processes. Superintendents' extensive use of values, as distinct from short-term goals, in solving both clear and unclear problems may be evidence of clear long-term general directions; their consideration of a small number of specific action sequences may suggest that they are sensitive to both the unanticipated issues that will arise as they begin the solution process and the futility of excessive prior planning.

Conclusion

It would be tempting, but inadvisable, to overinterpret the results of this study. Because the collection and analysis of protocol data is time consuming, expensive, and effortful, the study only provided data about the thinking of a small number of superintendents. Furthermore, as Ericsson and Simon (1984) have pointed out so well, protocol data vary widely in their ability to capture thought processes depending on how they are collected. Additional types and amounts of such data are needed to bolster confidence in results of the current study. With this in mind, we sum up the study, offer several additional interpretive observations, and point to areas for future research.

At the outset, the need for this study was rationalized on the grounds that descriptions of overt administrative behavior by themselves contribute little to either understanding administrative practice or improving it. Such understanding and improvement, it was argued, depended on a better appreciation of how administrators think about the wide variety of problems they face in the wide variety of contexts they encounter. An information-processing orientation to problem solving was adopted as a general framework for the research. This orientation had been used in our previous and ongoing research with principals and Schwenk (1988) has argued for the value of such a perspective in understanding the strategic decision making of senior executives.

The specific framework used to generate research questions for the study was a model of problem-solving components which emerged from a study with principals (Leithwood and Stager, 1989, 1986). The components of the model included interpretation, goals, values, constraints, and solution processes. Results of the present study appeared to be interpretable within this overall model with one addition, not yet discussed. Throughout their simulated problem solving, superintendents exuded an unmistakable air of self-confidence. This was more evident in what they did not say than what they did say. For example, none of the superintendents, in spite of identifying certain problems as complex, difficult, unclear, or messy, expressed any doubt about being able to manage these problems, nor did they show any signs of anxiety or tension. The same air of assurance was evident among expert (but not typical) principals in the study described in Chapter 3, as well. We are not the first to notice this quality; Klemp and McClelland (1986) identify it as a "generic competence" for senior managers indicated by the manager who: "sees self as prime-mover, leader, or energizer of the organization; mentions being stimulated by crises and other difficult problems; sees self as the most capable person to get the job done" (p. 41). As well as adding self-confidence (or mood) as a component to the general model, further theoretical and empirical work needs to be devoted to clarifying the relationships among the model's components. So far, these relationships have not been explored in detail.

Data related to specific components of the model indicated similiarities as well as differences between expert principals and superintendents. Some of these differences appear to be a function of work context. For example, because superintendents have considerable resources for problem solving, they can assume the routine availability of adequate information which principals have to more self-consciously seek out. Furthermore, since there appears to be much that is similar in the problem solving of superintendents and senior managers in other fields, this lends support to the idea that one's position in the organization (work context) may be a significant factor in accounting for variation in problem-solving processes. Other differences may be a function of experience. Superintendents, for example, show more signs of "opportunistic planning" if not "strategic opportunism" than do principals. Perhaps they have better learned the importance of fundamental directions (as their use of values suggests) and the capricious nature of their environment (which makes backward planning frequently a waste of time).

Another observed difference between superintendents and principals might also be due to experience. Whereas expert and typical principals solved well-structured problems similarly, there were significant differences between them in the solutions to ill-structured problems. In contrast, the superintendents in our sample showed no such distinction between well- and ill-structured problems for several components in the problem-solving model. Even for the problems they called "very complex," there was very little evidence of grappling with dilemmas. (This might also be a manifestation of their observed self-confidence.) It is as if the superintendents are able to translate difficult problems into familiar scenarios which can then be treated as routine problems. In fact, at the end of their solutions to the least-clear problems, two superintendents stated that the problems were not so hard after all.

On the whole, the results of this research indicate that senior school administrators appear to operate more like senior managers in other fields than like principals. In contrast to principals, superintendents spend more time interpreting the problem, use more values or principles to direct their problem solving, have fewer explicit "product" goals, and plan fewer steps in the solution process.

One interpretation of these differences is that superintendents are more concerned with the process of problem solving than with the actual details of the solution. Whether this is a function of work context, experience, or personality (the game is more fascinating) remains to be seen. Nevertheless, it seems that superintendents behave as if they believe that, if the process is right (and they work hard to ensure that it is), the outcome will be fine. One superintendent captured this sentiment well:

> And that's a key role for the director, is finding things, just looking at things with this broad look, that nobody else has in the system. Nobody else can have the broad look that the director has, and that's one of the most important parts of the director's role, is to have a finger in every pie. You've got to know what's going on. . . . So you don't look at the detail, but you can see the gestalt, and you can try to find things that will not fit.

In terms of future research directions, two have already been identified. One direction is simply to increase sample sizes and the variety of data used. A second direction involves exploring, more explicitly, relations among components in the problem-solving model. This is likely to involve developing a series of lower-order models, an example of which is provided by Hambrick and Brandon (1988). They conceptualized the relationship between values and solution processes by initially hypothesizing both direct ("behavior channeling") and indirect relationships (values affect solution processes through their influence on whether and how "stimuli" are perceived). Finally, this study assumed that all superintendents in the sample had comparable expertise. In fact, this is not any more likely than it would be in relation to any role, and we developed our own opinions about the relative levels of problem-solving expertise possessed by the eight superintendents in the sample. If the aim of improving superintendent problem solving is to be taken seriously, it will be necessary to undertake future research with superintendents who are known to be exceptionally expert at what they do. In Chapter 6 we describe the results of one such study.

Chapter 5

Processes Used by Expert and Typical Principals to Solve Problems in Groups

Much of the problem solving engaged in by educational admin-istrators occurs in a social context; that is, with one or more other people. In this chapter, we report the results of a study that compared the group problem-solving processes of expert and typical elementary school principals. Experts' group prob-lem-solving processes, we argue to begin with, seem likely to give rise to forms of leadership practice typically thought of as "transformational."

Whereas this chapter touches on the links between leader-ship thinking and practice, we address this link much more di-rectly in Chapters 10 and 11.

Originally published as K. Leithwood, and R. Steinbach. 1991. Indicators of transformational leadership in the everyday problem solving of school ad-ministrators. *Journal of Personnel Evaluation in Education,* 4, 221–244. Reprinted with permission.

What principals do depends on what they think, and what they think is a product of interactions between their environments and their unique intellectual biographies, beliefs, values, dispositions, and traits. The reality of the principalship is, in this sense (to use Berger and Luckmann's, 1967, words) "socially constructed." Why do principals act as they do? Why do two principals respond to similar challenges in their schools in quite different ways—very helpfully in some cases and unhelpfully in many others? How can principals be assisted to provide better leadership? Given the potential contribution of principals to the quality of education in their schools (e.g., Leithwood, Cousins, and Begley, 1990), these are crucial questions to those concerned about school improvement. Answering these questions requires a better understanding of how the subjectively defined reality of the principal's world is constructed.

The present study is part of an ongoing research program investigating administrators' problem-solving processes; it is one way of learning more about what and how principals think. Other studies in the program have examined administrators' problem classification and management processes (Leithwood and Stager, 1986; Leithwood, 1988); developed a grounded model of administrative problem solving (Leithwood and Stager, 1989; Leithwood and Steinbach, 1990); examined the flexibility of principals' cognitions (Stager and Leithwood, 1989); inquired about the role of values in problem solving (Begley, 1987; Campbell, 1988); and described the nature and number of problems expressed by principals over an annual school cycle (Leithwood, Cousins, and Smith, 1989). Differences in problem-solving processes due to differences in role or organizational context (Leithwood and Steinbach, 1991) have also been examined.

In some of this research, we have attempted to look at differences in the problem-solving processes of "expert" and "typical" principals. As in the research of many others using expert versus novice designs (reviewed by Alexander and Judy, 1989), our long-term purpose has been to clarify those aspects of expertise that might become a productive focus for selection, evaluation and professional development of principals. Aspects of our previous work have had such a focus in relation to principals' solving problems individually (e.g., Leithwood and Stager, 1989; Stager and Leithwood, 1989). The present study extends this work to the problem solving of principals in groups. Evidence from our previous studies indicated that group, as distinct from individual, problem solving was increasingly valued by all principals as they gained experience. Also, it was used more frequently by expert principals than it was by typical principals and more often by superintendents than by principals (Leithwood and Steinbach, 1991). In the present study, we explored two general questions: What are the extent and nature of differences between expert and typical principals' processes for solving problems with their staffs? and, How do differences in principals' problem-solving processes explain, in part, differences in their impact on schools? We attempted to answer this second question by comparing data about principals' problem solving to a set of theoretical concepts associated with our understanding of "transformational leadership."

Framework

Because in earlier chapters we described our general information-processing orientation to understanding problem solving, this aspect is not reiterated here. Described instead are two more specific refinements to such an orientation warranted by our previous work and especially useful in guiding the present study. One refinement is the addition of a sixth component (Affect or Mood) to our model of administrative problem solving (Interpretation, Goals, Principles, Constraints, Solution Processes) described in Chapter 4. Affect is defined as the feelings, mood, and sense of self-confidence the principal experiences when involved in problem solving. This model provided the basis for comparing expert and typical principals' problem-solving processes (see Chapter 3, as well as the problem solving of superintendents in Chapter 4). A second refinement of our framework was to assist in investigating the relationship between principals' problem-solving processes and principals' impact on schools; this refinement consists of theoretical constructs associated with transformational leadership.

Theoretical Constructs Associated with Transformational Leadership

Arguably, the most significant focus for school reform at present in both Canada and the United States is to truly professionalize teaching (e.g., Fullan and Connelly, 1987; Little, 1988). Often referred to as teacher "empowerment" (e.g., Maeroff, 1988), such professionalization is associated with greater discretion for teachers to shape their own work, a central role for teachers in significant school-level decisions, more peer involvement in personnel assessment, and the like.

Whereas much thought has been devoted to what teacher empowerment could mean for teachers, its implications for school-level administrators has been largely neglected (Bolin, 1989). In our view, the term *transformational leader* evokes intuitively compelling images of what such implications might be. Bennis and Nanus (1985) view leaders as transformative when they are able to "shape and elevate the motives and goals of followers (p. 217)." Such leadership, they suggest,

> is collective, there is a symbolic relationship between leaders and followers and what makes it collective is the subtle interplay between the followers' needs and wants and the leader's capacity to understand . . . these collective aspirations. (p. 217)

Like Bennis and Nanus (1985), we were intrigued by the promise of transformational leadership in schools but anxious to demystify it. In this study, therefore, we looked for specific practices, especially among effective principals, that could be viewed as evidence of transformational leadership. Our data seemed a potentially powerful source of such evidence since group problem solving is the kind of collective activity central to transformational leadership.

Our own previous research suggests that group, as distinct from individual, problem solving is preferred by more-experienced, more-effective, and more-senior administrators (e.g., Leithwood and Steinbach, 1990). This evidence also suggests that the reasons for valuing group problem solving, consistent with other research on the matter, were threefold. Some forms of group problem solving contribute to better solutions to immediate problems, long-term growth on the part of participants, and greater motivation and commitment on the part of those involved to implementing such solutions—all aspects of transformational leadership. Taking these reasons as starting points, we adopted several additional theoretical constructs to help direct the search for evidence of transformational leadership.

Better Solutions through "Collegial Rationality"

"Bounded rationality" offers a powerful theoretical perspective from which to appreciate how collaborative problem solving can lead to better solutions. The phrase, initially coined by Simon (1957), was intended to draw attention to the limitations in a person's capacity to process information in the face of the complex demands placed on that processing by frequently encountered problems. The limited capacity of short-term memory was of particular interest to Simon and others who elaborated the idea. As Shulman and Carey (1984) explain, however, bounded rationality focused exclusively on individual cognition and did not adequately recognize how individuals "participate in jointly produced social and cultural systems of meaning that transcend individuals" (1984, p. 503). Because human rationality, "whether bounded or not, is practiced in the context of social exchange and human interaction" (p. 515), a view of people as collectively rational is offered as a better conception of problem solving in many life circumstances. From such a view, problem solvers use others to compensate for their own limitations. They do this by transforming, redefining, and distributing parts of the problem task to others in the working group in an opportunistic way according to each individual's unique abilities. More specifically, under ideal collaborative problem-solving conditions, better solutions seem likely to be the result of, for example:

- a broader range of perspectives from which to interpret the problem;

- an expanded array of potential solutions from which to choose;

- a richer, more concrete body of information about the context in which the problem must be solved;

- the reduced likelihood of individually biased perspectives operating in the solution process.

When such conditions prevail, "Humans liberate rationality from its bonds through the collective work of civility" (Shulman and Carey, 1984, p. 518).

Empirical evidence in support of the value of collaborative problem solving can be found in the extensive body of research on peer interaction (see Webb, 1989, for a review of this research). This research unpacks, in more detail, forms of group interaction most helpful in reaching productive outcomes. Schoenfeld (1989) provides a useful, personal case study of how a collaborative research setting fostered achievements not possible for him to accomplish working alone.

Long-Term Growth of Participants through the Creation of a "Zone Of Proximal Development"

Vygotsky's (1978) concept of a "zone of proximal development" has been used in research on peer interaction to help explain how such interaction may stimulate individual development among participants (e.g., Damon and Phelps, 1989). This concept also seems valuable in helping to understand why and under what conditions group problem solving by administrators and teachers may contribute to their long-term growth. According to Vygotsky, an individual's independent problem solving is a function of processes in which he/she has participated in the past—for the most part processes involving interaction (or collaboration) with others. In this sense, an individual's independent problem-solving capacity, at a given point in time, is an internalization of previously experienced, collaborative problem-solving processes; it is the individual's actual developmental level. The zone of proximal development:

> is the distance between the actual development level as determined by independent problem solving and the level of potential development as determined through problem solving . . . in collaboration with more capable peers. (Vygotsky, 1978, p. 86)

In the context of administrator-teacher collaborative problem solving, the long-term growth of participants seems likely when, for example:

- the process used by the group is actually superior to the individual's independent problem solving and the individual participants recognize that superiority;

- there are opportunities for the group to reflect consciously on the process in which they are involved, to evaluate it, and participate in its refinement;

- individual members of the group compare their own independent problem solving with the group's processes and identify ways of increasing the robustness of their own independent processes.

Joseph Schwab's (1983) conception of curriculum deliberation is based on a set of premises very similar to those captured in the discussion of collegial rationality. He also argues that teacher involvement in the kinds of deliberations which he advocates lead to a form of long-term growth critical to his conception of teaching as a complex and demanding art. Teachers, from this view, are required to make decisions hundreds of times a day and, as Shulman (1984) notes, their options arise differently every day with every group of students. No theoretical principles or abstract guidelines are sufficient to the task faced by teachers under these circumstances. What is required, rather, is a deep understanding of their purposes and how such purposes may be accomplished flexibly and often opportunistically. Such understanding arises through thoughtful and extensive deliberations about the nature of instruction, the school curriculum, and other problem areas that teachers are expected to address at higher stages in their development (Fullan and Connelly, 1987; Leithwood, 1990).

Increased Commitment through "Shared Goals"

There is much evidence in support of the claim that at least some forms of involvement or collaboration in problem solving lead to greater commitment by participants to implement solutions arising from such problem solving (e.g., Ettling and Jago, 1988). Under what conditions of involvement does commitment arise and why? Conventional wisdom has it that it is simply the participation in the solution process that leads to greater commitment to the solution itself. Though this is no doubt true, we see that the reason for the increased commitment is due to the concept of shared goals. This commitment occurs because: (1) individuals' goals are prime motivators of their behavior; (2) individual goals are arrived at, in part, through social interaction; (3) certain characteristics of goals are more motivating than others; and (4) some forms of social interaction produce such goal characteristics better than others—in particular, forms of social interaction which lead to shared goals.

When individuals commit themselves to explicit goals, "perceived negative discrepancies between what they do and what they seek to achieve create dissatisfactions that serve as motivational inducements for change. . . . Once individuals have made self satisfaction contingent upon goal attainment, they tend to persist in their efforts until their performances match what they are seeking to achieve" (Bandura, 1977, p. 161).

Certain characteristics of goals contribute to their role in motivating behavior. Relatively explicit goals provide a clearer basis for self-evaluation than do ambiguous goals. Moderately difficult goals are more motivating than those which seem trivial because of their simplicity or those which seem unrealistic because of their difficulty. Relatively immediate or proximal goals (or subgoals) serve as greater stimulants to action than do remote goals, especially when there are competing demands on one's attention.

Goals are actively constructed by the individual through social interaction. The nature of such interaction is substantially influenced by the context (or culture) in which people find themselves.

Rosenholtz's (1989) research provides evidence of this influence on teachers. In her study she showed that in school contexts, which she described as "static" (dominated by norms of self-reliance and isolation), teachers' goals were, for example, idiosyncratic, focusing on maintenance activities and interaction with others about social issues or discipline problems. School contexts described as "moving," in contrast, appeared to foster shared goals focused on student learning and interaction with others about instructional improvement. In "moving contexts":

> principals interacted with teachers to shape their school reality, to construct school traditions . . . goals about the importance of students' basic skills came to be commonly shared. (Rosenholtz, 1989, p. 39)

Shared goals, in Rosenholtz's formation, constitute the initial foundation on which to build teacher commitment, certainly about instructional practices, and for the confidence to participate in further collaboration.

Collaboration with one's colleagues seems likely to generate not only shared goals but also goals which have highly motivating properties. Interaction requires one to put one's purposes in words and to be clear enough to explain one's purposes to others. Furthermore, the public nature of such interaction creates pressure to set goals which seem worthwhile to others and therefore are not likely to be trivial. Continuous interaction about shared goals supplements, through the evaluation of others, one's own evaluation of discrepancies between performance and desired achievement. Finally, because they are determined in a deliberative manner (with the aid of others), such goals are less likely to be remote or unrealistic.

The multicomponent model of administrative problem solving, along with the three sets of theoretical propositions outlined in this section, served as guides for the study's data collection and analysis.

Method

Data for the study were provided by nine elementary school principals, four designated as "experts" and five designated as "typical." Stimulated recall methods in the context of a staff meeting were used to generate principals' talk about their problem-solving processes (see Chapter 1 for a description of the value of this method). These responses were audio taped, subsequently transcribed, coded, and content analyzed.

Designation of expertise was made on the basis of two criteria—independent judgments of two senior administrators and ratings of effectiveness on *The Principal Profile* (Leithwood and Montgomery, 1986). For a detailed description of this process, see Chapter 3.

At the beginning of data collection, both groups of principals had approximately the same amount of experience in school administration (about 16 years). The experts' schools had an average of 506 students; the typical principals' schools averaged about 150 fewer.

In this study, data were collected at three points in time. Prior to the staff meeting which provided the context for group problem solving, principals were interviewed about the background of the problem they would be working on, what they expected and wanted to happen at the meeting, and what they were planning to do. An audio tape recording was made of the entire staff meeting, usually about 1 1/2 hours in duration. Finally, after some preliminary instructions, the principal and interviewer listened to the tape of the meeting together, stopping frequently to ask or offer information about intentions and thought processes. This discussion was recorded on a separate tape and it is this tape that was subsequently transcribed.

Results

Using the six categories associated with our model of administrative problem solving, all relevant statements in the transcripts were coded. Every effort was made to determine the meaning of each statement from the context in which it appeared, and statements ranged from a sentence to several paragraphs in length. Similarly coded statements were then analyzed in part by using results from previous studies as organizers; the most dominant use of this strategy was in relation to the category *Principles/Values*. We also tried to be sensitive to new ways of organizing the data within categories and to any limitations of our previous ways of organizing.

The reliability with which data from the protocols was coded was determined by two independent judges who assigned a random sample of 25 protocol excerpts to our coding categories. There was 84 percent agreement between the two judges.

Each principal in the study was attempting to solve a different problem. There was little evidence that the problems being addressed by effective principals differed in terms of structure or complexity as compared with the problems being addressed by typical principals. In all cases, the problems seemed to be challenging. The challenge was sometimes provided by the problem's history. For example, planning for a two-day professional activity session at the end of June in one school was complicated by the teachers' expressed dissatisfaction with previous professional activity days. This dissatisfaction focused on some fairly significant decisions about how the professional activity time would be spent—whether an external facilitator would be involved, what proportion of the time would be spent on school goal setting, and the like. In other instances, the problem itself, independent of its history, provided the challenge. This was likely the case for staff trying to decide whether or not and how to implement a "house system," since they had no previous related experience. These problems had significant elements that might be labelled "unstructured," as unstructured problems have been defined in our previous research (see Chapter 3). Principals did not have a significant amount of problem-relevant knowledge, built up through previous experience, on which to draw, and the goals to be achieved were ill-defined. This is important since those previous studies also found that differences in problem-solving processes between effective and typical principals were much more visible in response to unstructured as compared with structured problems.

A Comparison of Expert and Typical Principals' Problem Solving

Table 5.1 summarizes similarities and differences between expert and typical principals in relation to each component of their problem solving.

Problem interpretation. Expert and typical principals differed significantly in their approach to problem interpretation. For the most part, these are differences in degree. Evidence from the five typical principals revealed no signs of conscious reflection on their own problem interpretation processes. Although such reflection was not extensive on the part of expert principals either, one explicitly talked about the importance of having a clear interpretation of the problem: "To me the critical part is identifying what the problem is . . . and the problem is different for different people."

Expert and typical principals did vary substantially on the extent to which they took into account the interpretation others had of the problem they were addressing. Two of the four experts explicitly checked their own assumptions and actively sought out the interpretations of their staff members as well. In contrast, none of the typ-

Table 5.1   Principals' Problem-Solving Processes with Others: A Comparison of Expert and Typical Principals

COMPONENTS	EXPERT	TYPICAL
Interpretation	• understands importance of having a clear interpretation of problem	• no conscious reflection on this matter
	• seeks out and takes into account the interpretation others have of the problem	• assumes others share same interpretation
	• immediate problem usually viewed in its relation to the larger mission and problems of school	• tendency for problems to be viewed in isolation
	• has a clear interpretation which they can describe to others and rationalize	• less clarity about their interpretation; difficulty in explaining it to others
Goals	• has multiple goals for problem solving	• has multiple goals for problem solving
	• shares own goals with others involved in problem solving	• shares own goals with others involved in problem solving
	• has goals for both the problem and the meeting in which collaborative problem solving occurs	• has goals for both the problem and the meeting in which collaborative problem solving occurs
	• strong concern for the development of goals both the principal and staff can agree to	• concerned with achieving only own goals and getting staff to agree to those goals
	• less of a personal stake in any preconceived solution; wants the best possible solution the group can produce	• often strongly committed to a preconceived solution and attempts to manipulate group problem solving so as to result in support for the preconceived solution
Principles/ Values	• order of frequency of mention of value categories included Professional Values, Basic Human Values, Social and Political Values, and General Moral Values	• order of frequency of mention of value categories included Professional Values, Basic Human Values, Social and Political Values, and General Moral Values

Table 5.1 *Continued*

COMPONENTS	EXPERT	TYPICAL
Principles/ Values	• most frequently mentioned specific value was Specific Role Responsibilities • made a mean of 21 value statements • high use of specific values: Respect for others, Participation, Consequences for clients, Knowledge—in that order	• most frequently mentioned specific value was Specific Role Responsibilities • made a mean of 16.6 value statements • high use of specific values: Consequences for clients, Respect for others, Loyalty, Happiness— in that order
Constraints	• accurately anticipates obstacles likely to arise during group problem solving • plans in advance for how to address anticipated obstacles should they arise • adapts and responds flexibly to unanticipated obstacles which arise • obstacles not viewed as major impediments to problem solving	• does not anticipate obstacles or identifies relatively superficial obstacles • rarely considers in advance how to respond to those obstacles that are predicted
Solution Process	• has well-developed plan for collaborative problem solving (meeting) • provides clear, detailed introduction to problem and its background to collaborators • outlines clearly the process for problem solving (e.g., how meeting will be conducted) • carefully checks collaborators' interpretations of problem and own assumptions	• rarely plans for collaborative process and may value "spontaneity" • introduction of problem unclear and occasionally missing altogether • not likely to share plan for meeting with collaborators if plan exists • assumes others have same interpretations of problem; does not check

Table 5.1 *Continued*

COMPONENTS	EXPERT	TYPICAL
Solution Process	• without intimidating or restraining others, clearly indicates own view of the problem and relationship with larger problems	• argues stubbornly for own view or "orchestrates" meeting so that it supports such a view
	• remains open to new information and changes views, if warranted	• adheres to own view in the face of competing views
	• assists collaborative problem solving by synthesizing, summarizing, and clarifying as needed and by keeping group (gently) on track	• limited action to assist collaboration and may seriously underestimate time required for collaborators to explore problem as principal has done
	• ensures that follow-up is planned	• rarely considers plans for follow-up
Affect	• always appears to be calm and confident	• usually appears calm but frustration may occasionally become visible
	• hidden anxieties usually the result of inability to find a workable solution	• frequently feels frustrated, especially by unwillingness of staff to agree with principal's views
	• invariably treats others politely	• occasional signs of insecurity about own ability to solve problems
	• uses humor to diffuse tension and to clarify information	• uses humor to diffuse tension and to clarify information

ical principals did this and three of the five assumed that their staff had the same interpretation of the problems as they had.

Another difference in problem interpretation between expert and typical principals concerned the context in which problem interpretation took place. Most expert principals viewed the immediate problem they were addressing in the context of the larger mission and problems of their schools. For example, one effective principal noted in his introduction to the topic:

Discipline is a school thrust [and] the PA day [we had on it] was too brief. We need to equip ourselves with more strategies, refine our skills, because of the greater challenges we [now] face in the classroom, for example, the integration of special kids.

Finally, a particularly striking difference between expert and typical principals was the degree of clarity they had about their interpretation of the problem and their ability to both describe their interpretation to their staffs and to indicate the reasons they had for such an interpretation. An expert principal said, for example:

Earlier in the fall we had a discussion about a house system and some of the ideas were of some concern to one division more than another. I don't think you were really able to come to a decision that it should be school-wide and yet there was a feeling that it might very well work out that way. . . . We took it to a lead teacher meeting . . . with some guidelines I had. We've done some revising of those guidelines and what I will give you is an outline of that and some of the ideas behind it. Hopefully, then the meeting will come to you as a house system that could really work for (this school). I favor for that to happen if it can— under the whole philosophy we have here of lots of participation and low key amount of competition.

This does not really deal with school teams . . . We're talking about in-school activities and its not just sports teams and I think that's part of what S is after too. Each of you will get a sheet with a revised set of guidelines and thoughts and S will carry forth from here.

Typical principals frequently were unclear about their interpretations and had difficulty explaining the reasons for the interpretations they held.

Goals. Expert and typical principals shared many similarities in this component of their problem solving. Both had multiple goals for problem solving—usually five or six goals in relation to any given problem. For example, in response to the problem regarding survey results one principal voiced these goals:

- Share the findings [of the survey conducted];

- Identify one, two, or three areas that we see as targets;

- Relate these target areas to overall school goals that will be formulated shortly;

- Invite staff input;

- Look for agreement among the group members, not for solutions.

Furthermore, both groups of principals made a point of sharing their own goals with others involved in problem solving. Eight of the nine principals set goals not only for the problem to be solved but also for the meeting in which collaborative problem solving was to occur. One typical principal established goals only for the problem and gave little or no attention to the process for problem solving.

There were two differences between expert and typical principals with respect to goals, however. One of these differences concerned the relationship between the principals' goals for problem solving and the goals that other staff members held. Expert principals indicated a strong concern for the development of goals that could be agreed on by both themselves and their staff. For example:

I want this to go, quite frankly I do, but I want it to be something that they have set up the way they can make it work. It's not something I intend as principal to give out great big awards for; it's something that I want the teachers to feel comfortable that they are able to build a program.

Typical principals, in contrast, were concerned only with achieving their own goals and with persuading their staffs to agree with them about what those goals should be. As one principal said, "I think I got them [the teachers] to identify the several key areas that are relevant from my point of view."

The second difference between expert and typical principals was the stake held by the principals in a preconceived solution. Typical principals were often strongly committed to such a solution prior to entering the "collaborative" problem-solving process and constantly manipulated the process in an effort to gain support for that solution. Expert principals, on the other hand, had much less stake in any preconceived solution. They wanted the best possible solution the group could produce and took steps to ensure that such a solution was found. For example, one principal said: "I can either see it happen or let it wash through and say it was a good try, maybe another time. I'm willing to go with it either way."

Values.   In Table 5.2 we provide examples of statements coded in relation to each of the value types included in the values classification system alluded to earlier in the chapter. In Table 5.3 we report the number of principals who made statements about each value, the frequency of such statements, and the percentage of such statements in relation to the total number of statements. These data are reported for principals, as a whole (n = 9), as well as separately for expert principals (n = 4) and typical principals (n = 5).

As we indicate in Table 5.3, the nine principals as a whole made a total of 167 statements coded as values (mean = 18.8). Of the total number of value statements made, 46 percent were coded in the Professional Values category, 25 percent in the Basic Human Values category, and 23 percent in the Social and Political Values category. Six percent of the value statements were coded as General Moral Values. Within these four value categories, the six specific values mentioned most frequently included, in order, Specific Role Responsibilities (40), Respect for Others (27), Consequences for One's Immediate Client (26), and Participation (17). Both Sharing and Loyalty, Solidarity, and Commitment were mentioned an equal number of times (11). Specific Role Responsibilities were mentioned substantially more often than were the other values. Respect for Others and Consequences for One's Immediate Client were in the midrange in terms of frequency among the six mentioned most frequently.

In addition to the responses of principals, as a whole, data in Table 5.3 compare typical and expert principals. Because there were five typical principals in the sample and only four expert principals, the numbers in brackets concerning the frequency of statements reported for typical principals is an adjusted number (4/5 the raw frequency). This number, referred to in subsequent text, provides a more meaningful basis for comparison with the frequencies reported for expert principals.

Expert principals expressed about 17 percent more value statements than did typical principals, with a mean of 16.6 statements for typical principals and a mean of 21 statements for expert principals. There were very few differences, however, between expert and typical principals in terms of the proportion of values associated with each of the four major value categories. The primary differences between typical and expert principals were in the frequency with which they mentioned specific values within the four categories. Specific Role Responsibilities were mentioned most frequently by both groups and the frequency of mention does not differ substantially between expert and typical principals. The order of mention of specific values among typical principals with respect to other specific values,

Table 5.2 Examples of Protocol Statements Coded in Relation
to Each Value

VALUE	EXAMPLES OF STATEMENTS CODED IN RELATION TO EACH VALUE
1. Basic Human Values	
1.1 Freedom	[That's a] school rule. We don't have many. I think that's the only mean rule I have.
1.2 Happiness	I was really pleased with the result and the way people seemed to be happy with it.
1.3 Knowledge	They wanted more information and I'm glad to hear that.
1.4 Respect for Others	She can turn kids around like that. She's a good teacher.
1.5 Survival	—
2. General Moral Values	
2.1 Carefulness	[I wanted to] make sure she had all the bases covered.
2.2 Fairness	We have teachers who tend to take on more than their fair share—others not jumping in.
2.3 Courage	Does anyone want to take the risk to make a comment?
3. Professional Values	
3.1 General Responsibility as Educators	So that was going to be a problem for me if they [assemblies] weren't educationally sound.
3.2 Specific Role Responsibility	I purposely stayed out of it [so as not to unduly influence the group].
3.3 Consequences (immediate clients)	We have a lot of special education kids here and I want to be sure that they're not missed.
3.4 Consequences (others)	We have to address this as a group not just with staff but with parents and the community at large.
4. Social and Political Values	
4.1 Participation	Staff really need to be there and to be part of the process.
4.2 Sharing	I think a characteristic of this staff is to be honest and open. They'll tell you right from the shoulder what they think.
4.3 Loyalty, solidarity, and commitment	Hopefully we're going to have everybody on board.
4.4 Helping others	—

Table 5.3 Statements in Protocols Coded as Different Types of Values: Expert and Typical Principals

Values	Expert Principals No. of Prs. (n = 4)	Freq.	%	Typical Principals No. of Prs.	Freq. (n = 5)	%	Total Principals Freq.	%
1. *Basic Human Values*								
Total	4	22	26	5	20 (16)	24	42	25
1.1 Freedom	1	1	1	0	0 (0)	0	1	1
1.2 Happiness	0	0	0	3	6 (4.8)	7	3	3
1.3 Knowledge	2	8	10	0	0 (0)	0	8	5
1.4 Respect for Others	4	13	16	5	14 (11.2)	17	27	16
1.5 Survival	0	0	0	0	0 (0)	0	0	0
2. *General Moral Values*								
Total	3	4	4	4	6 (4.8)	7	10	6
2.1 Carefulness	2	2	2	2	2 (1.6)	2	4	2
2.2 Fairness	2	2	2	2	3 (2.4)	4	5	3
2.3 Courage	0	0	0	1	1 (.8)	1	1	1
3. *Professional Values*								
Total	4	37	44	5	39 (31.2)	47	76	46
3.1 General Resp. as educators	3	6	7	2	2 (1.6)	2	8	5
3.2 Specific Role Resp.	4	20	24	5	20 (16)	24	40	24
3.3 Consequences (Imm. clients)	4	11	13	5	15 (12)	18	26	16
3.4 Consequences (others)	0	0	0	1	2 (1.6)	2	2	1
4. *Social / Political Values*								
Total	4	21	25	4	18 (14.4)	22	39	23
4.1 Participation	4	12	14	3	5 (4)	6	17	10
4.2 Sharing	3	6	7	2	5 (4)	6	11	7
4.3 Loyality, Solidarity, Commitment	3	3	4	2	8 (6.4)	10	11	7
4.4 Helping Others	0	0	0	0	0 (0)	0	0	0
TOTAL	4	84	100*	5	83 (66.4)	100	167	100*

* Because of rounding off the percentage may add up to more than 100 percent.

however, includes, in order, Consequences for Immediate Clients, Respect for Others, Loyalty, Solidarity and Commitment, and Happiness. In contrast, the order of specific values for expert principals was Respect for Others, Participation, Consequences for Immediate Clients, and Knowledge. Whereas knowledge was mentioned by two expert principals a total of eight times, no typical principals mentioned this value. There seemed to be substantial differences between expert and typical principals in their use of the value Participation, also. Participation constituted about 14 percent of the value statements for expert principals as compared with only about 6 percent of the value statements for typical principals.

Constraints.   As we indicate in Table 5.1, expert principals were better able to anticipate the obstacles likely to arise during group problem solving. Typical principals either did not anticipate obstacles (one principal) or they identified relatively superficial obstacles. Even when they did anticipate obstacles, typical principals rarely considered, in advance, how they might respond to those obstacles should they arise. This is in contrast to expert principals, who planned carefully in advance for how they would address anticipated obstacles (three out of four principals). In addition, expert principals adapted and responded in a flexible way to unanticipated obstacles. For instance, during the stimulated recall one principal said: "The point he is making which I hadn't taken into account . . . I'm bringing up discipline, so obviously it's interpreted that I'm not happy with discipline in the school." The principal went on to say during the meeting: "I am glad that point has been raised. By doing this, I'm not saying that things are falling apart. People are on top of things and I appreciate that. At the same time, it's something we must continually be at. . . . " He then provided a personal example of a difficulty he had in handling a discipline problem.

Expert principals tended not to view obstacles as major impediments to problem solving in the same way that our previous evidence has suggested typical principals do. Furthermore, whereas expert principals were concerned to learn and build on the perception of their teachers, typical principals viewed differences in their perceptions and those of their teachers as frustrating constraints. This is not surprising given their preconceived ideas about what goals were to be achieved at the meeting.

Solution processes.   The greatest differences between expert and typical principals were found within this component of their problem solving. Typical principals rarely planned for collaborative problem solving. In contrast, experts developed careful plans, as is evident in these remarks:

> [First] I'll share with them what the problem is for me. . . . [Then] I'll have them working in small groups to identify the problem or what they see as the problem—brainstorm some ideas of what they think the problem is. . . . After we have a look at what the problems are we can look at some potential solutions.

During the process of collaborative problem solving, usually in the context of a staff meeting, expert principals ensured that the stage for effective collaborative problem solving was set by providing a clear, detailed introduction to the problem and its background. This was not a matter given much attention by typical principals, one of whom provided no background at all to his staff. Although one typical principal did develop a clear plan for problem solving at the meeting, he did not share that plan with his staff; most of the expert principals shared not only the background to the problem but the process that they were suggesting for how it would be solved—how the meeting would be conducted, for example.

Part of the process for conducting the meeting, on the part of expert principals, was the careful checking with staffs regarding their interpretation of the problem and the extent to which their assumptions were shared. Typical principals invariably assumed that others had the same interpretation of the problem which they held and did not check to see whether or not that was the case. Because of the prior commitment typical principals had to a set of goals and a problem solution, in meeting with their staffs they tended either to argue overtly for their own view of the solution or manipulate the meeting subtly so that it supported such a view. One typical principal remarked: "I did cut off one person in the group who spoke only once, and tried to solicit more time to pursue all the data but that was not part of my agenda." This principal also deflected the need that teachers had to vent feelings of disappointment or outrage (over prior results in a survey): "I went through that stage and now look at it as a reality. . . . Let's not stay with the raw numbers here; let's get past that." Other principals changed topics or called on teachers who used the strategies the principal wanted to be accepted.

Expert principals were able to make clear their own view of the problem without intimidating or restraining their staffs. In addition, they were open to new information and, if such information warranted it, were prepared to change their views of what the solution should be.

Experts, in contrast with typical principals, facilitated collaborative problem solving by synthesizing the views of others, summarizing progress in the meeting from time to time, providing clarification as needed, and gently prodding the group to keep on task.

None of the typical principals considered how to follow up on decisions made during the meeting, whereas this consideration was raised by three of the four expert principals.

Affect.   Both expert and typical principals usually appeared to be calm and confident during the problem-solving process with their staffs; one typical principal's frustration was visible on one occasion. There were substantial differences, however, in the amount of anxiety or frustration actually experienced (but not demonstrated) by principals. This was evident in their discussion following the staff meeting. In that context, three of the five typical principals expressed some frustration over the meeting. Their source of frustration was the unwillingness of the staff to agree on what the problem should be: "Inside me I say, your question is not relevant. It has nothing to do with what we're doing. Damn it, I don't need that. . . . Outside I hope I didn't show it."

One principal also showed some signs of insecurity about his own ability to solve problems collaboratively: "I guess the problem that I had in the first place was to find a problem for you to see. So I guess the kind of thing I want is some feedback [about] how I conduct meetings on all problems."

Expert principals exhibited few signs of frustration although one seemed mildly frustrated at his own inability to help the staff arrive at a suitable solution.

Expert and typical principals made use of humor to diffuse tension and to clarify information during collaborative problem solving.

Indicators of transformational leadership

In the framework section of this paper we developed three theoretical constructs to help guide the search for evidence of transformational leadership. These constructs suggested that evidence of transformational leadership could be found in the means used by principals to (1) generate better solutions to school problems (including teacher evaluation problems), (2) develop teachers' commitment to implementing such solutions, and (3) foster long-term staff development.

In the context of group problem solving, we anticipated that those benefits occur as a result of a principal's ability to nurture "collegial rationality," develop shared, explicit, moderately challenging, achievable goals, and create a "zone of proximal development" for themselves and their staffs.

The left-hand column of Table 5.4 summarizes specific conditions, identified in earlier discussion, associated with each theoretical construct. The right-hand column draws information from Table 5.1 (features of expert principals' group problem-solving processes) likely to satisfy these theoretical conditions.

In Table 5.4 we suggest that expert principals' problem-solving processes potentially satisfy all but one of the theoretical conditions (2.3, encouraging individual staff members to evaluate their own problem-solving processes against the standard provided by the group process). This suggests that the everyday act of solving problems in groups offers principals significant opportunities for exercising transformational leadership but that typical principals do not make use of this opportunity. It also suggests that even expert principals can become more transformational by devoting more attention to encouraging individual staff members to reflect on their own problem solving.

Summary and Conclusion

We conclude with several observations concerning research methods and a consideration of the significance of the data which has been reported. Of the variety of methods proposed for collecting verbal protocol data, most of which we have used in our own previous research, the stimulated recall method used in this study yielded by far the richest set of data, from our point of view. Those pursuing lines of research similar to our own would be advised to give this method careful consideration. This method might also be useful in principal evaluation. Since group problem solving is a frequent occurrence, effective behavior in this arena would be essential. The results of this study suggest guidelines for establishing degrees of expertise.

The design of this study conforms loosely to the expert/novice design employed in much problem-solving research (Alexander and Judy, 1989). This design too often amounts to a comparison of the problem solving of "experienced" and novice groups, however. Our "typical" principals would certainly qualify as experienced and on some counts would be considered "expert" (in solving structured problems, for example). Yet, as this study demonstrated, substantial

Table 5.4 How Expert Principals' Problem-Solving Processes Produce Better Solutions, Long-Term Staff Growth, and Enhanced Commitment

CONDITIONS FOSTERING IMPACT	HOW EXPERTS MEET CONDITIONS THROUGH GROUP PROBLEM SOLVING

1. Collegial Rationality

1.1 broader range of perspectives from which to interpret problem	• actively seeks out staff interpretations; is explicit about own problem in larger perspective
1.2 expanded array of solutions	• assists group discussions of alternatives; ensures open discussion; avoids commitment to preconceived solution
1.3 better information about context	• actively listens to staff views; clarifies and summarizes information during meetings
1.4 avoidance of biased perspectives	• keeps group on task; does not impose own perspective; changes own views when warranted; checks out own and others assumptions; remains calm and confident

2. Creating a Zone of Proximal Development

2.1 group processes superior to individual processes	• plans carefully, in advance, for how how group problem solving will occur • actively facilitates group problem solving • anticipates and plans for constraints
2.2 conscious reflection on group process	• outlines explicitly to the group the process for problem solving • plans for follow-up • keeps group on task (gently)
2.3 self-evaluation of individual	[not addressed]

3. Commitment through Shared Goals

3.1 increase explicitness of goals	• shares own goals for problem solving; interprets problem in relation to larger mission of school
3.2 develop moderately difficult goals	• encourages staff discussion of goals; interprets problem in relation to larger mission of school • strongly values consequences for Immediate Client
3.3 foster interaction about goals	• values Respect for Others and Participation • strong concern for arriving at goal consensus

differences exist between typical administrators and those carefully defined as expert through the application of a rigorous set of standards for their professional practices. It is especially crucial to clarify these differences if, as is often the case, the long-term purpose for such research is to provide objectives for the development of expertise or to assist in the selection or approval of school administrators.

One purpose of the study was to explore differences between expert and typical principals' problem-solving processes. Results suggested that there were many such differences and that these differences appeared to be nontrivial in nature. Differences appeared in each component of the problem-solving model used as the basis for comparison. At least two quite fundamental attributes of expert principals' problem solving help explain differences found within components of the model. Expert principals demonstrated a high degree of metacognitive control; this was evident, for example, in their ability to monitor the effects of their own behavior and change that behavior when warranted. Expert principals, in addition, provided evidence of holding beliefs which Baron (1985) has suggested are fundamental for good thinking, in general. For example, experts clearly believed that thinking often leads to better results and that staff members working together could think better than when they were working alone. Typical principals behaved as if they did not believe this to be the case. In this sense, a significant part of the explanation for differences in problem solving may be found in administrators' intentions as distinct from their skills or abilities. Should further research confirm the importance of such beliefs and intentions in explaining a significant portion of variance in administrative problem solving, new dimensions would need to be added to current attempts at training in problem solving. Currently such attempts focus almost exclusively on skill development.

A second more theoretical and speculative purpose for the study was to begin to demystify the intuitively compelling concept of transformational leadership. This was done by searching for concrete group problem-solving practices linked theoretically, at least, to our own embryonic understanding of such leadership. Three theoretical constructs were introduced to help explore the data from this perspective: collegial rationality, the zone of proximal development, and shared goals. A high degree of consistency was found between expert principals' group problem-solving processes and the conditions associated with these constructs for generating better solutions, greater commitment, and long-term staff growth. Practices associated with transformational leadership were particularly clear in the solution processes of expert principals. The central quality of these processes is reasonably well captured in the phrase "authentic dialogue," the kind of dialogue Bolin (1989) views as central to empowering leadership. Expert principals were open-minded, honest, careful, attentive to the group's needs, and attentive to their thinking. This was in stark contrast to the solution processes of typical principals. As Bolin observed:

> Strategies of conquest, divide and rule, manipulation through human relations techniques and cultural invasion are not uncommon in administrative practice. They are problematic in a democratic society, however, because they are based on an oppressive leadership model. (Bolin, 1989, p. 86)

Such oppressive models are the antithesis of what will be required in a professionalized teaching force. Discovering the specific practices and beliefs which give meaning to transformational leadership is an important research task. Helping aspiring and incumbent administrators acquire these practices and beliefs is the challenge to be met through school district personnel practices. In Chapter 11 we report one of our efforts to further explore the meaning of transformational leadership and the thinking which gives rise to it, and in Chapter 10 we provide additional information about principals' group problem-solving processes, as well as their relationship to overt leadership practices.

Chapter 6

Processes Used by Expert Superintendents to Solve Problems in Groups

Building directly on the results of Chapter 5, in this study we set out to determine how comparable were the group problem-solving processes used by expert superintendents and those reported (in Chapter 5) for expert principals. We did not find what we expected. More precisely, some aspects of superintendents' problem solving were clearly similar to the results for principals reported in Chapter 5, but we found evidence of superintendents striving to accomplish several purposes not evident in our data from principals. These purposes we termed "transforming ideas into organizational reality" and "fostering organizational learning."

A version of this paper with a somewhat different focus will be published in *Educational Administration Quarterly*, 1993, 28(3).

In the Framework section of this chapter we provide the most detailed account of our multicomponent model of problem solving available in the book.

Peter Vaill (1989) claims that today's executives "live in a world of permanent white water" (p. 2), a world in which few assumptions are beyond scrutiny and the environment sometimes appears chaotic. In such a "contingent" world, well-rehearsed, routine, managerial behaviors provide the solution to a rapidly decreasing proportion of the potential problems lurking in the choppy waters executives navigate daily. It is the prevalence of wicked or ill-structured problems, just below the surface of the water, that explains why even a light breeze often results in whitecaps, and, sometimes, apparently benign problems turn out to be deceptively wicked. Such a perspective explains the need for executives to have a repertoire of general problem-solving skills, along with a considerable store of knowledge about their specific businesses, to help them to cope with unpredictable and new problems.

The study of senior executives' problem-solving processes has been underway for some time in organizational settings outside of education (see, for example, Srivastva, 1983; Schwenk, 1988; Argyris, 1982), but little systematic attention has been devoted to the thinking and problem solving of senior educational administrators. The study described in this chapter was one in a series aimed at redressing this neglect. Prior studies in the series have focused on school principals (see especially Chapter 5 of this text) as well as the individual problem solving of superintendents (e.g., Leithwood and Steinbach, 1991a, and Chapter 4 of this text).

Among the results of our prior studies is evidence that as educational leaders become more "expert," more experienced in their roles, and move to more senior positions, they rely more extensively on solving their problems in collaboration with groups of colleagues, rather than by themselves (Leithwood and Steinbach, 1990). Indeed, some leaders are able to use the context of group problem solving not only for developing productive solutions to their problems and enhancing the subsequent implementation of those solutions, but also for fostering powerful forms of staff development (Leithwood and Steinbach, 1991b, and Chapter 5 of this text). In addition, a growing body of evidence argues for much greater attention to the nature and role of values in executive problem solving, a matter addressed most directly in Chapter 8; such values appear to be pervasive and variations in their nature and use are closely related to variations in executive expertise (Begley and Leithwood, 1989; Hambrick and Brandon, 1988). To explore these tentative findings further, the study described here asked: How do superintendents solve problems in groups? And, in particular, what is the nature and role of superintendents' values in their group problem solving? What purposes are being served by superintendents when they engage in collaborative problem solving with their senior colleagues?

Framework

This study was guided by information-processing approaches to problem solving and the multicomponent model of executive problem solving briefly described in Chapter 3. In this section we outline several key features of such an information-processing orientation; we also identify additional, selected features of such an orientation, in the context of extending the description of the main elements of our problem-solving model begun in Chapter 3 and further nudged along in Chapters 4 and 5.

An Information-Processing Orientation to Problem Solving

Information-processing orientations to problem solving are embedded in a broader theory of how the mind works. This theory consists of hypothetical structures and relationships which explain why people attend to some aspects of the information available to them in their environments, how their knowledge is stored, retrieved, and further developed, and how it is used in solving problems (see, for example, Gagné, 1985; Newell, Rosenblum, and Laird, 1990; Rumelhart, 1990). From this perspective, problems are defined as circumstances in which a gap is perceived between a current state and a more desirable state (Gagné, 1985; Hayes, 1981). When both states are clearly known and the procedures to follow (or operators) to get from one to the other are also known, a problem is considered routine or well structured. Lack of knowledge about any of these three elements in the "problem space" (Newell and Simon, 1972) makes a problem more ill-structured. Hence, both the objective complexity of the problem and the relevant knowledge possessed by the solver combine to determine the degree of novelty or structure of a problem.

Information-processing orientations to problem solving devote considerable attention to the concept of "expertise" and the patterns of thought which distinguish between those who possess expertise and those who do not. Expertise is associated with both effective and efficient problem solving within a particular domain of activity (such as leading a school system). Research across many domains suggests, for example, that experts excel mainly in their own domains, perceive large meaningful patterns in their domains, solve problems quickly with few errors, and have superior short- and long-term memories. Experts also represent problems at deeper, more principled levels than do novices; they spend more time than novices interpreting (as distinct from solving) problems. In addition, experts are able to monitor their own thinking much better than are novices (Glaser and Chi, 1988). The amount of domain-specific knowledge possessed by experts and the way it is organized is offered as the primary explanation for these attributes (Van Lehn, 1990; Nickerson, 1988–1989). General problem-solving processes or heuristics, in the absence of such knowledge, are not considered powerful tools for problem solving. Rather, such processes help people to gain access to useful knowledge and beliefs that they otherwise may have overlooked (Bransford, in press).

Well-structured problems, usually those repeatedly encountered by expert executives, are solved with little conscious thought. The problem is recognized as an instance of a category of problems about which the executive already knows a great deal. As Herbert Simon (in press) argues:

> any expert can recognize the symptoms, the clues, to the bulk of the situations that are encountered in his or her everyday experience. The day would simply not be long enough to accomplish anything if cues didn't do a large part of the work for the expert.

Such recognition permits the executive access to all of the knowledge he or she has stored in long-term memory about how to solve that category of problem. Because no comparable store of knowledge is available for ill-structured problems, however, the executive needs to respond in a more deliberate, thoughtful manner. As executives face a greater proportion of ill-structured problems, better understanding of these deliberate, thoughtful processes becomes increasingly important (Day and Lord, 1992; Schwenk, 1988), as does enhancing the expertise with which they are carried out. Furthermore, the degree of discretion and the cognitive demands placed on executives appear to increase the higher their position in the organization (Mumford and Connelly, 1991; Hunter, Schmidt, and Judiesch, 1990), in part because of the extended time horizons over which solutions to their problems must be planned and the accompanying abstractness of the thinking that necessitates (Jaques, 1986). This makes learning more about the problem solving of senior executives especially worthwhile.

Components of a Problem-Solving Model

There are two general categories of processes involved in problem solving: understanding and solving (Hayes, 1981; Van Lehn, 1990; Voss and Post, 1988). Understanding processes serve the purpose of generating a superintendent's internal representation of the problem—what she or he believes the problem to be. Solving processes aim to reduce the gap between current and desired states—how the executive will transform the current state into the more desirable goal state. Understanding and solving often interact during the course of problem solving as feedback from initial steps taken toward a solution builds a richer understanding of the problem. Both sets of processes require searching the contents of memory for existing knowledge which may be helpful in either understanding or solving the problem.

The multicomponent model of executive problem solving which served as a framework for collecting data in this study includes two components which primarily address understanding: Interpretation and Goal Setting. Two other components are primarily concerned with solving: Constraints and Solution Processes. Components of the model labeled Principles/Values and Mood seem equally relevant to both understanding and solving. This section provides an explanation of the cognitive processes encompassed by each component. In addition, characteristics of expertise in relation to each component are described, based on our own research with educational administrators. Those characteristics of expertise selected as a focus of attention in the present study are designated with an asterisk (*).

Processes Designed Primarily for Understanding Problems: Interpretation and Goals

Interpretation. Executives are bombarded with much more information from their environments than they can possibly think about (Simon, in press). Furthermore, because this information frequently presents itself as an untidy "mess" rather than a clearly labeled set of possibilities, there may be a host of potential problem formulations. Problem interpretation is an instance of giving meaning to and evaluating such information (Kelsey, in press). Meaning is created when newly encountered information is compared with those "schema"—organized contents of long-term memory—which the executive thinks might be relevant (Van Lehn, 1990). Such schema have two parts: one for describing the problem and the other for describing the solution. Nonroutine or ill-structured problems may be difficult to understand for several reasons. For example, more than one schema could apply to the problem, giving rise to the need for a sometimes trial-and-error search for the most workable schema; two or more schema may have to be combined in order to adequately cover the whole problem.

The complex process of understanding ill-structured problems is aided by the use of problem categories which are learned from experience. As Chi, Feltovich, and Glaser (1981) explain, "categorization of a problem as a type cue[s] associated information in [one's] knowledge base" (p. 22). The search for and combining of schema can be limited to stored schema considered relevant to the problem category. A series of studies by Cowan (1986, 1988, 1990, 1991) suggests, for example, that executives normally distinguish between strategic and operational problems, and between technical and human problems. Different processes seem to be used to solve each of these categories.

Problem interpretation involves not only making sense of information by comparing it to existing schema, it also requires evaluation: the perception of a discrepancy between the executive's understanding of current reality and a more desirable reality. As Cowan (1990) points out:

> This dynamic highlights the importance of an evoked problem concept in directing attention . . . , in cuing related knowledge to assist interpretation . . . , and in constraining search and solution activity . . . Once executives categorize a situation as a particular problem, causes are related to the initial categorization . . . , as are reformulation, . . . [and] the search for solutions. (pp. 366–367)

Our evidence from educational administrators suggests that, as compared with nonexperts, experts:

- develop a relatively clearer understanding of the problem before attempting to solve it;

- devote more time and effort to the initial formulation of ill-structured problems; and

- are more inclined to view the immediate problem in its relationship to the broader mission and problems of the organization.*

Goals. Understanding an ill-structured problem sufficiently well to solve it usually requires decomposing it into pieces that are more manageable (Newell, 1975; Hayes, 1980). This begins to transform the often abstract, general interpretation of an ill-structured problem into a set of more-precise goals which can serve as targets for problem-solving activity (Voss and Post, 1988). Given these more-precise goals, the executive is better able to compare the current state with the goal at each stage of the process, as is normally possible with well-structured problems (Greeno, 1978). Similar to what is accomplished through problem classification, such goals also provide relatively direct access to stored knowledge relevant to solving the problem without the need for more elaborate, time-consuming, and possibly inaccurate search processes necessitated by vague goals (Greeno, 1980).

Expert as compared with nonexpert educational administrators:

- adopt a broader range of goals for problem solving;*

- when solving problems in groups, have less personal stake in any preconceived solution. Rather, their aim is to arrive at the best solution the group can produce;*

- more often establish staff development as one explicit goal, among others, for solving problems in groups.*

Processes Designed Primarily for Solving Problems: Constraints and Solution Processes

Constraints. The distinction between well structured and ill-structured problems is a matter of degree. How much an executive already knows that is relevant to solving a problem is one factor in determining the extent to which a problem is well-structured. Another equally important factor is the number of constraints that must be addressed in solving the problem (Reitman, 1965; Voss and Post, 1988). Once goals are set, much of problem solving involves recognizing and dealing with constraints to accomplishing those goals. Often constraints arise, or are encountered, only in the midst of solving a problem. These may be obstacles (absence of something required in order to continue) or errors (an action taken which caused an inappropriate result); they may also be distractions (Shank and Abelson, 1977)—for example, some other problem requiring immediate action comes to the executive's attention. And, in the case of multi-step problem-solving processes, the actions taken at a prior step become constraints on possible actions at later steps. For example, in order to cope with the problem of a deficit budget, a superintendent may request all central office unit heads to cut back five percent on their projected spending for the current year. One unit head refuses to do so—a constraint facing the superintendent in solving the deficit problem. Threatening to fire the unit head unless he or she complies makes "voluntary restraint" among units an unlikely strategy for coping with the deficit problem in subsequent years.

As compared with nonexperts, our prior research suggested that expert educational administrators:

- more adequately anticipate many of the constraints likely to arise during problem solving;

- show a greater tendency to plan, in advance, for how to address anticipated constraints;

- respond more adaptively and flexibly to constraints which arise unexpectedly;* and

- do not view constraints as major impediments to problem solving.

Solution processes. The overt or covert steps or actions taken in order to achieve goals for problem solving is our meaning of "solution processes." Such actions or steps result from a deliberate search through memory for relevant procedural schema. These are structures in the mind about how to perform certain actions, a set of instructions for action—for example, how to develop a budget, how to resolve a conflict with a trustee, how to ensure one's position is made clear in a two-minute radio interview.

Procedural schema take several forms, each more or less appropriate to different problem conditions. One set of conditions occurs in the face of problems or subproblems that are relatively well structured. Under this set of conditions, procedural schema of most use take the form of "scripts" (Shank and Abelson, 1977), well-rehearsed sequences of actions leading to a desired goal. They may be quite elaborate, including long causal chains of actions and an anticipated role for many other people, but, because they are so well-rehearsed, they are also fairly rigid. Unanticipated deviations from the script (e.g., errors, distractions) require novel responses to be grafted onto the script. Such responses may be thought of as microscripts, a type of script that seems relevant, also, when solution processes are developed more spontaneously, during action. Reflection-in-action, to use Schön's (1983) term, involves intuitive and rapid search processes through memory for guides to short sequences of action or microscripts.

A second set of conditions occurs when the executive is faced with more ill-structured problems or subproblems. Under such conditions, searches through memory are unlikely to locate a script that will solve the problem. The more likely outcome of such a search will be a "plan" (Shank and Abelson, 1977; Suchman, 1987). A plan describes the choices available to the executive as she attempts to accomplish a goal. A plan may include a number of different scripts connected in novel ways (Van Lehn, 1990).

For a plan to be developed by an executive as a guide to solving an ill-structured problem, the executive must still possess considerable, problem-relevant knowledge, although that knowledge initially is not organized as efficiently as a script for solving the problem. Under a third set of problem-solving conditions, executives may not possess even this initially inefficiently organized knowledge. When existing stores of problem-relevant procedural knowledge are not available, executives must rely on a third type of structure called general "heuristics." These include such content-free procedures as brainstorming, means-end analysis, use of analogies and metaphors, collecting more information about possible steps, and trial and error (Rubinstein, 1975; Brightman, 1988; Hayes, 1981; Newell and Simon, 1972).

Our previous study of school principals solving problems in groups (Leithwood and Steinbach, 1991b, Leithwood and Steinbach, in press) found that, as compared with nonexperts, experts:

- had well-developed plans for collaborative problem solving (meeting);*

- provided a clear, detailed introduction to the problem and its background to collaborators;*

- outlined clearly the process for problem solving (e.g., how the meeting will be conducted);*

- carefully checked collaborators' interpretations of the problem and their own assumptions;*

- without intimidating or restraining others, clearly indicated their own view of the problem and its relationship with larger problems;*

- remained open to new information and changed views, if warranted;*

- assisted collaborative problem solving by synthesizing, summarizing, and clarifying as needed;*

- had strategies for balancing the need to keep the group on track (focused) and allowing discussion;* and

- ensured that follow-up was planned.*

Processes for Understanding as well as Solving: Values and Mood

Values. A value is an enduring belief about the desirability of some means or action. Once internalized, a value also becomes a standard for guiding one's actions and thoughts, for influencing the actions and thoughts of others, and for morally judging oneself and others.[1] Conceptualized in this way, values have a pervasive role in problem solving. They shape one's view of the current and desired goal state and figure centrally in the choice of actions to reduce the perceived gap.

To explain how values play such a role, it is necessary to situate them within two structures in the mind. One structure acts as a repository of one's goals and aspirations, as well as at least some of one's values. The purpose of this structure is to evaluate perceived information from the senses, deciding which to ignore and which to process further because of its potential relevance to one's goals, aspirations and values. Such a structure is sometimes referred to as the "executive"; in Anderson's (1983) Act* theory, the function is performed by a "working memory." Situating values in an executive or working memory structure helps explain the pervasive but indirect effects which superintendents' values have on their actions; they provide perceptual screens which, as Hambrick and Brandon (1988) explain, allow the superintendent to "see what he wants to see" and "hear what he wants to hear." The superintendent who values efficiency and frugality in the running of schools may not "hear" the community's expressions of willingness to spend more money on better education for its children.

Values also seem likely to exist, in two forms, in long-term memory. In one form, they are embedded as integral parts of superintendents' organized knowledge structures (schema) about their organizational worlds, including procedures for how to solve known problems in that world. This is their implicit form. Although values in this form are an important part of superintendents' domain-specific knowledge, superintendents often may not be consciously aware of such values and the strength of influence of their implicit values on their actions. Values also may be stored as independent structures in the mind—their explicit form. Superintendents are likely to be consciously aware of their values in this form and, hence, have more control over the influence of such values. Whether in their implicit or explicit forms, values stored in long-term memory have direct effects on superintendents' thoughts about what actions to take—a "behavior channeling" effect (Hambrick and Brandon, 1988). Nevertheless, even when values are in explicit form, their effects on a superintendent's actions are mediated by the amount of discretion the superintendent possesses. Superintendents' actions are formed from thoughts about many matters in addition to their explicit values. But it is difficult for superintendents to escape from the influence of their implicit values and the values which act as perceptual screens.

Our own research with educational administrators concerning the nature and role of their values in professional problem solving, described in more detail in Chapter 8, suggests that experts in comparison with nonexperts:

- are more aware of their values;
- use their values more regularly in solving problems; and
- use values as substitutes for knowledge in solving ill-structured problems.

This research has also resulted in a classification of values used by educational administrators. Incorporating elements of Hodgkinson (1978), Beck (1984), and Hambrick and Brandon (1988), these value categories are described later in the chapter.

Mood. Knowledge is stored in the mind in several forms, words and pictures, for example. Furthermore, what is meant by "knowledge" goes considerably beyond the purely cognitive content implied by the term. In addition to values, as discussed above, other affective states or feelings will also be integrated as part of knowledge structures. A superintendent not only has in mind a procedure for facilitating the decision making of trustees, she also has associated (and therefore unavoidable) feelings about carrying out the procedure—despair, elation, fear, boredom, and the like. Both the nature and strength of their feelings shape the mood experienced by superintendents during problem solving. Additional feelings, for example, pressure and uncertainty coming from the context in which problem solving occurs, also contribute to the superintendent's mood. Research on social cognition suggests that, along with personal goals and the knowledge one possesses, mood has an important influence on the degree of cognitive flexibility the superintendent is able to exercise during problem solving. Showers and Cantor (1985) explain flexibility as:

> (a) adjusting interpretations in response to situational features; (b) taking control of [one's] thoughts and plans; (c) seeing multiple alternatives for interpreting the same event or outcome; and (d) changing [one's] own knowledge repertoire by adding new experiences and by reworking cherished beliefs, values, and goals. (p. 277)

Intense moods reduce such flexibility, thereby limiting problem-solving effectiveness. Consistent with this explanation, in our research with educational administrators (e.g., Chapter 9) we have demonstrated that, in contrast with nonexperts, experts:

- are better able to control intense moods and remain calm during problem solving;

- are more self-confident about their ability to solve ill-structured problems;* and

- treat staff with respect and courtesy during the meeting and the interview, i.e., show consistent and genuine respect.*

Method

Data for the study were collected through stimulated recall interviews conducted with seven "reputationally effective" superintendents. A letter was sent to every superintendent in Ontario (called Directors) requesting them to nominate five superintendents who they believed had reputations with their peers as being particularly effective on the job. They were advised to use whatever criteria they considered relevant. One hundred and eleven ballots were sent out and 74 were returned. The 11 top-ranking nominees were then invited to participate in the research. Ten agreed. Subsequently, three others dropped out for a variety of reasons (health, time, change of heart), resulting in a sample size of seven.

Data Collection

Participants were asked to audio tape a portion of a regular meeting with their senior administrative colleagues, usually six to eight people, in which they would be dealing with a problem the superintendent expected to be particularly controversial or "swampy." They were asked to select a nonroutine or complex problem because expert practitioners tend to deal with routine problems in a somewhat automatic fashion which makes it difficult to discern their thought processes.

Following the meeting, the superintendents were interviewed. Using the tape of the meeting to stimulate recall, superintendents were asked to comment on what they were thinking at various points. Both the superintendent and the interviewer stopped the tape frequently to ask questions or to offer information about intentions and thought processes. This discussion was recorded on a separate tape, which was subsequently transcribed carefully to eliminate all identifying characteristics. These transcripts, along with the record of the original meeting, provided the data for the present study.

Data Analysis

Elements of expertise identified with an asterisk in the previous section served as a focus for coding interview data collected from the superintendents included in the study. These elements emphasize the Solution Processes component within our model because of expectations created by our prior research about the more critical aspects of group problem solving. Also examined were superintendents' uses of problem-relevant knowledge, and degree and quality of self-reflection. In all, 18 codes were used to analyze the interview data.

For this study, each transcript was divided into relevant statements made by the superintendent. Two researchers (neither of whom was the interviewer, to maintain objectivity) worked together to code the interviews according to the 18 elements. Researchers initially coded each protocol independently and then discussed and resolved any discrepancies.

Results

The study was intended to address three questions: How do superintendents solve problems in groups? What values influence their problem solving? and, What purposes are being served by such problem solving? Results of our data analysis are reported as a response to each of these questions. Where possible, we point out similarities and differences with the results of our other recent research.

How do Superintendents Solve Problems in Groups?

In Table 6.1 we report the number of statements found in the verbal protocols of superintendents which were coded according to each of the 18 components selected from our problem-solving model; statements reflecting superintendents' values are reported separately (Table 6.2).

A superintendent's response for each component potentially might vary widely in its level of expertise, judged in comparison with the results of our previous research. However, the seven superintendents included in the study were selected because they had reputations, among other superintendents in the province, for being effective, and, in fact, all superintendents in our sample exhibited the kinds of thinking attributed to the expert problem solvers in our previous work. With the exception of one item (which will be addressed later), the superintendents displayed expert-like processes in relation to each component of our problem-solving model (Table 6.1 does not speak to this).

Given such uniformly expert processes, evidence in Table 6.1 clarifies which components of problem solving received most and least attention (number of statements made) by superintendents in their thinking-aloud about their conduct of the meetings with their senior staffs.

More than half the responses (58 percent) are accounted for by just six of the 18 problem-solving elements; one of these elements was part of problem Interpretation: views immediate problem in relation to the larger mission and problems of the school system (rank 4: item 1.1). Examples of superintendents' talk illustrating this process include:

And that's what was going through my mind. Here was an opportunity to again reference that second strategic direction. I point to an area [school-based decision making] where we can start to move.

We have as part of our philosophy "people before things," involvement in decision making, and yet here we are still solving the problem.

A second, frequently coded element concerned Constraints: anticipates obstacles, responds flexibly to unanticipated obstacles which arise and does not view obstacles as major impediments to problem solving (rank 5: item 3.1). Superintendents commented, for example:

There may be some awkward silences as we sort of look around and [think] what do you want us to say today? But really we have to be able to make a move somehow.

Now there's a conflict between S and S and they will go after each other. His question is unclear and sounds like he's setting him up. So I now start to focus on whether there's a set-up and whether I need to do anything.

Two frequently coded elements were part of Solution Processes. One of the elements involved superintendents assisting collaborative problem solving by synthesizing, summarizing, and clarifying as needed (rank 2: item 4.6); for example, this is how one superintendent summarized a rather lengthy and complicated staff recommendation: "Your words reflect the need for some inservice, even for them."

As part of their frequently mentioned Solution Processes, without intimidating or restraining others, superintendents clearly indicated their own view of the problem or opinion about the issue (rank 6: item 4.4). As one superintendent said:

D: You've said that it's the responsibility of the [Educational Assistant] from time to time to demand a right guaranteed by the contract.

S: That's right.

D: Would you agree that we have some responsibility to create a climate in which (a) it's not particularly difficult to do that [demand own rights] and (b) it's improbable that you have to in the majority of the cases demand your rights.

Table 6.1 Statements in Protocols Coded as Different Components of Problem Solving (values omitted)

PROBLEM-SOLVING COMPONENTS	TOTAL FREQUENCY	MEAN	PERCENT OF TOTAL	RANK
1. Interpretation				
1.1 Immediate problem viewed in broader context	32	4.6	7	4
2. Goals				
2.1 Less of a personal stake in preconceived solution	9	1.3	2	16
2.2 Broad range of goals	29	4.1	6	7
2.3 Staff development an explicit goal	16	2.3	4	12
3. Constraints				
3.1 Responds flexibly to unanticipated obstacles	32	4.6	7	5
4. Solution Processes				
4.1 Has well-developed plan	14	2.0	3	13
4.2 Provides clear introduction	12	1.7	3	14
4.3 Outlines the process for problem solving	7	1.0	2	17

4.4	Indicates own point of view without intimidating others	32	4.6	7	6
4.5	Remains open to new information	12	1.7	3	15
4.6	Summarizes, synthesizes, clarifies, etc.	56	8.0	12	2
4.7	Balances need to keep group focused and need for open discussion	21	3.0	5	10
4.8	Checks for consensus, agreement, understanding	27	3.9	6	8
4.9	Ensures that follow-up is planned	19	2.7	4	11

5. Affect/Mood

5.1	Always appears calm and confidant	3	0.4	.01	18
5.2	Genuine respect and courtesy shown to staff	54	7.7	12	3

6. Other

6.1	Use of problem-relevant knowledge	22	3.1	5	9
6.2	Self-reflection	58	8.3	13	1

D: One of the real underlying issues is who decides what the responsibility of the [Educational Assistant] should be? And they seem to be saying overtime is better than lieu time because [then] we know that we are needed. And that seems to be a question of, you know, who defines when and where they're needed. Is it the teacher, the principal, or them? *I think the principal.* Am I making sense in that analysis?

Superintendents consistently showed respect and courtesy toward their senior colleagues, not only during the meetings but in our interviews with them after (rank 3: item 5.2). For example:

I really appreciate all the backup. It really helps me.

[S] is just now, after being in the role for a year and a half, getting comfortable with the group.

I cheer him on. This is the superintendent of program. This chap has come a long way.

Although we coded such respect as part of Mood or Affect, it reflects a strongly held value (Respect for Others) and also seems integral to a solution process designed to foster collaboration.

Finally, the most frequently coded element of superintendents' problem solving were indications of self-reflection and self-evaluation (rank 1: item 6.2). For example:

And I'm asking myself, while I hear that, whether our current organization and structure is adequate.

So while he was saying, "Here's the problem as I see it," I've identified another problem that I want to raise with him in terms of how we get secondary school programs written, rewritten, refined, and perhaps it's time to reconceptualize.

What goes on in my head is, wow, conceptually we've got a difficulty here which won't affect the memo but is something I have to store for future reference.

Superintendents planned extensively for their meetings. Nevertheless, the extent of mention of these self-reflective processes suggests that a high level of effort on their part was invested in the meeting; these meetings seemed to be crucial to them. They also worked hard at learning as much as possible from the meetings.

A disproportionate amount of attention was focused on Solution Processes in our coding because we believed this might constitute the focus of attention for the superintendents with their groups. This belief appeared to be unwarranted from the frequency count alone, however. Two of the nine possible Solution Process items were ranked in the top six, but the remaining seven together accounted for only 24 percent of overall responses. Taking into account the third ranking of the Interpretation item, these data are consistent with previous evidence suggesting that experts devote considerably greater attention than do nonexperts to Problem Interpretation, thereby reducing the demands placed on Solution Processes. Nonexperts attempt to compensate (in vain) for inadequate attention to Problem Interpretation by devoting substantially more effort to Solution Processes (Glaser and Chi, 1988; Reynolds, 1992; Leithwood and Steinbach, in press).

How, then, do superintendents solve problems in groups? Our evidence suggests, in sum, that superintendents' problem-solving processes appeared to be highly expert in comparison with principals, for example. Especially attended to were efforts to help their colleagues to place the immediate problem they were addressing in a broader context and to anticipate and address constraints. They also conducted the meetings so as to ensure the contribution of most in attendance; planning carefully in advance for how the meeting would be conducted. Without intimidating others, they made sure their opinions were known. Furthermore, they were especially reflective about the meetings, both during the meetings and after the meetings were finished; they monitored progress in the meetings very closely but only intervened personally when the process began to stall or no one else was willing or able to further the groups' progress. The superintendents were explicit about their own efforts to learn as much as possible from the meeting.

The Nature and Role of Superintendents' Values

In Table 6.2 we report the frequency of occurrence, in the protocols, of statements coded according to the four categories of specific values: Basic Human Values, General Moral Values, Professional Values, and Social and Political Values. Values were ranked according to how frequently they were used.

Forty-two percent of all values statements were coded as Professional Values. Almost as many (40 percent) were coded as Basic Human Values. Relatively little use was made of either Social and Political Values (11 percent) or General Moral Values (5 percent). Such extensive reliance on Professional Values and little reliance on General Moral Values is consistent with trends evident in our other

Table 6.2 Statements in Protocols Coded as Different Types of Values

CATEGORIES OF VALUE	NO. SUPTS (N = 7)	FREQUENCY	%	RANK
1. *Basic Human Values*				
TOTAL	7	189	40	(2)
1.1 Freedom				
1.2 Happiness				
1.3 Knowledge	7	95	20	2
1.4 Respect for Others	7	94	20	2
1.5 Survival				
2. *General Moral Values*				
TOTAL	5	23	5	(4)
2.1 Carefulness	4	13	3	6
2.2 Fairness	5	10	2	7
2.3 Courage				
2.4 Honesty				
3. *Professional Values*				
TOTAL	7	193	42	(1)
3.1 Gen. Resp.: Educator	1	1	1	9
3.2 Role Resp.	7	127	27	1
3.3 Consequences: Imm. Clients				
3.4 Consequences: Others (system)	7	65	14	4
4. *Social and Political Values*				
TOTAL	7	49	11	(3)
4.1 Participation	7	33	7	5
4.2 Sharing	2	4	1	9
4.3 Loyalty, Solidarity, Commitment	5	11	2	7
4.4 Helping others	1	1	1	9

studies described in Chapter 8. We also show in Table 6.2 the ranking of specific values. Role Responsibility and Respect for Others are among the most frequently cited with Knowledge ranked second. Consequences for Others and Participation are additional specific values ranked relatively highly.

Raun and Leithwood (in press) concluded that pragmatism (Consequences), participation, and duty (Role Responsibility) were prevalent value themes in their data. The present study provides additional support for the prevalence of these themes.

What Purposes are Served by Superintendents' Group Problem Solving?

In order to determine how superintendents solved problems in groups, we relied on a microanalysis of their verbal protocols using codes explicitly derived from our problem-solving model. To address the question of purposes, we offer a more holistic and more speculative interpretation of the data, based less directly on our model and its related coding system. Instead of the frequency of mention of brief, coded statements, our focus was on the meaning of larger units of superintendent talk. We searched for the explicit or apparent purposes which superintendents attached to their problem solving with groups. We also searched for patterns of thought not likely to be evident in a component-by-component analysis of that problem solving.

The impression of purposes being pursued by superintendents, created by our holistic analysis of their group problem solving, was unexpected. Based on a previous study of expert principals solving problems in staff meetings (Leithwood and Steinbach, 1991b), we anticipated that superintendents would be attempting to find better solutions to their problems than would be likely were individuals to solve the problems by themselves. Instead, superintendents in this study usually brought to their meetings a well-worked out solution to the problem on the agenda. As one superintendent explained:

> I'm very pleased because it's going exactly where I wanted it to go and it's coming from them. I'm not telling them what we're going to do; they are telling me what I'm going to do, but they are telling me what I want to hear.

This is the anomaly found in our coding (Table 6.1, item 2.1). Like our typical principals (but unlike our expert principals), superintendents had a preconceived solution in mind and the few statements coded as 2.1 reflected flexibility around how the solution would be played out. So, we wondered, why have the meeting? Was it only to serve the purpose, usually shunned by experts, of manipulating the group into agreeing on a predetermined solution so that members of the group would be motivated to implement it?

Based on both explicit talk and inferences about likely effects of their processes, we concluded that superintendents were attempting to accomplish two purposes. Their immediate purpose was to "transform ideas into organizational reality" (Daniels, 1990, p. i); their long-term purpose was organizational learning (e.g., Senge, 1990).

Transforming ideas into organizational reality. The problems superintendents were solving with their colleagues in our study were primarily operational or maintenance problems (vs. strategic problems) and the context for solving these problems was usually a regularly scheduled meeting. Daniels (1990) claims that "what effective [leaders] are doing in regular meetings is exercising the organization's formal power" (p. iii). Such meetings, according to Daniels, are not intended for solving problems. They are a step beyond that: their purpose is to ensure that those responsible for putting solutions into practice understand and agree with the solution: This is "the step by which the organization's intelligence gets integrated into its operations" (Daniels, 1990, p. iii). In this respect, it is not so much that leaders are not solving problems but that the nature of the problems they are solving has shifted. In regular meetings, then, at least part of the problem is how to ensure that everyone responsible for implementing the solution knows, in general, what is to be done and, in particular, what that means for their own practices. Our evidence suggests that superintendents incorporated into their solution processes four strategies to ensure that ideas were transformed into practice. These strategies included:

- Deciding on the specific nature of the action to be taken. Most superintendents used several strategies to help ensure complete agreement around the solution. Reflecting the value "Solidarity," it was important to them that everyone in the group "speak with the same voice" or carry the same message to the people with whom they worked. One way this happened was to ensure agreement on the details of the overall actions to be taken. For example:

  I'm information gathering. I want to have a clear picture from the players so that everybody is talking the same language. That was really what I was after.

  What I'm trying to do . . . I need my team with me so that we're going in [to the meeting] with a common understanding of what the outcome is to be and how we're going to do it.

The problem here was to make sure that everybody understood those items and gave them appropriate weight.

And thirdly, I wanted to be sure we all understood and agreed with the final position that I was articulating, making sure we all had a common understanding of what had been agreed to.

- Being clear about the nature of the superintendents' actions for implementation. Another way of ensuring that everyone spoke with the same voice was to develop, with the group, those specific actions the superintendent would initiate to implement the solution. For example, one superintendent explained:

  The point there was to engage them in planning how I would respond to the people who had initially brought the concern [Educational Assistants]. And that's how the rest of the meeting is cast. It's in terms of their helping me plan what I'm going to say when I go back to them. Writing a script for me.

  Another asked his colleagues:

  Do I make it a quiet presentation? Do I make it a passionate presentation?

- Being clear about the nature of the actions to be carried out by other members of the group. Speaking with one voice was also fostered by explicitly working with the group on the actions other members of the group would take. For example:

  Okay, as a summary then, you're going to do some editing. This will go to the next principals' meetings—both of them. The [assistant] superintendents will follow up with one-on-one kind of interview with them and give them the support as we outlined in [point] five.

- Developing a viable implementation plan but remaining flexible in the face of alternative proposals offered by others. As a kind of "fail-safe" mechanism, superintendents usually had thought through the implementation problem and identified, in their minds, a viable course of action. Such mental rehearsal seems likely to have prepared the superintendent for a role in the meeting of ensuring that the group does not fail to anticipate important obstacles and/or is unable to generate useful implementation steps. However, possibly reflecting their valuing of Participation, superintendents did not rigidly adhere to their own preconceived plans in the face of other good suggestions. For example:

> I never have a clear idea what to expect exactly. I've got a general framework for what I anticipate happening in the meeting. But if the meeting is working well, there is a lot of spontaneous stuff going on. It's not like the thing is well planned out like a play or something like that. So there is lots of good discussion. But yes, overall, we accomplished what I hoped would be accomplished. . . .

Previous evidence (Leithwood and Steinbach, 1991b) concerning the group problem solving of expert principals demonstrated efforts by them to ensure that follow-up to group problem solving was planned (unlike their nonexpert colleagues). The present study, however, suggests much greater attention by superintendents to this aspect of the problem, perhaps reflecting the swampier nature of the implementation problem at the district or system level, rather than the school level.

Fostering organizational learning. Peter Senge (1990) conceives of learning organizations as:

> organizations where people continually expand their capacity to create the results they truly desire, where new and expansive patterns of thinking are nurtured, where collective aspiration is set free, and where people are continually learning how to learn together. (p. 3)

Most superintendents made explicit statements about their long-term purposes reflecting the aim of organizational learning. One said, for example:

> We want to confirm leadership in the school and we want to clearly signal that things are under control, that problems are getting solved appropriately. We want to set the stage for addressing the longer-term problems in the future, getting to the long-term sorts of solutions.

Beyond such talk about their purposes, processes used by superintendents to solve problems in groups addressed conditions necessary for group learning. What is required to foster group learning and how did the superintendents manage it? Senge (1990) views group (or team) learning as "the process of aligning and developing the capacity of a group to create the results its members truly desire" (p. 236). This happens when the group is able to think insightfully about complex issues by tapping the resources of many minds. There is also a need for innovative and coordinated action: Senge speaks of " 'operational trust' . . . each group member remains conscious of other group members and can be counted on to act in ways that complement each others' actions" (p. 236). Learning teams also foster other learning teams "through inculcating the practices and skills of team learning more broadly" (p. 237).

There is evidence in the verbal protocols of superintendents attempting to meet Senge's three conditions for group learning in several ways. Two superintendents reveal how they tap the mental resources of those in their groups in these comments:

> [S] is sometimes intimidated by program and instructional intellect and I . . . wanted to indicate to [him] that what he had to say was extremely valuable at that stage. If I allowed it to happen, he would wait until the end and that's becoming a pattern of his . . .

> reacting to your body language, your facial expression . . . so that we can make sure that people don't miss an opportunity to meaningfully communicate. I watch that fairly carefully.

> Can we just hold off on the strategies? I haven't heard from M. She's indicated she wants [to speak]. Then we'll come to that.

Examples of how superintendents encourage innovative and coordinated action is provided by these comments:

> the role I play frequently is making sure that we get all the data out on the table and listened to before we go ahead and make a decision.

> I see my role then as prodding, prompting, facilitating, encouraging . . . causing people maybe to stretch themselves a little bit further than where they were . . .

> Let me explain a little bit about this. My way of operating is that I very much trust the ability of a group if it is functioning well to make really good decisions. So I leave a lot of power with the group and really pick my spots very carefully on something

that I would try to impose on the group without getting their consensus or approval on it.

Superintendents showed little evidence, however, of fostering other learning teams. Only one superintendent alluded to this:

> my role is to make them as effective as possible. Therefore I feel that I have to do that in every respect, not only as they conduct their daily work, or entertain all their leadership assignments, but also as individuals.

Group learning requires both dialogue and discussion. Dialogue, "the free and creative exploration of complex and subtle issues" (Senge, 1990, p. 237), requires participants to suspend assumptions and to regard one another as colleagues: it also requires a facilitator who helps maintain the dialogue. The verbal protocols of superintendents show them thinking about providing such facilitation:

> if I can't read the group and work for them to keep contributing, then I shouldn't be in the role.

> right, this is exactly what should happen. That superintendent should be speaking up and raising that question and that's what the group will expect to have happen.

In addition to dialogue, Senge claims that "discussion" is a condition for group learning—the presentation and defense of different views and a search for the best view to help solve the problem. The intent of discussion is not to win, not to have your views prevail. Rather it is to clarify the meaning and consequences of the available alternatives to assist the group in finding the best solution to its problem. Superintendents encourage such discussion in several ways. For example:

> And I want to hear . . . just some opinions this morning about how you feel about the situation and what kinds of moves that we're really going to have to take.

> I went through all the items and paused long enough on each one to give people a chance [to talk].

> One of my theories of a meeting is that you have to let the talk go on long enough to get everything that wants discussing out

on the table. You make everything discussable by allowing somebody to introduce it.

Summary and Conclusion

The study asked three questions: How do superintendents solve problems in groups? What is the nature and role of values used by superintendents in their problem solving? and, What purposes are superintendents attempting to serve through solving problems in groups? Verbal protocols collected using stimulated recall techniques with seven reputationally effective Ontario superintendents, each solving problems with a group of their senior colleagues, provided data for the study. Using evidence from principals as a basis for comparison, the superintendents' problem-solving processes appeared to be highly expert (with the exception of having a preconceived solution in mind).

As expected, values were pervasive in the problem-solving processes of superintendents. In support of earlier studies, superintendents appeared to be largely influenced by the consequences that their problem solving would have on stakeholders in their organizations (pragmatism). Participation and their own sense of role responsibility (duty) were the other two values most evident in superintendents' problem solving.

Superintendents appeared to be using their group problem-solving processes for two purposes. The short-term purpose, using Daniels' (1990) phrase, was to transform ideas into organizational reality. This meant ensuring that the solution to problems was systematically reflected in the subsequent practices of the superintendents' senior colleagues, as well as in their own practices. A second, longer-term purpose was organizational learning, especially fostering the learning of the groups. Some of the conditions for organizational learning offered by Senge (1990) were used as a basis for interpreting those processes used by superintendents likely to serve this purpose.

Processes used by superintendents to solve problems in groups serve a number of leadership functions, some of which have been made clearer by this study. To the extent that educational systems continue to restructure in ways similar to other large organizations, it seems especially important to continue the effort to better understand group problem-solving processes. In order to meet the demands for change and to respond opportunistically to unanticipated events, organizations are becoming structurally flatter (Naisbitt and Aburdene, 1987; Toffler, 1990). Much of the work of these organizations is being done in teams, with organizational learning as an explicit goal to help ensure their survival. These restructured organizations demand new forms of leadership based on collegial and expert sources of power. Referred to as transformational, such leadership will often be expressed through the exchange of ideas in groups. As Bill O'Brien claims:

> Being a visionary leader is not about giving speeches and inspiring the troops. [It] is about solving day-to-day problems with my vision in mind. (Quoted in Senge, 1990, p. 217)

Part 3

—◄○►—

Key Processes

Chapter 7

Problem Interpretation: How Administrators Classify and Manage Their Problems

This study examined aspects of the problem-solving processes of 11 "effective" secondary school principals: how they classified and managed their problems, broad problem-solving strategies, and influences on their problem solving. Intensive interviews were audio taped, transcribed, and content analyzed. Results identify criteria secondary principals used to prioritize problems, estimate their difficulty, and determine the involvement of others. In addition, results describe the broad problem-solving strategies of principals and influences on such processes. Comparisons are made with data from elementary principals and su-

This chapter is a modified version of K. Leithwood, and R. Steinbach. 1990. Characteristics of effective secondary school principals' problem solving. *Journal of Educational Administration and Foundations*, 5(1), 24–42. Reprinted by permission.

perintendents as a means of assessing the importance of organizational context in shaping administrative problem solving.

Chapters 3 through 6 each provided some evidence concerning the processes administrators use in problem interpretation; this is the process by which they extract a focus for their action from the buzzing confusion or mess in which they often find themselves. To argue that this process is crucial requires little empirical evidence; no degree of skill in the development of a solution, for example, will compensate for defining the wrong problem at the outset. Yet, problem interpretation processes used by administrators are not yet well understood. As Kolb (1984) observes:

> Previous attempts to describe executive behavior in problem solving or decision-making frameworks are too narrow, excluding a most important strategic executive function—finding and defining the right problems to work on. (p. 110)

In the study reported in this chapter we aimed to better understand administrators' problem interpretation processes in both their cognitive and organizational contexts. By cognitive context we mean those factors, including those in the external environment, that administrators actually think about as they frame their problems; administrators' general approaches to problem solving were also considered part of cognitive context. By organizational context we mean primarily the size of the organization in which they find themselves. This study was undertaken with principals of secondary schools and results are compared with evidence from two identical studies carried out previously, one with superintendents and one with principals of elementary schools (Leithwood and Steinbach, 1989; Leithwood and Stager, 1986).

Framework

Our theoretical description of what is involved in problem interpretation, outlined in Chapter 6, noted the density of information with which administrators are routinely bombarded. Problem solving is initially a process of screening, sorting, and prioritizing this information, using one's existing knowledge to evaluate the salience of such information in light of one's goals and aspirations. How problems eventually are labeled and classified may give rise to different solution processes. It certainly determines one's subsequent focus of attention.

In this respect, it seems important to know what influences administrators' problem interpretation; these influences are likely to shape the criteria used by administrators in evaluating the priority to be awarded to some potential problems in relation to others. Theoretically, the context in which problems are solved appears to be one of several important determinants of problem solving (e.g., Fredericksen, 1984; Shulman and Carey, 1984). Typically, context has been conceptualized largely in terms of whether or not the problem was solved alone or with others. However, Clark and Peterson (1986) have noted differences in teachers' problem solving before as compared with during classroom interaction. This observation lends support to context as an important variable in explaining problem solving but suggests the need to view it more comprehensively than has been the case so far; number of people involved and timing may be only two of many aspects of context shaping problem-solving processes.

Greater clarity with regard to the influence of organizational context on administrative problem solving has immediate, applied value also; one such value resides in the direction provided for the preparation of administrators to work in different contexts. Previous studies of differences between elementary and secondary school principals (reviewed by Leithwood, 1986) have identified at least a dozen differences that would be consequential in the preparation of a principal. But, because these studies are small in number, of uneven quality, and inconsistent in the differences which they identify, little confidence can be placed in them as guides to action. More research would be helpful.

Evidence reported in Chapters 3 through 6 suggests that, as compared with nonexperts, experts develop a relatively clearer understanding of the problem before attempting to solve it. They also devote more time and effort to the initial formulation of ill-structured problems and are more inclined to view the immediate problem in its relationship to the broader mission and problems of the organization.

The present study was intended to extend these results by asking a series of five questions: (1) On what bases do school administrators determine priorities among problems? (2) On what bases is the difficulty of the problem judged? (3) How do school administrators decide when to involve others in problem solving? (4) What broad strategies for problem solving are used by these administrators and what influences those strategies? and (5) Does organizational context influence problem interpretation processes?

Method

Eleven secondary school principals from three urban/suburban school systems were included in this study. These principals were identified as highly effective on the basis of a three-step screening process. In the first step, two central office administrators from each school system were asked independently to identify those secondary principals they considered to be exceptionally effective. Next, those recommended by both judges were provided with information about the general purpose of the study and asked if they would be willing to participate. The third step involved rating the effectiveness of the principals in terms of a four-stage, research-based conception of growth in principal effectiveness called the *Principal Profile* (Leithwood and Montgomery, 1986). Data were collected by an interviewer who did not know the reputational ratings of the principals in the sample. In this step, analysis of data from a 2.5-hour standardized interview permitted principals' overall effectiveness to be estimated on a four-point scale. There were only two principals whose reputational ratings were discrepant with their *Profile*-based ratings. Therefore, the latter ratings were used in those cases.

The eleven effective secondary school principals had an average of 5.5 years of experience in that role, and were in schools with over 1,000 students. All had vice principals.

Data were collected through an interview which included two sets of questions. The first set, somewhat open-ended in nature and followed by detailed problems, focused on principals' reflections on their own problem solving, how it had changed with experience, and factors (such as values and beliefs) perceived to influence it. The second set elicited information about how principals selected, from the myriad problems they encountered, those to which they assigned time and priority.

The interview instrument and procedures for its use were identical to those in two previous studies, used for comparison. One of these studies collected data from six highly effective and 16 typical elementary school principals drawn from three Ontario urban/ suburban school systems. Data for the second study were collected from the superintendents of eight Ontario school systems which varied widely in size and geographical location. The superintendents' effectiveness was not assessed in any way. Data were collected in the present study by a researcher who had not been involved in the interview leading to the Profile ratings and who was unaware of the reputational rating of the principals. Interviews averaged about one and one-quarter hours; they were audio taped and subsequently transcribed. These interview records were then coded and the content analyzed.

Results

Data from interviews with secondary principals concerned three aspects of their problem solving: the classification and management of problems; broad problem-solving strategies; and influences on problem solving. In this section, each aspect of problem solving is described separately. The ways in which these results are similar to or different from results of our studies of elementary principals and superintendents are noted.

Problem Classification and Management

Data about problem classification and management addressed specific questions about (a) how principals determined the priority they would award to problems, (b) what features of problems were considered by principals in estimating problem difficulty, and (c) the bases upon which principals determine the involvement of others in problem solving. In Tables 7.1, 7.2, and 7.3 we summarize results for each of these questions and provide illustrations, from the interview transcripts, of principals' talk related to these questions.

All principals in the study provided evidence of having some explicit problem-sorting process and most appeared to use the process regularly and systematically. In Table 7.1 we indicate the eight bases or criteria used as part of these processes for determining how much priority to award a problem. Among the criteria identified by almost all principals were numbers and nature of people involved (2) and the urgency or time frame for finding a solution (4). About half of the principals mentioned the availability of others to whom to delegate problem solving (1) and their own conception of their responsibilities as principals (5). What is seen as important by others (7) was mentioned by only one principal; three to five principals mentioned the remaining criteria (8, 6, 3).

These data share much in common with our previous data of effective elementary principals. Both sets of principals had an explicit problem-sorting process and elementary principals used four of the eight criteria outlined in Table 7.1. Data from the present study suggest, however, that effective elementary principals are more directly concerned about the impact of problems on school programs. Whereas secondary principals were not unconcerned about programs, they were more explicitly concerned with how the problems fit with their role responsibility, relationship to long-term plans, and the avoidance of problem escalation. Principals labeled typical in our previous study of elementary principals shared with the one secondary principal in the present study a concern for what is seen as important by others.

There are even stronger similarities between results of this study and data from our previous studies of superintendents. Both sets of administrators shared all eight criteria for problem sorting. This is the case if the strong concern of superintendents about the visibility of a problem is interpreted as a concern for what is seen as important by others—especially by trustees—and if superintendents' concern about relevance to board policy is equated with the secondary principals' interest in long-term plans.

In Table 7.2 we indicate that secondary principals estimated the probable difficulty of a problem using seven criteria in total. Although all principals could readily indicate their criteria, there was not much consensus among them. Impact on staff (personnel problems, 2) was the criterion identified by the largest number of principals (four). At least two principals identified the criteria remaining: availability of clear procedures; number of people involved in a solution; the possibility of value conflicts arising; whether the solution would be acceptable to all (a win-win solution); and whether those affected by the solution would accept it (be reasonable even if the solution did not favor them). The extent to which the problem could be solved within the school, and therefore be controlled, was also a basis for estimating problem difficulty.

Our previous data from elementary principals were similar in respect to only three of the seven criteria: availability of clear procedures; impact on staff (problems affecting people directly and likely to have significant emotional content); and numbers of people required to solve the problem. On the other hand, superintendents, according to our previous data, used all of the same criteria as secondary principals in their estimates of problem difficulty. The extent of a problem's impact across the school or school system was a criterion associated with problem difficulty by elementary principals and superintendents, but not by secondary principals.

Effective secondary principals indicated consideration of six issues when deciding whom to involve in problem solving (Table 7.3).

Table 7.1 Bases on Which Secondary School Principals Determine Priorities among Problems

BASES FOR AWARDING PRIORITY	ILLUSTRATIVE COMMENT
1. Number of staff capable of handling the problem	"I say to myself, 'Am I the right person to be doing this?' And that thought process is really important to me, in terms of deciding what to do . . . and what problems to farm out."
2. Number (and nature) of people involved in or affected by problems	"[I am] very aware of the impact that problem solving is going to have on students, teachers, parents, . . . trustees, parents, . . . superintendents . . ."
3. Content of the problem	"I separate every problem that I deal with as an educational or noneducational issue. If it's an educational issue, I will do everything I can to deal with it. If it's a noneducational issue, I will pray that it goes away, and 90 percent of the time it does."
4. Time frame for finding a solution	"I try to look at and to budget my time for [problems] that I see have . . . long implications and those that are going to require . . . my undivided attention to do them. So I guess I'm prioritizing them according to what I see as long-range effects."
5. Fit with principals' conception of role	"it doesn't take me more than 30 seconds, in hearing the problem, to know whether this is my responsibility or whether there is someone much closer to this, who should be dealing with it."
6. Relationship to long-term plans	"[problems] divide themselves into two groups . . . (1) lower-level—basic operations things and (2) the kinds of higher-order things reflected in [the principal's] goal package."
7. What is seen as important by other people	"I probably frequently decide my priorities on the basis of what needs are seen as most important by other people, as I am terribly responsive to that . . . "
8. Avoidance of problem escalation	"there are certain things you had better deal with quickly . . . or you may get some spin off that you hadn't anticipated."

Table 7.2 Bases on Which Secondary School Principals Determine Difficulty of Problems

BASES FOR DETERMINING PROBLEM DIFFICULTY	ILLUSTRATIVE COMMENT
1. Availability of clear procedures	"[easy problems are] things like budget allocation in as much as I have done it for a long time . . . I know how to negotiate with the people who are responsible for the various accounts . . . "
2. Impact on staff—morale, etc.	"The most difficult issues are issues of personnel performance. No question."
3. Number of people required to solve	"something that falls into the area of administrivia . . . they're the easiest ones to solve because you don't involve the interaction of all those people. As soon as you get all of the people involved, with their diverse views, problem solving becomes a complex issue."
4. Likelihood of value conflicts	"I guess the easiest problems to solve are problems that do not have a values component to them."
5. Likelihood of a solution all can accept	"The easiest problems are problems whose solutions . . . will be acceptable [to those affected]."
6. Type of people affected by problem	"easiest to solve are [problems] where I am dealing with people . . . who have some flexibility."
7. Degree of control over solution	"[easy problems] are in-house . . . we have control of the resources and the people being involved. It becomes more difficult . . . as you move out."

The first issue to be considered by most principals was whether or not the time required for a solution permitted any involvement of others (2). Many problems faced by principals have an undeniable urgency attached to them that precludes consultation with others—

Table 7.3   Bases on Which Secondary School Principals Determine the Involvement of Others in Problem Solving

BASES FOR DETERMINING PROBLEM DIFFICULTY	ILLUSTRATIVE COMMENT
1. Problem difficulty	"if it's a swamp type problem I'll try to get my data from as many of the sources as possible, so that I can make the best decision or so the group can make the best decision."
2. Time available for a solution	"sometimes we are limited by time and time makes the decision for us . . . it's whatever data you can gather within the time frame."
3. Importance of finding best solution	"you involve people when they can be honestly influential to the solution."
4. Amount of relevant knowledge possessed by others	"it's a matter of some process to involve input data from the prime stakeholders . . . the department heads' [group] within a school is a very key group to me . . . [because] they are working closely with staff."
5. Impact of problem on others	"when an issue involves their own working success, then they must be involved. You don't make decisions that will change a person's mode of operation without letting them tell you whether it's feasible or not, in their mind."
6. Need for ownership of the problem	"I was trying to work through a cycle that would get them to take some ownership."

emergencies affecting student safety, for example. Three issues considered by respondents were related, one way or another, to the need for information. These were problem difficulty (1), importance of finding the best solution (3), and the amount of relevant knowledge possessed by others (4). The two remaining issues reflected concerns about the implementation of the solution. If a problem affected someone quite directly, principals believed that person ought to be part of solving it (5). More directly, if a person was going to have to change their practices as a consequence of the problem solution, the likelihood of their doing so was greater if they had participated in finding the solution (6).

The first four bases for involving others in problem solving in Table 7.3 were the total set identified by superintendents in our previous study. Unfortunately, we do not have comparable data from elementary principals on this matter.

This section, in sum, has identified the criteria used by secondary principals in awarding priority to problems, determining how difficult it will likely be to solve a problem, and deciding on whether or not to involve others in the problem-solving process. On these matters, the problem solving of secondary principals appeared to have much in common with the problem solving of both superintendents and effective elementary principals. Differences which were evident among the three groups of administrators could be interpreted as a function of their span of control. As the units for which the administrators were responsible became larger, the importance of student program-specific criteria for classifying and managing problems, for example, became diluted, although not displaced by other criteria.

Broad Problem-Solving Strategies

Data concerning the broad problem-solving strategies of secondary school principals described aspects of their overall style, identified a sample of specific, frequently used strategies, and clarified the role of knowledge in their problem solving.

The three aspects of secondary principals' overall style evident in the data were identical with those described in our previous study of effective elementary principals. All eleven of these principals had a highly collaborative approach to solving all but those problems they considered to be trivial or mechanical. As one principal said:

> There are very large decisions, and I'm trying to think of one—there are almost none—that would not be made by a group of people. And normally that group of people would be the group that's interested in making a decision . . .

As part of their overall style, seven of the eleven respondents could be viewed as front-end risk takers but careful information collectors;

they were prepared to define a problem, initially, as quite complex, for example. This involved the risks associated with the difficulty of finding a solution or being critical of an aspect of the school's program which might lead to defensiveness on the part of staff, something typical elementary principals were rarely willing to do. Once a problem was defined in such a way, however, effective principals were extremely careful about collecting relevant information. For example:

> if I have to discipline a teacher, it's very humane. It's based on the data . . . and the facts are there and the conclusion is derived from the facts (and no public hangings).

Ten of the secondary principals also had an overall problem-solving style characterized by a high degree of self-conscious reflection. They were articulate about how they solved problems and showed signs of extensive metacognitive control. This is clear in the remarks of a principal who said:

> when I consider alternative solutions to a problem . . . [each] will have tentative solutions. I will very quickly try to take those as branches on a tree and . . . think through, in my own mind, what will happen if I pick each one.

Previous data from superintendents about their overall problem-solving styles suggest that their styles were also characterized by collaboration, front-end risk taking, and reflectivity. In addition, however, they placed much greater stress on situating specific problems within the big picture, which superintendents believed they saw better than did others.

Most secondary principals (ten of eleven) indicated that they used the same four specific strategies that previous data suggested were used by superintendents and elementary principals. Two of the strategies were direct extensions of results reported earlier in the chapter (and were strategies also used by superintendents): the use of a deliberate model for problem solving on the basis of their reflection on their problem-solving processes, and participation. Both are part of the broader collaborative style of principals. The two remaining strategies are more distinct. One such strategy included applying the same, basic processes to almost all problems; for example, diagnosing the impact of the problem on different groups; getting feedback from others, clarifying one's priorities and vision and then using them directly in problem solving and communicating with others as effectively as possible.

Finally, secondary principals, as with their effective elementary counterparts and superintendents, developed organizational structures to help in problem solving. Such structures included, for example: regularly meeting with Department Heads, using administrative props ("I have, for example, an alphabetical listing of everything an administrator has to do . . . in this building"), and administrative teams ("one of the reasons it went well was the planning process that had gone on. So the administrative team is one particular factor and I think it's a critical factor").

Superintendents used problem delegation as a strategy more than principals did; secondary principals used this strategy more than elementary principals.

Nine of the eleven principals identified types of knowledge and skill which they considered to be crucial to doing an effective job. Only one or two respondents identified each type. These types included:

- The specific context in which one works:

> to select the issues in any professional context, you have to know a lot about the forces impinging on that context . . . human and financial resources . . . community expectations . . . the potential of your staff . . . demands on the curriculum . . . That's just a partial list.

- Knowledge about fundamental characteristics shared by most schools:

> I really think that if I'm having any success at all, it's because I have been in so many different school settings . . . and I'm able to see the similarities.

- Skill in acquiring new information when needed:

> I've learned how to ask the questions, the right questions, that give me the information that I need.

- Knowledge about the educational process:

> first and foremost, we need to understand what learning is about, what kids are about, what programming is about. Without [that knowledge] . . . we're making decisions based on other things that aren't as important.

- Skill in administrative routines:

> the basic operations of running a school . . . the lower-level mechanical thing that one has to do.

• Knowledge of human nature:

> what makes them tick . . . [so that you can help them] . . . see that there is a problem and then work toward the kind of structures you're going to put in place to arrive at the best solution.

Specific sources of information identified by the eleven principals included: research, particularly as disseminated through face-to-face contact with researchers (one respondent); all those with a stake in the problem (one respondent); informal networks of other school administrators; formal professional development programs (one respondent) provided by the school system; students; teaching and nonteaching staff in the school; and members of the community such as senior citizens (three respondents).

The types of knowledge considered crucial by secondary principals, as well as sources of knowledge, overlap considerably with results from our earlier studies of superintendents and elementary principals. Unlike either group of principals, however, superintendents stressed the importance of having a breadth of knowledge about as many aspects of their system as possible. They also talked about how hard they had to work at acquiring and maintaining such knowledge; this difficulty seems likely to be a function of the size of their system, as compared with the principals' system, and the greater possibilities for superintendents to delegate problems to those with the appropriate depth of knowledge to solve the problem.

In sum, results reported in this section identified secondary principals' overall style of problem solving and some of the specific strategies which they used frequently. Results also described the types and sources of knowledge these principals considered to be of most value for their problem solving. A comparison of these results with elementary principals and superintendents showed considerable similarity. Most differences emerged in relation to superintendents who relied more on placing problems within the big picture in order to find a solution. Superintendents also used delegation more frequently as a strategy than did principals, especially elementary principals.

Influences on Problem Solving

Results of the present study concerning influences on secondary principals' problem solving were highly consistent with results of our previous study of elementary principals. Four categories of influences were evident in both sets of data: increased experience, personal values, the larger school system context, and principals' attitudes toward problem solving. Our data from superintendents can also be classified in this way but they were not as extensive as the data from either secondary or elementary principals.

Nine of the eleven secondary principals in the study cited influences which were classified as increased experience. As with the administrators in our previous studies, effective secondary principals provided evidence of greater reflection on their problem-solving processes with experience. An outcome of greater reflection for one respondent, for example, was clarity about how he worked best:

> I operate best on a one-to-one. I am not so good in staff meetings . . . and I know that. I am always good with a small group, reasonably good with heads and definitely [I] know I'm good with the individual.

As well, most principals believed they had refined their processes as a result of experience. Such refinements invariably included a more collaborative approach to problem solving. Often this meant outright delegation:

> in the time that I've been here, I made fewer of certain kinds of decisions than I did when I came because someone else is making those decisions now. It's not me.

One principal also described the role that visualization had come to play in his problem solving:

> [I] try to visualize the outcome . . . you never visualize it as it will eventually turn out. But that doesn't really matter . . . it would be nice to do that but one needs to at least take a look into a crystal ball and get some idea of what the possible . . . scenarios are. And if you can do that you at least have a general sense of direction . . . you've got some kind of goal that will help you move toward.

One principal talked about the relative ease with which previously experienced problems could be solved, as compared with novel problems. Increased experience reduces the number of completely novel problems that one encounters, although effective administrators remain sensitive to the unique features of largely familiar problems.

Whereas evidence from superintendents on the effects of experience suggests strong similarities with what was reported by principals, superintendents cited a much greater need to resolve increasingly diverse sets of problems and to do so from multiple perspectives. This seems like a predictable difference in light of the broader responsibilities faced by superintendents.

The second category of influences on administrative problem solving was personal values. Other recent studies have suggested that such values are a pervasive part of effective elementary principals' and superintendents' problem-solving processes (see Chapter 8).

These studies also indicate a wide range of values used by administrators. Begley and Leithwood (1989) found, for example, that principals used all three classes of values in Hodgkinson's (1983) typology: values of preference, values of consequence, and moral values. Furthermore, increased effectiveness in the role, more experience, and more problem-relevant knowledge were associated with greater reliance on values of consequence for students, in particular. Data from this study are consistent with such results. Respondents were able to articulate their values quite clearly and used their values as explicit instruments in problem solving. This is evident in one principal's explanation of how he responded to differences among staff concerning their basic stance toward instruction of the less academically talented students in the school:

> I . . . had a value conflict, for example, with those teachers who tended to be at the right wing . . . I'm not entirely at the other end of the spectrum saying, o.k., all we need is nurturing. . . . My concern is, we need to find better ways to try and respond to those kids and at least be able to say that, within our resources and . . . capabilities, we did the best we could with what we had before we just threw up our hands and said "well let them go."

At least four of the respondents used their sense of role responsibility and that of their staffs as a value to influence their problem solving. For example:

> There will be some problems that I think it's imperative that the principal as school leader handle . . . there are times when the principal must be seen as the person who is taking the ball or is supporting the group.

Although most principals spoke about how they resolved value conflicts, one respondent was clearly faced with value conflicts with which he felt powerless to deal. These were conflicts between the value he attached to a highly individualized form of education and the type of program his school was able to provide students. He spoke of keeping "a very leaky ship afloat" and his disenchantment in not being able to change the system ("When I first became principal, I thought I was going to change some of those things . . . but I learned that I couldn't"). As a consequence, he said, "I probably live with some pretty severe value conflicts."

A third category of influences on the problem solving of all secondary principals in the study was the broader school system context in which they worked. One element of this context, also identified by elementary principals, included board policies, procedures, and other requirements. The effect of these influences could be either positive or negative. As one principal noted:

> It's a pretty highly centralized system. I'm a great respecter of the people in the system but I'm not a great fan of some aspects of the system . . . there are enough procedures . . . that it's tough to get too far out of step. [It's] tough for you to be poor . . . [but] it's tough for you to be outstanding.

A second element of system context influencing respondents in this study, as well as elementary principals, was the combination of autonomy and high performance expectations for those in the principal's role. Four principals spoke of having "a certain amount of rope to either hang myself or do something with," of being able to "bring that unique programming" to the school. They also spoke, however, of their systems' expectations for such things as "good planning" and "meeting Ministry guidelines."

Finally, ten of the eleven secondary principals identified board resources as an element of school system context which have a positive bearing on their problem solving. Specific board resources that were identified included inservice education for administrators, access to legal advice on matters such as the termination of teacher contracts, and knowledge provided by people outside the system (such as researchers) and made available through efforts of senior administrators. Several principals also appreciated the models of effective administrative practice provided by their senior administrator colleagues.

Although superintendents, in one of our previous studies, identified influences related to school system context, the specific influences were at least partly different than those identified by principals. Such influences bearing negatively on superintendents included the unsatisfactory distribution of authority between trustees and the superintendent and dysfunctional school system structures. Positive influences included the ability of other staff to solve problems and the willingness of schools to behave autonomously.

Attitudes toward problem solving was the final category of influence on secondary principals' problem solving. Previous data from elementary principals and superintendents suggested that both groups of administrators (a) were aware of problem solving as an activity, as distinct from just doing it, and (b) enjoyed the challenge of new problems, often viewing them as opportunities to advance their own goals. These administrators were also self-confident about their ability to deal with problems, but realistic about the inevitability of making occasional mistakes. Data from secondary principals suggest that they shared many of these same attitudes. At least nine of the 11 principals demonstrated signs of each of the three attitudes. Awareness of the problem-solving process for one principal included the self-judgment that he did not do aspects of it very well:

As far as problem solving . . . [concerned with] . . . planning and decision-making, I would see myself as not doing that particularly well. I probably thrive on the chaos of the standard secondary school. I even like the chaos. I was superintendent for a couple of years and went wild with boredom.

Another principal expressed the view that the nature of the process was quite unique from person to person. A third respondent spoke of its ongoing nature: "once you reach where you think you want to be, then you start the process over again. It's a continual thing." The confidence and air of calm secondary principals brought to problem solving is evident in comments by this respondent: "I certainly don't want to give you the impression that we handle everything perfectly, but a little anticipation and communication goes a long way to solving these problems." Another principal also noted: "[as] you gain experience . . . [you know] that this is how it's going to happen, and not being flustered or trying to short cut the process."

Results reported in this section, in sum, provide evidence of four categories of influences on secondary principals' problem solving: increased experience, personally held values, the context of the larger school system, and principals' attitudes toward problem solving. In the case of each category, secondary principals appeared to be very similar to superintendents and effective elementary principals.

The small number of differences that were evident seemed to be quite obvious differences in roles and the particular demands created by such roles.

Discussion

What are the consequences of this study in relation to our original research questions? First, it seems likely that several different elements of organizational context shape, in an interdependent fashion, the way educational administrators solve their problems. This is evident in administrators' responses to direct questions on the matter as well as comparisons of problem-solving processes used by those in the three different roles that have been investigated. One of these elements is the level in the organizational hierarchy at which the administrator works. For example, superintendents differed from principals in their sensitivity to the public visibility and political content of problems in determining their priority. This seems to be explained by the proximity of superintendents to elected officials and their positions between education professionals and the public.

Another relevant aspect of organizational context is the size of the unit being administered. Secondary principals for the most part administered much larger schools than did elementary principals. This appears partially to explain, for example, differences between the two groups in their concern for control. Control was a strong theme—indeed, a value—clearly expressed by superintendents and to a lesser extent by secondary principals. It has also been identified as a central theme in research with senior managers in non-educational institutions (Quinn, 1988; Hambrick and Brandon, 1988). Although a concern for control seems a natural consequence of administering units of larger sizes and, therefore, more likely to fly apart, this may also help explain recent evidence supporting the greater efficiency and effectiveness of smaller schools and school districts (e.g., Walberg and Fowler, 1987). We speculate that energy devoted to control may easily consume some of the attention and effort otherwise available for matters which more directly bear on the quality of education being delivered to students.

Role responsibility is a third element of context that appears to shape administrative problem solving. Evidence about the importance of this element of context was available, for example, in differences between superintendents and principals in the type of knowledge they valued for problem solving. Whereas principals were more concerned with depth of knowledge, superintendents were more interested with breadth, that is, some knowledge about as many aspects of their organizations as possible, so that they had the big picture with which to work. Both Tobert (1987) and Kanter (1983) report similar findings from their research with senior executives in noneducational organizations. Tobert (1987) explains this interest in the big picture in terms of a model of management development. Managers at higher stages in this model are not just, or even primarily, concerned with the technical aspects of their work. Rather,

> they come to appreciate the importance of interpersonal relations, marketing, politics and so on. ... Such managers are committed to achieving results in a complex real world characterized by the collision of many types of logic, many scales of social systems and many different temporal rhythms. (p. 7)

Tobert (1984) suggests that such a "synthetic theoretical perspective" endows the executive with "the vigilance and the balance to foresee and to respond in a measured fashion to the otherwise unexpected" (p. 92). Without such a perspective, the executive's activities easily become fragmented.

In describing successful managers, Kanter (1983) also stresses their integrative capacities. "They aggregate sub-problems into larger problems, so as to recreate a unity that provides more insight into required action" (p. 29). While Tobert and Kanter both characterize concern for the big picture as a function of expertise, such concern also appears likely to be nurtured or to correlate highly with more extensive role responsibilities.

Finally, the availability of problem-solving resources or support seems to be an element of organizational context bearing on problem-solving processes. Superintendents used delegation as a strategy more than did secondary principals. The point seems to be that each group of administrators had different levels of support for decision making. In earlier studies, superintendents appeared to be clearinghouses for many problems, quickly deciding who ought to handle the problem before delegating it, not unlike practices reported for other types of senior managers. Secondary principals, unlike many elementary principals, at least had access to several other administrative staff.

How effective secondary principals classify and manage their problems and what broad problem-solving strategies they use were the second and third set of questions pursued in this chapter. Data reported in response to both these questions highlight the social character of most problems faced by principals and how that social character infuses both the interpretation and solution of such problems. Effective principals appear to appreciate implicitly what Berger and Luckman (1967) refer to as the social construction of reality. There is, in this sense, no objective reality for principals to rest on; even their strong commitment to information collection is a commitment to exploring understandings of events by different people involved in those events. The search for a solution seems mostly to be a process of negotiating a course of action which those involved believe to be reasonable, to satisfy their interpretation of the problem. Because developing such a course of action is made easier when people begin to share common perceptions, effective principals see collaborative problem solving as a crucial strategy for developing such perceptions. In this matter, principals appear to be on hard ground. A large corpus of evidence supports the superior quality, as well as acceptability, of even problems with substantial, potential conflict solved by a leader in collaboration with colleagues, as distinct from problems solved individually or in a one-to-one relationship (Ettling and Jago, 1988). Recognition of the importance of collaboration seems to grow with experience. In the early stages of their careers, all groups of educational administrators that we have studied spoke of making many decisions by themselves, of being decisive and having the view that this was expected of them. This stance toward the role is symptomatic of the fourth stage of Tobert's six stage model of management development ("the manager's role is to know everything," cited in Quinn, 1988, p. 6). In contrast, effective secondary principals behaved like Kanter's corporate entrepreneurs: "[they] get their projects done by crafting coalitions and building teams of devoted employees who feel a heightened sense of joint involvement and contribution to decisions (p. 241)."

Influences on problem solving was the final set of interests explored in this study. Organizational context influences have already been discussed; most frequently, they appear to frame the problem space for administrators in ways that may not be explicitly recognized by administrators. A much more explicit and active influence on administrators within that problem space seems to be their own values. Hambrick and Brandon (1988) also award considerable influence to managerial values, but they suggest that executives often have limited discretion and, as a result, organizational outcomes may have little correspondence to managerial values. Data from the present study of secondary principals and its companions (Begley, 1988; Campbell-Evans, 1988; Leithwood and Stager, 1989; Leithwood and Steinbach, 1989, 1991) suggest an even more pervasive influence of values than this, however.

This influence is most apparent in relation to unstructured or novel problems where values act, in part, as substitutes for problem-relevant knowledge. In addition, however, values may function as long-term goals for problem solving. In this capacity, values are sufficiently fundamental as guides to action so that they may be viewed as among the more powerful instruments available to administrators in shaping the big picture, in developing an integrative vision and purpose basic to the leadership which they provide to their organizations. Moreover, the value of values increases as administrators gain experience, become more expert, and assume positions of increased responsibility.

Conclusion

Our conclusion, as a whole, portrays effective administrative problem solving as a logically messy and decidedly social process. This finding calls into question the generalizability of previous research on problem solving which was primarily carried out in relation to nonsocial problems. This warning is also a challenge to take the problem solving of administrators as a serious object of inquiry. As Tobert (1984) observed:

> "Executive Mind" bespeaks an immense discipline relating the very sources of human aspiration to the ultimate ends of human action—an immense discipline which few persons imagine as a possibility . . . which still fewer persons actually undertake, which fewer yet master, and which virtually no institutions actively cultivate. (p. 85)

Chapter 8

The Nature and Role of Values in Administrators' Problem-Solving Processes

In Chapters 4, 5, and 6 in this text we demonstrate the pervasive role of values in administrators' problem-solving processes. Moreover, these chapters begin to clarify the types of values which most frequently influence such problem solving. Equally important, however, but not addressed in these chapters, are questions about how conflicts among competing values are resolved and what influences the development of administrators' values. Results of three additional studies are summarized to help answer these questions.

There is an extensive literature in the fields of management and administration concerned with decision making and problem-solving processes (e.g., Fox, 1987; Kepner and Tregoe, 1981; DeBono, 1985). By far the bulk of this literature is prescriptive in nature and assumes that such processes ought to be almost entirely rational: Kepner and Tregoe (1981) entitle their book, for example, *The New Ra-*

tional Manager. In contrast, a smaller but impressive body of literature has devoted theoretical attention to the role of values in
administration (e.g., Barnard, 1938; Weber, 1949; Simon, 1976).
This literature acknowledges, for administrators, what is considered
common-sense for people, more generally: that values are a critical
aspect of thinking and problem solving (Frankena, 1973; Rokeach,
1973). But in spite of this seemingly common sense proposition, the
empirical study of administration has traditionally "ignore[d] value
and sentiments as springs of human action" (Greenfield, 1986, p. 59).

In the early stages of our research on administrators' problem
solving we, too, ignored values. It was not until we began frequently
tripping over them in our data that we began to realize their central
importance. Following that realization, however, values were added
to our model of administrative problem solving and we began the
kinds of data collection reflected in Chapters 4, 5, and 6. In addition
to the work described in those chapters, three doctoral dissertations
with a similar focus and supervised by the first author have been
completed. The purpose of this chapter is to summarize what we
have learned about the nature and role of values from these half-
dozen studies. This summary addresses five questions:

- What role do values serve in administrators' problem solving?

- What types of values are reflected in the problem solving of
  administrators?

- What is the relationship between administrators' expertise
  and the values they use in their problem solving?

- How do administrators respond to problems that include (or
  are mainly about) value conflicts?

- Through what influences are administrators' values shaped?

Sources of Evidence: A Synopsis

Chapters 4, 5, and 6 in this book touch most directly on values, although their importance first occurred to us in the context of the
study reported in Chapter 3. In brief, the Chapter 3 study was carried out with samples of expert and nonexpert elementary principals with no preconceived expectations concerning values; this
study, however, does contribute information about the role of values
in problem solving. The study of superintendents in Chapter 4, provided evidence concerning the completeness of a taxonomy of values
built from our own prior evidence and a broad review of values liter-

ature. In Chapters 5 and 6 we described further testing of the extent to which this taxonomy captured the values which elementary school principals and superintendents, respectively, bring to bear on their problems.

Because the same taxonomy of values was used in three of these studies, a comparison of results offers some (very tentative) insights about whether or not values used for problem solving differ by administrative role. In addition, evidence about values in administrative problem solving is available from dissertations by Begley (see Begley and Leithwood, 1989), Campbell-Evans (1988), and Raun (forthcoming).

Begley.   Principals' decisions to adopt and promote the use of computers in their schools provided the context for Begley's study with elementary principals. Its purpose was to learn more about the nature of values related to such decisions, the relative influence of values in comparison with other factors on these decisions, and the relationship between school leaders' orientation to their role and the values which they used in decision making. Begley used Hodgkinson's (1978) conception of value types and relationships as a framework for collecting data from principals.

Interviews conducted with 15 elementary school principals (about two-thirds of the principals in one central Ontario school system) provided data for this study. Each interview lasted from 1 1/2 to 3 hours and was tape recorded and transcribed.

Campbell-Evans.   In addition to the purposes for Begley's study, Campbell-Evans inquired about how principals responded to problematic situations in which courses of action proposed by others (e.g., senior administrators) conflicted with their values. The values framework used in this study was developed by Beck (1984a, 1984b, 1984c).

All eight elementary and junior high school principals in a small urban school district in Alberta provided data for this study. These data were collected in three phases. Phase One included retrospective, audio-taped interviews with principals concerning two or three prior but recent decisions considered important by the principals; these data were analyzed before the second phase of data collection was initiated. Phase Two required principals to think aloud as they responded to five simulated problems presented by the researcher; these responses were also audio taped and transcribed. At the completion of think aloud responses, principals were asked to react to the accuracy of an analysis of their responses in Phase One. Each principal was given a written report of the identification and prioritization of values revealed in their Phase One interviews and their reaction was requested. Phase Three consisted of an interview designed to identify the level of expertise of each principal.

Raun. Adopting the values taxonomy described in Chapters 4 through 6, Raun inquired about types of values used by superintendents and factors influencing the development of those values. Evidence was collected through a survey with closed and open questions, responded to by 53 superintendents in Ontario.

With this brief description of the half-dozen studies on which our evidence is based, we turn to a discussion of the five questions outlined earlier.

The Role of Values in Administrators' Problem Solving

Orientation. Whereas research about the values of educational administrators is in its infancy, the values of business executives have been explored more extensively. Both theoretical and empirical insights from such research are helpful in the study of educational administrators' values, and similarities with results of the limited research in education are already apparent. Hambrick and Brandon (1988), for example, propose a conception of the links between values and actions (or problem solving, for our purposes) which begins to explain, with some precision, why values are critical in problem solving. Of the two links which they propose, one is direct. Values influence executives' actions directly when such actions or solutions are selected strictly because of their preference. Begley and Leithwood (1989) reported instances of such influence in principals' decisions about adopting computer technology in their schools. Leithwood and Stager (1989) also reported a form of direct influence of values on problem solving in their comparison of differences in how expert and typical principals solved ill-structured (knowledge-lean) problems. Experts were much clearer about their values, and, as a consequence, could and did use them as substitutes for more problem-specific knowledge, which would have helped them but which they lacked. The direct influence of values on problem solving is called "behavior-channeling" (England, 1967).

Indirect effects of executives' values on their problem solving, termed "perceptual screening," also are proposed by Hambrick and Brandon. In this case, values influence the perceptual saliency of stimuli; executives see or hear what they want to see or hear. Perceptual screening may have a dramatic influence on the problems executives choose to notice and how these problems are defined. Leithwood and Steinbach (1990) have reported significant differences between expert and typical secondary principals' definition of problems, partly due to differences in their value orientations.

Both the direct and indirect effects of values on problem solving, proposed by Hambrick and Brandon, are modified by the amount of discretion executives' environments permit. In general, the more discretion allowed executives, the greater the likely effect of executives' values. Assuming that discretion is greater in more senior roles, values are especially important to consider in the problem solving of superintendents. Hambrick and Brandon's (1988) model also suggests that when discretion permits, strongly held values will have a more direct influence on problem solving than will weaker values. Furthermore, particular types of values (e.g., duty) may influence problem solving in unique ways (e.g., cause executives to be more or less aggressive about their own values). Accordingly, a better understanding of superintendents' values—their nature and development—seems critical to a fuller appreciation of superintendents' problem-solving processes.

Results.   Three studies helped clarify the role that values play in school leaders' problem solving. Begley inquired about the role of values in their decisions about the adoption and implementation of computer technology in their schools. Results demonstrated a preeminent role for values in the adoption decision but a much less important role in the subsequent process of solving the implementation problem. For that problem, factors identified in school improvement research (e.g., building fit, user commitment) appeared to be more influential. These results appear to reflect a direct relationship between values and actions. That is, dominant or very strong managerial values are thought to be capable of dictating behavior without any (or much) regard for facts. Indeed, this study provides especially relevant support for this role of values since a number of school leaders in the study decided to adopt computers in the absence of knowledge about the consequences for students or others. As we noted earlier, this role for values has been termed "behavior channeling" (England, 1967).

Campbell-Evans examined the role of both internal influences (i.e., beliefs and values) and external influences (e.g., time, money) on school leaders' problem solving. Results argue for a more pervasive role for values than did Begley's results by suggesting that values give meaning to potential external influences and act as filters in determining whether potential external influences will be allowed to be actual influences. So, for example, factual information in a report available to a school leader relevant to some aspect of her work is more likely to influence that work if she strongly values Knowledge (a Basic Human Value) than if she does not. These results illustrate the second type of relationship between values and action suggested by Hambrick and Brandon (1988); this is an indirect relationship, referred to earlier as "perceptual screening" (England, 1967). Values influence principals' perceptions of events causing them to attend closely to some and ignore others altogether. These highly subjective perceptions then lead to action.

Finally, the study reported in Chapter 3 which compared the problem solving of expert and nonexpert school leaders, especially in response to ill-structured problems, found that, for experts, explicit values acted as substitutes for knowledge. An ill-structured problem, by definition, is one about which the solver possesses little problem-relevant knowledge. Unlike nonexpert principals, experts were relatively clear about their values and so were able to make use of them as guidelines for problem solving (e.g., "I may not know exactly how to solve this problem but whatever we do, we are going to be open and honest with everyone"). This role played by values when there is little problem-relevant knowledge appears to be the same role proposed by Barnard (cited in Hambrick and Brandon, 1988) when managers face the opposite—excessive knowledge about a problem. Values, he suggests, provide a moral code for sorting a bewildering load of information and options that may confront the manager. In the absence of such a code, the manager bogs down.

In sum, then, dominant values appear to play an especially explicit and important role (behavior channeling) at key points in the problem-solving process. But throughout, they also act, more subtly, as perceptual screens for determining what aspects of the wider environment will be considered, and they are substitutes for knowledge (or moral rules of thumb) in the face of novel problems.

These studies provide considerable support for the theoretical claims that have been made by Hodgkinson (1978, 1986), Greenfield (1986), and others about the importance of values in administrators' problem solving.

The Types of Values that Influence the Problem Solving of Administrators

Orientation. Whereas in previous chapters we described our values taxonomy, we provided only a sketchy description and were largely silent about its origins. A bit more about that seems in order before using the taxonomy as a basis for responding to this question.

A value, in Hodgkinson's terms, is "a conception, explicit or implicit, distinctive of an individual or characteristic of a group, of the desirable which influences the selection from available modes, means and ends of action" (1978, p. 121). Imbedded in this definition are attributes of values also evident in the work of Rokeach (1973), Kluckhon (1951), and Williams (1968). That is:

- a value is an enduring belief about the desirability of some means or end; and

- once internalized, a value also becomes a standard or criterion for guiding one's actions and thought, for influencing the actions and thoughts of others, and for morally judging oneself and others.

As Rokeach (1973) suggests, a person's value system is a learned set of rules for making choices and for resolving conflicts.

To inquire about the values used in superintendents' problem solving, we were guided by a classification of values developed in our previous work and summarized in Table 8.1. This classification of values is a synthesis and modification of two value frameworks: one proposed by Hodgkinson (1978), the other by Beck (1984a, 1984b, 1984c). Hodgkinson proposes three categories of values:

1. *Transrational values* grounded in principle;

2a. *Rational values* based on an individual's assessment of consequences, the attainment of what is perceived as right;

2b. *Rational values* based on an individual's assessment of consensus, again, the attainment of which is perceived as right;

3. *Subrational values* related to personal preferences or what is perceived as good.

Type 3 values represent an individual's conception of what is good. Such values are grounded in affect or emotion and constitute the individual's preference structure. They are self-justifying and primitive. Each of the remaining categories of values describes a level of right that, according to Hodgkinson, is higher than the one below it. Type 3 values, unlike the others, represent what is good as opposed to right.

Type 2 values are subclassified: Type 2b values attribute rightness to consensus or the will of the majority in a given collectivity. Type 2a values define 'rightness' in relation to a desirable future state of affairs or analysis of the consequences entailed by the value judgment. Type 2 values, as a whole, are rational, Type 3 values subrational, and Type 1 values transrational.

Hodgkinson argues that Type 1 values are superior, more authentic, better justified, or more defensible than the other types. Indeed, use of these "sacred" values in decision making, according to Hodgkinson, is the hallmark of the ethical educational leader. Such a leader "seeks to increase his own degrees of freedom (a Type 1 value) and the degrees of freedom of those who function under his ' aegis" (1978, p. 8). However, Hodgkinson also claims that values tend to lose their level of grounding with time, thereby reducing their authenticity or their force of moral insight. He is critical, for example, of what he sees as the widespread use of Type 2 rational values in administration and attributes it to a positivistic, impersonal view of organizations and a natural desire to avoid the messiness and unpredictability associated with use of other types of values. This tendency toward rational values is greatly reinforced by the characteristics of contemporary culture, according to Hodgkinson.

Beck's (1984a, 1984b, 1984c) categories of values, not developed with administration in mind, are based on the premise that a fairly common set of universal values exists. Priorities and emphases may shift over time and with respect to specific circumstances. Nevertheless, a set of Basic Human Values can be identified, since values arise from need and many individuals have similar needs. These values are part of human nature and the human condition (Beck, 1984b, p. 3) and include, for example, survival, health, happiness, friendship, helping others, respect for others, knowledge, fulfillment, freedom, and a sense of meaning in life. Some of these values are means to others, but this cluster of basic human values, according to Beck, is mainly ends-oriented. Furthermore, these values are interconnected and are continuously being balanced, or traded off, with others. A sense of fluidity, openness, and flexibility exists within this formulation.

In addition to Basic Human Values, Beck (1984a, p. 3) identifies four other categories of values: Moral Values (e.g. carefulness, courage, responsibility); Social and Political Values (e.g., tolerance, participation, loyalty); Intermediate-range Values (e.g., shelter, entertainment, fitness); and Specific Values (e.g., a car, a telephone, and a high school diploma). According to Beck's conception none are absolute. Values are to be considered within their own system rather than in isolation. They are both means and ends. Viewing a value merely as a means is to deny its intrinsic worth. Viewing it merely as an end is to make it into an absolute. Even the Basic Human Values category forms a set, each of which has considerable importance in itself, but must also be weighed against other values (Beck, 1984c, p. 4).

Results of research carried out using the Hodgkinson and Beck frameworks separately (Begley, 1988; Campbell-Evans, 1988) led to the four-category system of values described in Table 8.1. The first category, Basic Human Values, incorporates values at the apex of Hodgkinson's hierarchy which he calls principles. These are primarily terminal values; they refer to "end states of existence" (Rokeach, 1973, p. 160). The remaining categories are more instrumental in nature. They represent preferable modes of conduct although, as Beck (1984a) warns, the distinction between means and ends is difficult to maintain. People's values act as interdependent systems to influence their problem solving. Categories entitled General Moral Values and Professional Values include norms of conduct or guidelines for judging the ethics of an individual's actions. Professional Values, an addition to Beck's framework, includes values uniquely relevant to guiding decisions in one's work life; Hodgkinson's (1978) values of consequence are included here. As Bayles (1981) suggests, in order for Professional Values to be guides to ethical conduct, they must be consistent with and subordinate to Basic Human Values.

Social and Political Values, incorporating Hodgkinson's (1978) values of consensus, recognize the essentially social nature of human action and the need for individuals to define themselves in relation to others to make their lives meaningful. There is also a close link between the specific values in this category and the Basic Human Value of respect for others. The categories of values included in Table 8.1 do not include Beck's short- or intermediate-range values.

Other categories of values relevant to administrative problem solving also have been proposed. However, they share sufficient similarity with those outlined in Table 8.1, or are not sufficiently grounded in empirical data, so as not to challenge the defensibility of using the value categories in Table 8.1 as initial guides for our research. For example, from research on business executives, Hambrick and Brandon (1988) propose six categories of values important in their thinking, three of which have direct parallels in Table 8.1: collectivism (comparable to the two Professional Values in Table 1 dealing with consequences), duty (same as general and specific role responsibilities), and rationality (some similarity with Knowledge). The remaining three, Novelty, Materialism, and Power, are not in Table 8.1 nor are they evident in the results of our previous research with educational administrators.

Table 8.1   Categories of Values Used in Administrative Problem Solving (From Leithwood, Begley, and Cousins, 1992)

CATEGORIES OF VALUES	ILLUSTRATIVE STATEMENT
Set 1 Basic Human Values	
• Freedom	• Staff is not forced to supervise dances by the Education Act . . . I would not force people to do this
• Happiness	• Most people felt pretty good about those goals
• Knowledge	• I would collect as much information about the probable suspects as possible
• Respect for others	• In a blanket approach you could offend many teachers
• Survival	• I don't think you can let an issue like this dominate a lot of time
Set 2 General Moral Values	
• Carefulness	• [Check] to indeed see whether or not we have a problem
• Fairness (or justice)	• Make sure that some people who are a little unsure of themselves also have an opportunity to speak
• Courage	• Their responsibility is to speak out when vandalism occurs
Set 3 Professional Values	
• General Responsibility as Educator	• Your value system is interfering with the mandate that we have in education
• Specific Role Responsibility	• Staff have to feel they are supported by the office
• Consequences for students	• Kids deserve a certain number of social events
• Consequences for others	• There's an impression that . . . students aren't under control
Set 4 Social and Political Values	
• Participation	• Involve groups such as Head's Council, Special Education, Student Services
• Sharing	• Allow people to get things off their chests—talk about the problems they perceive
• Loyalty, Solidarity, and Commitment	• We [admin. team] have to be seen as being philosophically in tune
• Helping others	• Let's help each other [school and parent] deal with that child

Another classification of values, proposed by Ashbaugh and Kasten (1984), is grounded in evidence collected from a sample of principals. As with our framework, Ashbaugh and Kasten's categories were influenced by Hodgkinson (1978). They propose a category of Transcendent Values very similar to Hodgkinson's "transrational" and our General Moral Values categories. A category labeled Personalistic Values includes subcategories concerning personal style, human relations, and nature of schooling; the first two of these are very similar to our Social and Political Values. An Organizational Values category is also proposed; it overlaps with a significant proportion of what we have included in our category Professional Values.

Results.   In Table 8.2 we summarize the results of four studies, three with superintendents and one with principals, with respect to the ranking, based on frequency of statements coded in the verbal protocols, of values used in their problem solving. The table also reports the percentages of all value statements, in the Chapter 6 study, coded as instances of specific values in our taxonomy.

Forty-two percent of all values statements were classified as Professional Values. Almost as many (40 percent) were coded as Basic Human Values. Relatively little use was made of either Social and Political Values (11 percent) or General Moral Values (5 percent). Such extensive reliance on Professional Values and little reliance on General Moral Values is consistent with trends evident in the other three studies indicated in Table 8.2. Discrepancies across studies are apparent, however, with respect to Basic Human Values and Social and Political Values. In both cases, the Chapter 6 study and the Chapter 5 study share similar findings as do the Chapter 4 and Raun studies. Whereas there may be several other explanations for these similarities and differences, it is noteworthy that both Chapter 5 and 6 studies were carried out with expert administrators, although from different roles; the Chapter 4 and Raun studies included samples selected without reference to expertise, but from the same role.

In Table 8.2 we also show the rankings of specific values associated with each of the four categories. Role Responsibility and Respect for Others are among the most frequently cited values in the Chapter 6 and two of the three other studies. Knowledge, ranked second in the Chapter 6 study, was also a prevalent value in the Chapter 5 study, although this is not evident in the data used for Table 8.2. Finally, Consequences (for immediate) clients and/or the system at large) and Participation are additional specific values ranked relatively highly in most of the studies.

Table 8.2 Statements in Protocols Coded as Different Types of Values

Categories of Values	EXPERT SUPTS. (CHAPTER 6) %	EXPERT SUPTS. (CHAPTER 6) Rank	SUPTS. (RAUN) Rank	SUPTS. (CH. 4) Rank	EXPERT EL. PRS. (CH. 5) Rank
1. *Basic Human Values* TOTAL	40	(2)	(4)	(4)	(2)
1.1 Freedom			14	7	11
1.2 Happiness			11	13	
1.3 Knowledge	20	2	10	6	5
1.4 Respect for Others	20	2	1	7	2
1.5 Survival			17	13	
2. *General Moral Values* TOTAL	5	(4)	(3)	(3)	(4)
2.1 Carefulness	3	6	5	9	9
2.2 Fairness	2	7	3	2	9
2.3 Courage			18	13	
2.4 Honesty				9	
3. *Professional Values* TOTAL	42	(1)	(2)	(1)	(1)
3.1 Gen. Resp.: Educator	1	9	7	9	6
3.2 Role Resp.	27	1	16	1	1
3.3 Consequences: Imm. Clients			7	3	4
3.4 Consequences: Others (system)	14	4	3	13	
4. *Social and Political Values* TOTAL	11	(3)	(1)	(2)	(3)
4.1 Participation	7	5	13	3	3
4.2 Sharing	1	9	12	9	6
4.3 Loyalty, Solidarity, Commitment	2	7	2	3	8
4.4 Helping others	1	9	5	7	

Raun concluded that pragmatism (Consequences), participation, and duty (Role Responsibility) were prevalent value themes in her data. Our other studies provide additional support for the prevalence of these themes, especially for superintendents.

The Relationship between Administrators' Values and Expertise

Studies reported in Chapter 3 and by Campbell-Evans examined the relationship between school leaders' values and their levels of problem-solving expertise. These studies were "grounded" in the sense that there was little prior evidence to use as a basis for framing the research at the outset.

Principals included in Campbell-Evans' study (using Beck's values framework) were evenly divided into expert and typical groups. Evidence from this study suggested that, whereas both sets of principals shared a common core of values, a strong relationship existed between level of expertise and some specific values, most notably within the category Basic Human Values. Respect for others was the most frequently mentioned Basic Human Value by typical or nonexpert principals. For the experts, Knowledge was the most frequently mentioned Basic Human Value. Within the category of Social and Political Values, both sets of principals frequently mentioned Participation, but nonexperts made greater mention also of Sharing. Responsibility was the moral value mentioned most by both sets of principals. Nonexperts also identified Carefulness as a value in this category.

Principals in the study reported in Chapter 3 also were divided into expert and nonexpert groups. Comparing the responses of these two groups to structured problems revealed few differences with respect to principles and values. Three differences were evident, however, in responses to ill-structured problems. As compared with the nonexpert group, experts more frequently drew upon principles and values in their problem solving. Given current expectations for the role, the principles on which the experts drew also seemed more defensible: for example, greater attention was given to consequences for students. Finally, the expert group more frequently relied on Specific Role Responsibility as a value in approaching swampy problems; this finding is consistent with evidence collected from chief education officers (Chapter 4) and expert secondary principals (Chapter 7).

Our research suggests, in sum, that administrators rely on a common core of values in their problem solving, independent of their levels of expertise (and perhaps administrative level). This is the case, in particular, with General Moral Values and Social and Political Values. Since education is indeed a moral enterprise and therefore likely to attract people with similar Basic Moral Values, this is not surprising. Furthermore, principals are regularly in communication with many different groups of people and spend as much as three quarters of their time in personal communication (Martin and Willower, 1981). It would be difficult to avoid seriously acknowledging the influence of Social and Political Values in such an environment.

But there does appear to be evidence of relationships between expertise and both Basic Human and Professional Values. For example, nonexperts' preoccupations with school climate and interpersonal relationships seems consistent with the frequency of mention of the value of Sharing. Similarly, experts' concerns for the quality of the classroom learning environment seems consistent with the stress they give to Knowledge. These relationships provide tentative support for administrators' values as a partial explanation for, or a variable interacting with, their levels of expertise.

More specifically, results concerning the dominant values of experts are intriguing in light of Hambrick and Brandon (1988). Their review stimulated the suggestion that the more managers value rationality (what we have called Knowledge) the more their other values will operate through perceptual screening; this also appears to be the case as managers increasingly value duty (our Responsibility values). Since our evidence depicts the most expert administrators adhering strongly to both sets of values, a substantial direct influence of values on action seems likely. This assertion assumes considerable discretion for school leaders' to act in concert with their values since organizational constraints on administrators' actions will blunt the influence of values on action. Indeed, as school-based management creates more discretion for principals, their values are likely to become an increasingly productive focus of attention, especially for purposes of administrator selection.

How Administrators Solve Value Conflict Problems

This issue was addressed by the Campbell-Evans study and by the study reported in Chapter 7. Neither study was guided by an initial orientation provided by previous theory or research. No such theory or research could be found. As part of the Chapter 7 study, principals were asked to (a) describe a problem in which they had been involved which had a great deal of value conflict, (b) indicate the competing values, and (c) outline how they had dealt with the conflict.

Our understanding of responses to this question indicates that principals encountered two types of value-related conflicts. One type involved competition between two or more values for recognition in the formulation of a solution. Such competition took three different forms:

- Values conflicts between two or more people other than the principal with the principal acting as mediator (e.g., enrichment teachers and regular classroom teachers disagreeing about the meaning of treating students fairly in the context of an "honor week");

- Value conflicts between the principal and other staff members (e.g., general moral value of principal with respect to adultery in conflict with the values of two married staff members having an affair with one another; the principal was also quite concerned about the consequences for students);

- Value conflicts within the principal alone (e.g., principal caught between the need to act quickly to remove from the classroom a teacher accused of inappropriate behavior with an older student and the value of fair treatment and due process for the teacher).

A second source of conflict for principals was between their strongly-held set of values and their actions. This conflict was usually experienced as an inability to act in a manner consistent with held values. One principal, for example, held a strongly nurturant attitude toward his teachers and experienced considerable conflict in being unable to effectively counsel one teacher toward a consistent and productive career plan: "its a value conflict for me because I think she's making all the wrong decisions and it breaks my heart and I cannot do anything about it."

Principals also used two distinct processes for attempting to resolve value conflicts. The first type we called "deep and strong" because it appeared to be analogous to the solution processes of expert principals in response to other sorts of swampy problems. This process, used by about half of the principals to resolve conflicts between competing values, included taking considerable care and effort in the early stages to clarify the nature of the conflict; satisfying themselves that the problem could not be usefully interpreted as involving anything but serious value conflicts (i.e., avoiding such an interpretation where possible); and clarifying for themselves their own priority among the competing values. As part of the process, principals relied on formal, organizational procedures, where appropriate, for resolving value conflicts (e.g., teacher dismissal procedures) once they were clarified. Other less formal but systematic procedures such as information collection, collaboration with others, and consensus-reaching techniques were also used. When these procedures failed, as they sometimes did, principals capitalized on unanticipated opportunities (e.g., a parental complaint about a teacher).

The second type of conflict resolution process used by principals we labeled "surface and weak." In this process, principals often sought out others' interpretations of the conflict and consulted with others about solutions. Nevertheless, the cause of the conflict usually remained unclear (e.g., a teachers' erratic behavior, a teacher's lack of interpersonal skill), and possible courses of action were considered and tried sequentially (and, in one case, only half-heartedly). Principals using this process seemed less clear about their own relevant values and had fewer existing procedures to call on as supports for their own actions. Only one principal used a version of this process to resolve a conflict between two values. Three principals, however, used it in an effort to find a course of action consistent with their values. In no case did this process result in a solution satisfactory to the principal.

The Campbell-Evans study approached principals' resolution of value conflicts from a different perspective than did the study in Chapter 7. As a result, the two sets of research results are best viewed as combining to reveal a larger proportion of a still incomplete picture rather than two separate snapshots of the same complete picture. Whereas the Chapter 7 study included administrators' responses to value conflicts arising from problems within the school, Campbell-Evans' study examined conflicts created through the imposition of policy from outside the school. Principals were presented with a simulated demand from their districts to implement a policy which conflicted with some of their central values. This type of value conflict constrains alternatives for acting more severely than do the value conflict situations of interest in the Chapter 7 study. It required principals to weigh one specific value, Respect for Authority (Hambrick and Brandon's "duty"), against a range of personally held values which varied across principals in the study.

Seven out of the eight principals clearly indicated that it was their duty to implement the policy as written. Comments such as "you still follow the policy because it's policy," "you are bounded by Board policy," and "as an administrator, I must administer the policy," reflect the degree to which they felt committed to the implementation of official policy. Their individual preferences took second place to their Respect for Authority principle which compelled them to follow the policy as an initial action. In this study, Respect for Authority is difficult to separate from Specific Role Responsibility in the Chapter 7 study. One principal recalled a conflict which resulted from staff having no role in policy development. For another, a situation was perceived as unfair because of the demands placed on staff. In a third example, conflict arose from what the principal perceived as insufficient time available to meet the requirements of a new policy.

In spite of whatever differences principals had with the policy, however, they initiated its implementation. Then they began to deal with the conflict. A common first step of implementation initiated a series of events. While acting within the policy, all eight principals indicated that they would "do something," that is, some action would be taken. Action was, first, an expression of concern to significant others about the policy's content. In most cases this expression of concern involved the immediate school staff initially and then expanded to include the broader community of other principals and/or the superintendent or the elected trustees. The opinion of other principals was sought in five of eight cases through the forum of the principals' meeting. A desire to increase the understanding of staff was expressed by three principals. This expression of concern took shape through formation of school committees, working from within the policy toward change, working with the policy, working with staff, preparing a presentation for the Board, and letters to the Superintendent. In sum, principals dealt with the conflict by working with colleagues to change it. These actions reflect other important values which each principal considered. They readjusted their value structures and placed more emphasis on the values of participation and sharing, for example.

As a whole, these two studies suggest that when principals encounter value conflicts, their responses are more productive when the conflict itself is treated as a problem and subjected to the same (deep and strong) processes that would be used with other types of ill-structured problems. It also appears that even when conflicts arise between two unequal values (i.e., where one of the two values clearly carries more weight in the principal's value system), principals do not simply choose one and reject the other. Rather, they search for compromises.

Such processes for resolving value conflicts are similar to conclusions drawn by Toffler (1986) in her study of 21 non-school-based managers. Her results attribute importance to managers defining the elements of the conflict, assessing their own "Specific Role Responsibility" and using their imagination to identify a key factor on which the dilemma hinges or developing a mechanism to turn that key factor. When a key factor cannot be found, managers give greater weight to one value but also respond to the other as fully as possible.

Who and What Influences the Development of Administrators' Values

Orientation. Influences that shape the values used by administrators in their problem solving seem likely to be found in both their personal and professional life experiences. Prior evidence concerning these value-shaping influences is meager, however. For example, Miklos' (1988) review concluded that most studies of the recruitment, formal education, and employment of educational administrators have been doctoral dissertations about the experiences of women, only. Nevertheless, this research did offer some direction for our study. Most of this evidence was concerned with socialization processes: those processes by which an individual selectively acquires the knowledge, skills, and dispositions (including values) needed to effectively perform in a role.

Greenfield's (1985) research, with vice principals, suggested that values are more likely the product of informal experiences rather than such formal mechanisms as training. Formal programs designed for educational administrators traditionally have devoted little attention to values, ethics, or moral reasoning (Blumberg, 1984; Corson, 1985; Farquhar, 1981; Greenfield, 1985).

Leithwood, Steinbach, and Begley (1992) developed a framework for studying the socialization of school leaders based on research in several fields of study. This framework included the nature of administrators' experiences with school districts and their policies, formal education, and relationships with peers, subordinates, and superordinates. Further, they conceptualized the process of socialization as being divided into three stages: Initiation, Transition, and Incorporation. Five studies were done with school leaders seeking answers to four questions regarding their socialization experiences and their perceived usefulness in leaders' development. Many, but not all, socialization experiences were considered helpful by principals and vice principals, and there were variations among perceptions according to gender, geographical location, and whether people were already in administrative roles or working toward them. One of the specific suggestions for improvements that emerged from this research was the need for more opportunities for on-the-job leadership experiences where the skills and attributes required for the position could be acquired and practiced.

Ashbaugh and Kasten (1984) inquired directly about influences on the values used by school administrators to make difficult decisions. Results suggested that both personal and professional life experiences conspire, in a blended fashion, to shape administrators' values. Specific influences on values which they identified were religion, educational training, school district philosophy, and role models. Also shaping administrators' values were parents and mentors, experiences as a teacher, personal life events, and parental experiences.

This research is extremely thin and none of it addresses the development of superintendents' values, in particular. At best, it offers hunches about some possible influences on values, but no clear framework of the sort available to guide our inquiry about, for example, the nature of administrators' values.

Results.   Who are the people and what are the situations that have influenced the development and shaping of administrators' values? Our answer to this question is limited to the evidence provided by Raun in her study of 53 superintendents. In this study, participants were asked to consider a list of 18 possible influences (including both people and contexts), to select the ones which they considered to be important, and then to rank each one as being first, second, or third most important to them. They did not have to rank items on the list which they did not consider important. Ratings of first, second, and third most important were combined to determine the total number of superintendents who selected each influence, keeping personal and professional values separate. As Table 8.3 indicates, a substantially larger number of influences contributed to the development of personal as compared with professional values.

A small number of common influences appeared to contribute to the development of both personal and professional values. This becomes evident when the rankings of influences for the two categories of values are combined. Three of these influences are personal in origin: parents (overall rank = 1), spouses (overall rank = 6), and adult friends (overall rank = 7). Work contexts provide the origin of four of these influences: educational work experience and on-the-job leadership (tied for second overall); mentors (overall rank = 4); and peer groups (overall rank = 5). This suggests highly permeable boundaries around personal and professional values categories. Superintendents' practices, to the extent that they are influenced by values,

Table 8.3 Influences on Superintendents' Personal and Professional Values by Frequencies: Ratings of Importance (First, Second, Third) Combined

| VALUES | | | PROFESSIONAL VALUES | |
Influence Category	Frequency (Max. 53)	Rank	Influence Category	Frequency (Max. 53)
Parents	49	1	On-the-job leadership	31
Spouse	47	2	Peer group	31
Formal religious teaching	41	3	Mentor	30
Educational work experience	40	4	Educational work experience	30
Adult friends	36	5	Learning by observation	29
Mentor	36	6	Parents	28
On-the-job leadership	35	7	Professional development	28
Peer group	35	8	Adult friends	26
Professional development	34	9	Spouse	25
Learning by observation	34	10	Elementary teachers	24
Elementary teachers	33	11	Postsecondary teachers	23
Your children	33	12	Secondary teachers	22
Networking	28	13	Noneducational work	22
Other relatives	27	14	Formal religious teaching	21
Postsecondary teachers	27	15	Your children	21
Noneducational work	26	16	Networking	21
Secondary teachers	25	17	Other relatives	16
Childhood friends	24	18	Childhood friends	15

appear to be a product of their whole life experience. Such evidence would not support a claim that superintendents can keep their personal and professional lives separate.

Formal religious training had quite different impacts on the development of personal as compared with professional values. It ranked third as an influence on personal values but only fourteenth as an influence on professional values. This was especially surprising given the number of respondents (24 of 51) from Roman Catholic separate school systems where such teaching is held in high regard. A small number of influences appeared to have relatively little influence on the development of either personal or professional values. These included: childhood friends (overall rank = 18); other relatives (overall rank = 17); networking, noneducational work and secondary teachers (tied overall rank = 16). The low ranking of networking may be explained by the overwhelming proportion of males in the sample. Typically, women express much greater appreciation for networking than do men.

People are a category of influence, in Table 8.3, worth special analysis. Raun asked about which values were influenced by people. Most often mentioned as having influenced personal values were: parents, spouse, and adult friends. These people increased superintendents' sensitivity to Integrity and Honesty (both General Moral Values). People mentioned most often as having influenced professional values were colleagues, teachers, and mentors. Colleagues were considered to have influenced superintendents' sensitivity to Justice, while teachers and mentors were credited with influencing superintendents' sensitivity to Integrity (both General Moral Values). Comparing the values ranking in Table 8.2 with the values just mentioned, Integrity is ranked fourth in the framework, Honesty seventh, and Justice/Fairness third. Interestingly, in the context of problem solving, Integrity and Honesty did not appear to be very important. General Moral Values, development of which were influenced by the people mentioned above, may exist prior to other values and serve as a point of departure for the exercise of Professional Values.

How do superintendents, in sum, come to the values which they hold and think about while solving problems? Although people (parents, spouses, adult friends) are prominent influences in the development of values, it may be that they largely shape only superintendents' espoused value systems. Raun's evidence suggests that such people helped increase sensitivity to General Moral Values, in the main, and to a lesser extent Basic Human Values (especially Justice). But these were not the dominant values-in-use as superintendents solved problems. Rather, the work setting was the most powerful force in the development of values-in-use, an answer to questions about the influence of school districts raised as a result of Ashbaugh and Kasten's (1984) study. That is, superintendents' own direct experiences about what values are best, most sensible, successful, and the like in solving problems (through on-the-job leadership experiences, for example) may be the most powerful influence on the development of their professional values-in-use. This explanation of how values actually used in solving problems develop is the same as the explanation, offered by contemporary theories of situated cognition (Brown, Collins, and Duguid, 1989) and practical problem solving (Rogoff and Lave, 1984), of how authentic knowledge develops. Professionally-relevant values and useful, procedural knowledge develop through grappling with the authentic challenges of day-to-day leadership and administration.

Conclusion

A half-dozen studies summarized in this chapter have been used to answer questions about values in the context of administrators' problem solving. Concerning their role and significance, first, these studies depicted values as pervasive in the problem solving of administrators through their direct stimulation of action and their roles as perceptual screens and moral codes or substitutes for knowledge in response to ill-structured problems. Second, with respect to type of values and their relative weight, our evidence supported the comprehensiveness of a fourfold classification of values including Basic Human, General Moral, Professional, and Social and Political Values. Within these categories, administrators cited most frequently the specific values of Role Responsibility (duty), Consequences for Students (pragmatism), and Participation.

The studies also pointed to a plausible set of relationships between values and levels of expertise, although administrators did share a common core of values. Greater emphasis was placed on social values (e.g., sharing) by nonexperts, whereas knowledge and role responsibilities were dominant values for experts.

Conflict resolution strategies used by administrators in the face of competing values were of two types. The most successful strategies, "deep and strong," conceptualized value conflicts as problems in their own right and employed a set of deliberate problem-solving processes to resolve them. Less successful were "surface and weak" strategies which gave short shrift to problem interpretation or clarifying the source and nature of the conflict and used a sequential, trial-and-error procedure for determining the consequences of alternative solutions.

Evidence also pointed to both personal and professional sources of influence on the development of administrators' values, with professional sources exercising greatest weight. A number of implications for administrative development are inherent in the results of these studies.

Use values as criteria during the selection of school leaders. Although administrators' values may change, it is not likely that they will change quickly or easily (Hambrick and Brandon, 1988). Beliefs and attitudes will need to change in order to stimulate and reinforce value change. The challenge of change in administrators' values, to better serve the interests of the school, is best avoided, where possible, by selection processes which collect evidence about the nature of applicant values, the degree to which applicants are clear about their values and how well they are able to resolve value conflicts.

Redesign administrator socialization processes. Values develop more through the usually lengthy periods of informal socialization than through formal programs, but the socialization of administrators in most school districts is largely left to chance. More planful efforts to redesign socialization experience which will reinforce values important to future schools are called for.

Provide the discretion needed to act on one's values. When satisfactory steps have been taken to hire and/or develop administrators whose values are consistent with the needs of their organizations, it will be important to give them the discretion to act on the basis of those values. This may turn out to be an argument for more school-based management in one form or another. It is, at minimum, a call to design school districts in such a way that they support and enhance the work of expert school leaders.

These three implications for administrator development seem warranted given the limited research on which this chapter was based. Nevertheless, much more research is clearly necessary. It already seems clear that several of the questions raised in this chapter will be relatively easy to answer and others much more complex. For example, values clearly play a significant role in problem solving, but the nature of that role is by no means fully captured by our data. In order to build on our data in subsequent research, an explicit theory about the role of values in managerial thinking and action, such as Hambrick and Brandon's (1988), would be useful; their hypotheses offer productive starting points for subsequent inquiry.

Perhaps the most theoretically interesting and practically useful focus for subsequent study concerns the resolution of conflicting values. Such conflicts are a part of the everyday work world of school leaders and likely to remain so. Yet the few current texts intending to offer disciplined advice to administrators (e.g., Strike, Soltis, and Haller, 1989; Toffler, 1986) fall short of accomplishing that goal. Research describing an array of strategies used by expert administrators for resolving value conflicts would be helpful in future leadership development initiatives.

Pursuit of these implications for practice and research is likely to be a challenging but worthwhile business. As Hambrick and Brandon (1988) note:

to study executive values is to delve into the murkiest of organizational phenomena. Yet the role of values in influencing organizational processes, membership and outcomes is enormous. (p. 30)

Chapter 9

Cognitive Flexibility and Inflexibility in Principals' Problem Solving

Underlying expert human problem solving, many claim, is the disposition to think flexibly about problems. This study was intended to determine (a) whether principals' problem solving would demonstrate some of the same attributes of cognitive flexibility and inflexibility found in the problem solving of those working in other domains, and if so (b) to illustrate the nature of such flexibility in the context of school administration. Protocol data of several types were collected over a two-year period from 22 principals. Results identify such sources of inflexibility as cognitive errors, uncontrolled moods, and lack of responsiveness to opportunities in the problem solution. In each case, more

This study was originally reported as M. Stager and K. Leithwood, 1989. Cognitive flexibility and inflexibility in principals' problem solving. *Alberta Journal of Educational Research*, 35(3), 217–236. Reprinted with permission.

appropriate strategies are identified. Differences in flexibility
between expert and nonexpert principals are briefly reported.

In the studies reported in Chapter 3 through 8 we describe administrative expertise in terms of one or all of the six dimensions making up our comprehensive model of problem solving (problem interpretation, goal setting, values, constraints, solution processes, and mood). The virtues of such description are to be found in the detail. If one sets out to improve expertise, for example, the specific qualities or capacities provided by this detail provide clear goals to work toward. It is also useful, however, to consider whether there are any underlying characteristics or "dispositions" that help account for why some people display considerably more expertise than do others. Amounts of domain-specific knowledge possessed by problem solvers and their beliefs concerning the likely value of contributions made by colleagues (during group problem solving) are the most visible examples of such underlying characteristics identified in previous chapters. In this chapter, we report the results of a study with elementary school principals which explores a third underlying disposition—flexibility.

For purposes of this study, the attributes of flexibility in problem solving were defined on the basis of research carried out in other domains characterized by relatively unstructured problems. Two general questions were addressed: Does principals' problem solving demonstrate attitudes of flexibility and inflexibility similar to those found in the problem solving of people working in other domains? and, Do principals who engage in overt practices judged to be highly effective or expert demonstrate greater flexibility in their problem solving than their less-effective or less-expert peers? Answers to these questions provide a basis for helping to decide whether further inquiry about principals' cognitive flexibility is likely to be productive.

The choice of flexibility in problem solving as a focus for this study emerged most directly from our prior explorations of principals' problem solving. However, similar conclusions about the importance of flexibility have been reached independently by those working in a variety of fields. For example, Scribner (1986) points out that flexibility in meeting changing conditions (and what Schön, 1983, terms "informal improvisation") are well-documented aspects of practical intellect among dairy workers, assemblers, and warehouse employees. Results of Schwenk's (1988) review of research suggest that cognitive flexibility is central to successful strategic decision making on the part of senior managers in private corporations. As far as we are aware, however, only Glasman (1986), in addition to ourselves, has acknowledged its promise for understanding aspects of educational administration. Glasman asserts:

> The value of focusing on flexibility in judgement rendering should not be mysterious. After all, flexibility is required whenever there is uncertainty. What may be new to students of school leadership is that the work which Bruner and Simon began continues until this day, and its focus in cognitive psychology is on judgement research (e.g., Kahneman, Slovic, and Tversky, 1982). . . . Current cognitive psychologists who work on judgement rather than choice are sending the message that judgement under uncertainty is central. It is high time that students of school administration admit it too, and set out to examine it rather than be ashamed of it. (p. 167)

Framework

The framework for the study is based on several reviews of research carried out in related areas of social cognition. Showers and Cantor's (1985) review of research on social cognition provided the general outlines of the framework. This review examined the relationship between elements of motivation and cognitive processes central to problem-solving effectiveness, as depicted in Figure 9.1. The utility

Table 9.1   Showers and Cantor's (1985) Conception of the Relationship between Sources of Motivation and Problem Solving

MOTIVATIONAL ELEMENTS	FLEXIBLE COGNITIVE STRATEGIES
Goals	• Responsiveness to situations
Mood	• Active control
Knowledge	• Multiple interpretations
	• Change in repertoire

of this conception for interpreting evidence from our preliminary work and the comprehensiveness of research on which it is based were reasons for adopting Showers and Cantor's conceptualization, with some adaptation, into our framework.

Motivation, according to Showers and Cantor (1985), is a product of one's personal goals, mood states, and the knowledge one already possesses relevant to the problem at hand. Each of these sources of motivation guides one's interpretations of a problem and plans for how to respond to that problem. The relationship between these three sources of motivation and one's response to a problem is mediated by dimensions of one's thinking. These dimensions, within which Showers and Cantor define "flexibility," include: recognition and responsiveness to novel aspects of a problem; degree of active control over one's thoughts and plans; how one interprets a situation; and change in one's knowledge, beliefs, and values as a function of experience. Evidence reviewed by Showers and Cantor suggests that social problem solving is enhanced as one moves toward the flexible ends of each of these dimensions. Flexibility involves:

(a) adjusting interpretations in response to situational features; (b) taking control of [one's] thoughts and plans; (c) seeing multiple alternatives for interpreting the same event or outcome; and (d) changing [one's] own knowledge repertoire by adding new experiences and by reworking cherished beliefs, values, and goals. (p. 277)

The bulk of the evidence from research on social cognition, however, demonstrates more passive, less flexible ways in which prior knowledge contributes to one's interpretations and strategies. The inflexible end of the four dimensions of thinking include tending to cling to favorite interpretations and not be responsive to situations; exercising little active control over moods, self-defeating cognitions, and dysfunctional strategies; being trapped by perceptually salient and cognitively available stimuli; and having schemas and stereotypes in one's knowledge repertoire that are resistant to change. In applying the Showers and Cantor (1985) conception, we decided to concentrate only on the first three elements of flexibility and inflexibility because the fourth was concerned with a time frame too lengthy to capture in our study. In addition, although we used the terms *goals* and *moods* in the manner of Showers and Cantor, we took a somewhat different approach (explained below) to the role of knowledge, which is the third motivational element considered by these authors.

Two additional research syntheses were used to further elaborate on selected aspects of the Showers and Cantor formulation. Nisbett and Ross (1980) provide evidence related especially to the matter of knowledge and to the third aspect of inflexibility, "being trapped by perceptually salient and cognitively available stimuli." Although they do not deny the importance of motivation in situations where problem solving appears unsuccessful, they believe that there are additional explanations. According to evidence which they review, problem-solving failures often are "cut from the same cloth" as successes. That is, certain strategies are well adapted to deal with a wide range of problem situations (for example, recalling what you did the last time you encountered a similar problem) but become a liability when applied beyond that range (for example, when the current problem has unique features that must be addressed). Most of the evidence in support of this claim was generated in relation to problems which required some understanding of the normative principles that guide the professional scientist's formal inferences (for example, rules for deciding how "representative" is a sample of opinion data).

There are two general kinds of tools that people use in interpreting situations or in making inferences about them by "going beyond the information given." The first kind of tool, much studied by Kahneman, Slovic, and Tversky (1982), involves using two judgmental heuristics to make inferences—the availability and the representativeness heuristics. In the case of the availability heuristic, judgments about the likelihood of an event are based on the availability of past occurrences in one's memory. Frequently occurring events are usually easier to recall than those which occur infrequently, so availability is a good way of estimating probability. Unfortunately, this heuristic may also distort estimates of probability because other things besides frequency can increase the availability of an event in one's memory (for example, recency or vividness). The representativeness heuristic is used to estimate the likelihood of some state of affairs (for example, poor quality of a teacher's instruction) given knowledge of some other state of affairs (for example, the inattentiveness of a student during a lesson). Whereas this heuristic is an essential cognitive tool, it can mislead, for example, when it restricts the problem solver's attention to superficial causes of a problem or when it is used in conjunction with an incomplete understanding of cause and effect relations. The other kinds of tools to be used in addition to heuristics are knowledge structures: theories, beliefs, and other representations, in the problem solver's mind, of external reality. These knowledge structures, while often valuable, can mislead to the extent that they are incomplete or incorrect representations of external reality and to the extent that they preclude attention to the details of the actual object or situation at hand.

In combination, then, the three research reviews discussed above provided a set of categories for recognizing instances of cognitive flexibility and inflexibility among principals, as well as suggestions regarding the cognitive and motivational factors which may influence them.

Method

Data for this study were provided by reanalyzing the verbal protocols produced in studies reported in Chapters 3 and 5. Readers may wish to review the detailed description of methods in both of those chapters. We provide only a brief summary of those methods here.

Sample

Data were provided by 22 elementary school principals (one female, 21 males), six of whom we designated as an "expert group" and 16 of whom were designated as nonexperts. This designation of expertise was the result of a two-part procedure. Part one requested two senior administrators to provide a reputational rating of principals' expertise; part two involved comparing the results of a one-and-one-half-hour interview with each principal to a description of effective administrative practice derived from our prior research (Leithwood and Montgomery, 1986). Principals rated highly as a result of both procedures were designated as experts.

At the beginning of data collection, the six experts had an average of 15 years of experience in school administration, while the remaining 16 principals had an average of 17 years of experience. The experts' schools had an average of 506 students, and four of these schools had vice principals. The remaining principals' schools had an average of 350 students, and five of them had vice principals.

Data Collection

Protocol data were collected over a two-year period using three types of process-tracing methods (Hayes and Flower, 1983): retrospective reports, think-aloud methods, and stimulated recall. The last two of these methods have been shown to be reasonably free of the major threats to the validity of verbal reports (Nisbett and Wilson, 1977), including the distorted reporting of cognitive processes, incompleteness of description, and failure of respondents to rely on memory or to rely only on what can be retrieved from long-term memory. As Ericsson and Simon (1984) argue, both think-aloud and stimulated-recall methods primarily draw on the contents of respondents' short-term memory, and such memory for cognitive processes appears to be accurate. Retrospective reports, however, rely primarily on retrieval from long-term memory; their validity, therefore, is more suspect.

In total, data were collected from each principal four times over a two-year period; twice the data focused on their individual problem solving and twice their problem solving in groups.

Data Analysis Procedures

Transcripts were prepared for all interviews conducted. Results reported in this chapter are based on the analysis of these transcripts, along with the audio tapes of the group meeting sessions.

The specific data examined included principals' interpretations of and comments on their problem solving; observed solutions to hypothetical case problems; solutions as remembered and described by principals to actual problems they had encountered; principals' interpretations of and comments on their problem solving in group situations; and observations of principals in group problem-solving situations. Given our research purposes, any one of these categories of data taken alone has certain limitations. Relying only on solutions to hypothetical case problems would prevent our understanding of how principals clarify and interpret complex problems. As another example, there may be marked differences among principals in their willingness to recount the actual past situations in which they have been less than successful, and even in their ability to remember such situations. The triangulation of a variety of methods allowed us to search for patterns common across various types of data and helped to compensate for these potential limitations. However, because the possibilities of bias in the data were still sufficiently strong, the analysis was primarily concerned with identifying and explaining instances of flexibility and inflexibility per se and only secondarily with a comparison between experts and nonexperts.

We began the analysis of this large set of data by defining several categories of plausible cognitive or inferential errors, as such errors are defined in the work of Nisbett and Ross (1980) and others discussed earlier. This choice was based on considerable experience with our data as well as on a careful reading of relevant literature. These errors included:

1. *Overweighting vividness*: situations in which principals' judgments appeared to be unduly influenced by the vividness and/or emotional interest of information.

2. *Generalizing from a small or biased sample*: situations in which principals' judgments appeared to be influenced by a bias in sampling while collecting information.

3. *Overuse and misuse of knowledge structures*: situations in which theories or schemas are depended on so heavily that principals fail to attend to details of the actual situation at hand, or where such knowledge structures are poor representations of external reality.

Next, without knowledge of expert, nonexpert designations, two researchers read 30 of the first year's transcripts and noted (a) instances where these errors apparently were made, and (b) instances where a "more appropriate strategy" was articulated and the error avoided. When both researchers independently noted the same error or the same more appropriate strategy, the instance was recorded. Criteria used in judging instances of errors or more appropriate strategies were largely based on Nisbett and Ross (1980). For this study, then, correct strategies are primarily those that involve the use of a rule which formal scientists agree is appropriate in this situation. However, in several novel situations, the researchers, and in some cases two colleagues, made judgments based on a broad reading of the problem-solving literature. The latter judgments are necessarily considered somewhat tentative.

At this point, one researcher continued with the analysis of the remaining 14 first-year transcripts and audio tapes from the second-year interviews by identifying both errors and more appropriate strategies. The researcher, still unaware of expert, nonexpert designations, also noted any other instances throughout the interviews in which principals (a) appeared to be markedly responsive to specific aspects of the situation; (b) were clearly influenced by mood or aware of mood effects on problem solving; or (c) were clearly influenced by goals in problem solving or aware of their effects.

The data were then summarized, first in terms of the occurrence of various instances of cognitive inflexibility and flexibility, and then the apparent influences on them. Only then were differences between expert and nonexpert principals examined.

Results

Results from the analysis of the interviews are described in two sections. In the first and major section, the elements of inflexibility and flexibility identified for all 22 principals are presented (Table 9.2). In the second, contrasts are briefly drawn between the six experts and the 16 nonexperts in the study.

Elements of Inflexibility and Flexibility

Errors. The first instances of cognitive flexibility and inflexibility to be described are the more cognitive ones, that is, those observed when categories derived from Nisbett and Ross's (1980) work were applied. Unless noted otherwise, data reported in this and the two subsequent sections were based on all types of interviews. In Table 9.2 we summarize three major categories of influential errors (or inflexibility), along with the more appropriate strategies indicative of flexibility.

Errors in the first category, overweighting vividness, were made by six principals; all involved in some way making poor judgments regarding the determination of priorities among the various problems competing for their attention. In two cases, principals spent an excessive amount of their own time, at work and at home, trying to solve an extremely difficult and intractable personal problem of a staff member. In the remaining four cases, principals set priorities in their problem solving strictly in terms of the vividness of the problems. For instance, one principal thought that the only problems needing attention were the ones that were relatively vivid or highly apparent and stated that "I keep prioritizing. When there are no problems in the in-basket or walking into my office, I go and play with the kindergartens, do this and that."

There were several more appropriate strategies mentioned by a comparable number of principals as ways of dealing with the potential error of overweighting vividness. Some expressed the importance of deliberate planning and setting clear priorities as a way of avoiding the sort of reaction to vividness exemplified above: "I spend time on overall planning and analysis. I have learned not to jump and not to assume." Good planning also was a method used to pre-

Table 9.2   Elements of Inflexibility and Flexibility

INFLEXIBILITY	FLEXIBILITY
Errors	More Appropriate Strategies
1. *Overweighting vividness in setting priorities*	• deliberate planning and priority setting • conscious perspective on role of vividness
2. *Generalizing from a small or biased sample*	• encourage collective work from representative group
3. *Overuse and misuse of theories and schemas*	
(a) Fail to see that a situation is unique or different from others in the past	• deliberate vigilance for dangers
(b) Fail to determine actual causes of problem	• conscious of particular features of situation • deliberate awareness of need to search for nonsuperficial causes
(c) Fail to see there are new problems facing principals	• have opinion that there are new problems and can identify some
(d) Fail to modify a single approach or strategy in light of situational features	• conscious awareness of need for variability and flexibility in roles
(e) Use theories or schemas that do not accurately represent reality	• awareness of individual differences • hold theories that encourage flexibility and openness
Uncontrolled Moods	More Appropriate Strategies
• fail to examine alternative courses of action • focus on own negative mood	• recognize own limits in being able to solve some problems • conscious control of mood
Lack of Responsiveness	More Appropriate Strategies
• miss opportunities • fail to see other possible courses of action	• take advantage of opportunities in situation • vigilance for opportunities to meet goals, particularly those related to students

vent vivid crisis situations or to avoid dealing with too much emotional information: "I just quite frankly don't see a strong payoff in
spending time and energy raking up these feelings."

Some had a deliberate bigger picture perspective on issues that
could otherwise have been seen as vivid. One said, "this is a very poor
move, and even good teachers can sometimes make a mistake," and
from another, "I don't worry so much because I've found that you can
blow it the odd time."

Three principals made errors of the second type, generalizing
from small or biased samples. Each error involved collecting information from a restricted set of those people who would have some association with a decision. In one case, the principal based his
interpretation of and planning for an innovative program on limited
and biased information provided by strong advocates of the program.
In another case, the principal was aware that his information was
biased because he had deliberately chosen a group of only like-
minded staff to work with him in setting objectives. Despite this, he
seemed unaware of the dangers of disregarding other viewpoints.

A similar number of principals indicated use of a more appropriate strategy, that of strongly encouraging collective work from a
representative group of staff, as a method for avoiding such bias.
About his school cabinet, one principal noted: "They speak their
minds. They don't hold back and say just what they want you to
hear. . . . They come forward with information. With sharing like
that, things come forward I haven't thought of."

By far, the most numerous cognitive errors displayed in the interviews had to do with the overuse and misuse of theories and
schemas. As shown in Table 9.2, these are of five kinds. Fifteen principals made two or more of these errors, with some making several.
A similar number of principals mentioned at least once a more appropriate strategy to prevent or overcome such errors; however, only
six of them exhibited such strategies markedly.

One fairly common error of this type is failing to see that a situation is unique or different from similar cases encountered in the
past. In recounting difficult situations, several principals described
cases where they had failed to detect dangerous features in a situation. For example, one failed to detect that a parent complaint was
more serious than usual, and another failed to detect the real agenda
of a caller.

Another variant of this error is the tendency, observed in the
responses of some principals to the hypothetical case problem, to assume obstacles which are not necessarily present in a problem situation but may have been present in a similar problem encountered

in the past. For instance, based on past experiences, one principal assumed there would be "anger and hate and emotion" in a situation where several parents were requesting that their children be placed in a particular class, and that there would be "strong fear and emotion" in a situation where a principal had to enter a school in which the previous principal had been popular.

More appropriate strategies in this area included a deliberate vigilance for dangerous situations ("the ones that could blow up in your face") and a conscious awareness of the need to attend to the specifics of a situation, "clearly listening to the situation, the problem concern, and making sure the entire professional staff understands we've got a unique situation," or "I realized this was a serious variant of a familiar problem."

A similar, but less frequent, error was failing to determine the actual cause of a problem. Some of these errors, reported by principals noting that "hindsight is 20/20," concerned initial misinterpretation of others' motives in situations facing the principal, while others involved the use of superficial causal explanations.

The more appropriate strategy in this situation involved a deliberate awareness that things may not be as they seem at first. As one principal said, "It was not totally clear. It was tough to know. You don't often know if it's little stuff that is the problem, or if that's just an excuse for something major."

The better strategy also involves awareness that it is necessary to analyze consciously and thoroughly causes at the outset of problem solving. Another principal said "The principal has to hold people back from jumping to solutions . . . therefore let's analyze it and let's start looking at some causes. . . . Only then do we look at possible solutions and their ramifications."

Another source of inflexibility involves the failure to see that there are new problems facing the principal because overreliance on a theory or belief that there are none prevents the observation of such new problems. This attitude or opinion was expressed by some principals when they responded to a particular question, in the first interview, regarding the existence of new problems. Typical statements were: "I don't sit and think 'How am I going to handle that problem?' because I've been solving the same problem for 20 years!"; "I've never found a problem that was unclear. My steps are usually right 100% of the time"; and "No brand-new problems come to mind. I sometimes say 'I was doing this exact thing 20 years ago.' "

A more appropriate strategy with regard to this matter appears to be a conscious awareness of and vigilance for the new problems that face schools and principals. Principals who realize this indicate that "there's always something new," that "there are always new problems coming up," and tend to be able to immediately back up this opinion with concrete examples:

> Although there are always standard problems you deal with in a school . . . I have found that problems have changed in that they are more complex. Education has a much different profile, we are under attack much more than we were, and there is a much greater accountability factor. Due to the complexity of society today—and education can't divorce itself from it—life is more complex so education has to be more complex. . . . I have to be more of a lawyer. I have to be more facile not just with the Education Act but with other bills that relate to that, that have an impact on that. Since knowledge is increasing at a phenomenal rate, therefore my job's changing . . . as curriculum changes.

Another error or source of inflexibility involving overreliance on a knowledge structure is that of failing to modify a single approach or strategy in light of specific situational features. Principals who do this suggest, in speaking about their own practices, that they *always* use a particular approach, often one that is extremely useful in many situations. However, they do not suggest that they are aware of situations in which such an approach is inappropriate. Most of the responses concerned with this matter came from questions in the first interview regarding principals' perceptions of their own styles. Some involved a strong reliance on always staying within board policy or on a particular approach with which the principal feels confident. For example, one principal stated: "I like to gather a lot of information up front, and I like, I *love* the brainstorming process. I use it all the time." Another explicitly rejected alternatives to his own common-sense strategy:

> The actual turning to a set of designed problem-solving strategies doesn't turn me on, doesn't enter into the kinds of ways I solve problems. Although I know some of them, I tend not to use it. At PD [Professional Department] sessions, when I pick up two or three things and one contradicts the other, I tend to go back to my common sense experiential base and it works.

More appropriate and flexible practices involve conscious awareness of the need for variability and flexibility in one's practice:

> It's important to know the people, their strengths and weaknesses . . . being sensitive at the time to how close to overload they are, and when to ask them to give something, and when to not, when to back off, and when to share the burden around a bit.

One principal pointed out the need to have a contingency plan, because "as you get more experienced, you realize that almost anything can happen."

Particularly in the stimulated recall interviews, some principals displayed flexibility by indicating that they were aware of the requirement for variability in the role they played in group problem solving. In some cases, this involved categorizing clearly the type of problem being considered:

> I suppose that I look at problem solving in four basic areas when it comes to presenting a decision to staff. There are the "tell" decisions . . . that would just be done. There is the "sell" type . . . where I would have to sell my position to staff. Then there's the "consult" area, where I would like to consult with the staff and then let them know exactly that I'm consulting with them but I have to make the final decision. And then the final area, which is the highest level I think, are the "share" areas, where I would outline the problem to them: here are the parameters but *together* we are going to share in the overall plan. . . . I have openly told my staff that if they see me confusing the terms, blow the whistle and let me know.

In other cases, it involved changing one's role in the group in response to what was occurring. One principal, in commenting on what was happening in a staff planning committee meeting, said:

> I also want to mention that it's not up to me to focus the discussion. Often I sit back and become a participant, nothing more. People don't look to me necessarily on something like this to make a decision. They feel it's just as much their responsibility and they will focus the discussion. There are things that the principal and the vice principal do decide if there is not much to discuss, but at the staff planning committee, if it's a proposal or concept that is really the responsibility of the entire group, I back out as chairman and it just carries on itself.

Later in the meeting, the principal points out that he must play a different role:

> This is the principal talking. I have to talk about regulations. Now I'm not there as a participant but now I have to ask questions. She made a statement that I just couldn't let go. As a principal, I've got something I have to be responsible for.

The final kind of error regarding the inappropriate use of knowledge structures involves using theories or schemas that do not accurately represent reality. The examples of inflexibility or error with respect to knowledge structures which we have outlined up to this point involve misapplication of particular schemas when the more cautious or critical application of the same schemas would have served the principal well. Nisbett and Ross (1980) point out that there are particular schemas—especially those involving stereotypes—which are "so lacking in foundation and predictive value that they almost invariably serve the user badly" (p. 40). There were a number of instances where principals made strong generalizations about their staff. For example, one said, "Teachers can't take complaints; they'll fall apart emotionally," while another said, "Teachers don't like to open themselves up and have people come into their classrooms."

Another suggestion of erroneous schemas came from the metaphors and analogies used by some principals. One regarded an educational system as analogous to a military organization; another referred to some students as "the cream" and others as "the dregs"; and a third spoke of his staff as "my horses . . . I can't go anywhere without them."

Examples of more appropriate schemas came from principals who displayed a clear awareness of individual differences among staff members, of their competences and circumstances at any time. One principal stated that people move at their own rates, and all the research shows that you cannot get all of them up to level X at the same time." Another, in referring to a staff member who was experiencing some extreme personal stress, indicated that:

> There has to be a lot of understanding on my part and the staff's. We all have to be special with her. I don't treat everyone the same. Fairness is one thing, and consistency is another, but understanding is probably more important. We are different and we all have our own situations, and I think you have to work with that aspect.

This principal was aware not only of special needs of staff but also of their accomplishments, strengths, and philosophies of education;

this was also evident from a number of comments that he made during the stimulated recall interview session.

Another category of statements was much more compatible with cognitive flexibility and provided a contrast with the inflexible stereotyping described earlier. These statements included well-articulated beliefs or theories about the value of collective work in problem solving. Like the negative, stereotype statements, these involved generalizations about all staff, but they were generalizations of a different quality. It seems plausible to suggest that principals who act on beliefs such as these will empower their staff members by increasing the possibility that most, if not all, will contribute to group problem solving. Principals who believe in the more negative generalizations ("teachers want to do their own jobs, unassisted, and principals do too") seem likely, we speculate, to prevent even those individuals who are interested in working on collective problem solving from doing so; their inflexibility may in a sense generate a self-fulfilling prophecy. Examples of the apparently more empowering beliefs are: "I have a strong belief that everyone has something to contribute. I believe in letting the person take the risk" and "I believe that people have a mindset toward doing things better. I make it clear to staff that if they can see a better way of doing things, let me know and my nose won't be out of joint."

Mood-related Inflexibility.   Instances of inflexibility in the previous section were those primarily influenced by cognitive factors. Those described in this section are associated with more motivational influences.

There were several instances in which principals' moods produced considerable inflexibility and failure to examine alternative possible courses of action as judged, after the fact, by the principals themselves. In some cases, this led to poor choices of action. In one case, a principal decided to write letters rather than seeing an irate parent in person, a choice he later regretted: "I didn't want to see him again . . . he kept harassing me . . . continuing to put pressure on me . . . So I refused to see him in person."

In other cases, a concern with one's own mood and emotion had distracted the principal from more appropriate concerns and choices. One principal had a continuing concern with his own emotional state throughout the interviews, and made a series of comments such as, "I'm really not afraid of anyone, but now I guess I'm afraid of him," "I'd enter the situation with apprehension," and "My stress level is pretty low, I have tremendous confidence, but if I have no solution, my stress level can *really* go up." Another principal repeatedly spoke of his "frustration" with the staff.

More appropriate strategies for dealing with mood influences were demonstrated by a considerable number of principals. As was the case for those concerned with not overweighting the vividness of certain information, a sense of one's own limitations in the type and number of problems it is possible to solve appears to be helpful in avoiding emotions such as frustration. For example, "There are some problems you can't do anything about. They are just too massive. It may have taken years to get that way, so how are you going to turn that around in a few hours?"

A considerable number of principals were aware of the need to keep their moods under control in group problem solving: "You have to have a process where you can get people to air their concerns and then work through the concerns in a fashion that is as impersonal as possible."

A smaller number indicated awareness of the need to keep their own mood under control when solving a problem alone. One said:

A principal has to be a person who doesn't panic particularly easily, because so many things can go wrong, nothing ever goes exactly as planned, no matter how careful . . . You have to keep thinking, all the while. That's one of the things that makes a good principal, one who can keep thinking and readjusting his or her thoughts as situations arise.

And another said:

You have to know how to deal with things that are urgent and not panic, but use plans and click them in calmly. You know you don't have to solve any problems yourself.

Part of the more appropriate approach involved tackling problems with an air of calm confidence. One principal described his style: "As my wife said, 'When a situation arises, you don't seem to get all flustered . . . you are cool, don't get emotional.'" He went on to say:

I don't worry as much as I used to . . . you know you can make a negative statement. . . . I have enough self-confidence that I think it's better that I should speak up and say what I think than worry about whether someone will put an obstacle in my way.

Goal-Related Flexibility: Responsiveness to Possibilities in Situation.   In the previous sections, the instances which were clearest in the analysis and reporting were negative occurrences, indicators of

cognitive inflexibility. In this section, the instances which are clearest are positive occurrences, indicators of cognitive flexibility.

Among certain principals, particularly in their remarks during the stimulated recall sessions, there were six clear examples of a phenomenon which we termed (after Hayes-Roth and Hayes-Roth, 1979) opportunistic planning, where the problem solver makes decisions that follow up on selected opportunities that present themselves in the situation or "takes advantage of opportunities." For instance, one principal who was dealing with the problem of improving staff resources for disciplining students solved two other problems in the process. First, he became immediately aware during the group discussion that his vice principal had a serious personal concern with some facets of the discipline situation and made a deliberate point of discussing it with him alone very soon. Also, in considering the overall problem, he indicated the availability of a Ministry resource document for assisting with solutions and, while formulating a process for dealing with the discipline situation and introducing the document, he realized that the approach being developed would have great potential utility as a model for introducing the other documents which arrived in the school with great frequency.

In addition to these situations in which principals demonstrated specific strategies for taking advantage of an opportunity presented, some principals displayed an explicit awareness of interpreting problem situations as opportunities. One pointed out the possibilities for image building in several hypothetical case problems and in several problems that he had actually experienced.

This appears to be part of a more general vigilance by some principals. Particularly when faced with unstructured or unclear situations, these principals look for those specific aspects of the situation which will allow them to meet their goals, especially those to do with staff and students. These principals have a number of goals in mind and are extremely responsive to the possibilities in any situation for meeting such goals, especially their most important goals. For instance, one principal said: "Whatever it is we do, it has to be based on whatever we're doing for kids. That belief helps me make decisions. . . . When I look at a problem, one of the first questions I ask myself is, 'How will this benefit students?' "

Evidence of unresponsiveness was of two sorts. First, in the stimulated recall interview, there were two clear cases of missed opportunities, which the researchers noticed (although the principal, listening also, did not). Second, there were several instances in which principals seemed to be so focused on their own narrow goal that they were blind to any other possibilities in the situation. In contrast to a colleague who was well aware that a system which focused too much on avoiding mistakes is one which will be inflexible and have poor solutions, one principal described his approach to problem solving as "I know what they will support. You follow policies and procedures set down." The most dramatic example of this narrowness and inflexibility occurred during a stimulated recall interview. The principal was so consumed with "getting his own way" in a decision that he failed almost entirely to hear the strong opposition of most staff. When he stated that he wanted to get "good" information, he meant that he wanted to get information that agreed with his. There were also cases in which the principal failed to be responsive to possibilities in the situation because of an absence of *any* clear goals.

Expert and Nonexpert Patterns

The main purpose of this study was to identify and illustrate instances of inflexibility and flexibility in the practices of school principals; it was not primarily to focus on comparisons between experts and nonexperts in this domain. However, the marked differences in the patterns displayed by these two groups merit brief attention.

Before considering these results, it should be noted that only some of the principals in both the expert and nonexpert groups were good informants, whereas about half the group overall made few statements indicative of either inflexibility or flexibility. In general, the good informants seemed to be at the extremes of the expertness distribution.

Among the expert group, four of the six principals clearly demonstrated a variety of instances of flexibility and the other two a smaller number of such instances; none of these six experts showed any instance of inflexibility. Among the nonexpert group, five of the 16 demonstrated a marked variety of instances of inflexibility and no instances of flexibility. Another nine of the nonexpert principals demonstrated some instances of inflexibility and a few instances of flexibility. Of the remaining two nonexperts, one indicated no instances of inflexibility and a few of flexibility, whereas the other showed some inflexibility but considerable attention to flexibility. That is, the data were clearest, most informative, and least inconsistent for the expert and nonexpert extremes.

In summary, experts avoided errors, controlled their moods, and were responsive to opportunities in the situation. Nonexperts, at least those at the least-effective extreme, made errors, were unable to control their moods, and were unresponsive to opportunities available in the problem setting.

Discussion

In this study we found evidence for three main elements of cognitive flexibility. First, such flexibility involves a total avoidance of cognitive errors and an ability, noted by many authors (e.g., Morine-Dershimer, 1986; Nisbett and Ross, 1980; Schön, 1983) to make fine discriminations among details of particular situations. Second, cognitive flexibility involves controlling one's negative moods and approaching problem situations with an air of calm confidence. Klemp and McClelland (1986), in studying characteristics of intelligent functioning among managers, found that the competence of self-confidence was absolutely essential and served to drive the other intellectual competences. Third, cognitive flexibility involves being responsive to the possibilities in the situation, affording a clear illustration of what Sternberg and Wagner (1986) would regard as practical intelligence. These authors use Neisser's (1976) definition of "intelligent performance in natural settings . . . as responding appropriately in terms of one's long-range and short-range goals, given the actual facts of the situation as one discovers them" (p. 137).

It should be noted that cognitive flexibility never involves being over-responsive or spineless. According to other data we have collected, expert principal problem solvers have core values, beliefs, and goals that are inviolate. That is, they display extreme cognitive flexibility, but they are always guided by a coherent set of values (Begley, 1988; Leithwood and Stager, 1989; also Chapter 8 of this text).

Our data indicate that at least several types of cognitive flexibility and inflexibility, found among other widely disparate groups, can also be found among elementary principals as they do their work. These data also illustrate the forms such flexibility and inflexibility may take in the specific domain of elementary school administration. Such findings are potentially significant for the improvement of administrative performance. For example, identifying errors, in the Nisbett and Ross (1980) sense, creates the possibility of designing specific training in the use of more appropriate strategies. As another example, principals might also be assisted in becoming more sensitive to their overuse of otherwise helpful heuristics. Several crucial questions must be answered, however, before such potential can be pursued. One question concerns the teachability of error avoidance and other aspects of problem solving. We are optimistic that this is possible, to some degree, and describe one effort to do this in Chapter 12.

In our view, a second question points to the major limitations of the present study; that is, our adoption and application of criteria for defining cognitive flexibility and inflexibility (including errors) without any direct evidence of the relationship between such criteria and the problem-solving effectiveness of principals. The question is: Does flexible cognition, as Showers and Cantor (1985), Nisbett and Ross (1980), and others define it, actually make a principal a better administrative problem solver? Our modest attempt to address the question in this chapter involved briefly comparing samples of expert and nonexpert principals. That comparison suggested a much higher incidence of cognitive flexibility among expert principals. But, this evidence is correlational in nature and hence only weak support for the importance of such flexibility for principals' problem solving. Further research is needed to understand fully the role that cognitive flexibility plays in expert administrative problem solving.

Part 4

‑◂◉▸‑

The Relationship between
Thought and Action

Chapter 10

Problem-Solving Expertise as an Explanation for Variations in Instructional Leadership

How do practices used by principals to foster school improvement differ? Do differences in the nature of the thinking or problem solving of principals offer an explanation for variations in principals' practices? What is the nature of these differences? To answer these questions data were collected from the principals and primary division teachers in 12 schools implementing British Columbia's Primary Program. Results suggested that differences in principals' practices can be explained reasonably well by thought processes of principals when solving problems individually and in collaboration with their staffs.

In this chapter we bring together separate sets of data reported in two previous papers (Leithwood, Steinbach, and Dart, in press; Leithwood and Steinbach, in press). Our purpose is to make the case that variations in the instructional leadership practices of principals, variations of significant consequence for the success of school improvement efforts, can be largely explained by the nature of principals' problem-solving processes. The implications of this argument, we believe, are self-evident and quite important; one powerful strategy for increasing the productivity of school improvement efforts is to assist school administrators in developing greater problem-solving expertise.

Evidence reported in this chapter comes from a larger study conducted with a selected sample of principals in British Columbia, Canada, who were attempting to improve their schools through the implementation of a major Ministry of Education policy initiative. Called the Primary Program (1990), this initiative aimed to restructure the first four years of schooling through such organizational changes as ungradedness, continuous progress, and dual entry periods to kindergarten. Instructional changes were premised on a constructivist image of learning and aimed at the type of active participation of students in their own learning evident, for example, in "whole language" approaches to instruction (e.g., Watson, 1989). Anecdotal reporting to parents, greater parent involvement as partners in instruction, and a concern for better meeting the needs of a culturally diverse population of students were among some of the other elements of the Primary Program. The program was, itself, part of a broader set of policies (Year 2000, 1989) to be implemented through the end of secondary school over a ten-year period.

From the full set of data collected for our larger study, we report in this chapter primarily those data relevant to three general questions:

- Do differences in problem-solving processes explain differences in leadership practices?

- Are variations in school improvement leadership practices associated with variation in group problem-solving processes?

- Within which aspects of group problem solving do principals demonstrate greatest variation?

Framework

Principals' Leadership Practices

Do principals make a significant contribution to the improvement of schools? Based on the results of research reported over the past 15 years, the answer is: "some do but many do not." This research, recently reviewed by Leithwood, Begley, and Cousins (1990), has begun to generate the information required to explain the substantial variation in principals' impact on schools. One obvious explanation for variation in principals' contribution to school improvement is offered by research describing differences in the methods they use for this purpose (Hall et al., 1984; Blumberg and Greenfield, 1980; Salley, McPherson, and Baehr, 1978; Leithwood and Montgomery, 1986; Hoy and Brown, 1986; Blase, Dedrick, and Strathe, 1986; Brady, 1985). Four distinct patterns of practice are evident in this research, which Leithwood, Begley, and Cousins (1990) have summarized as follows:

> Leadership style A is characterized by a focus on interpersonal relationships; on establishing a cooperative and genial "climate" in the school and effective, collaborative relationships with various community and central office groups. Principals adopting this style seem to believe that such relationships are critical to their overall success and provide a necessary springboard for more task-oriented activities in their schools.

> Student achievement and wellbeing growth is the central focus of leadership style B. Descriptions of this class of practices suggest that while such achievement and wellbeing are the goal, principals use a variety of means to accomplish it. These include many of the interpersonal, administrative, and managerial behaviors that provide the central focus of other styles.

> Compared with styles A and B, there is less consistency, across the four dozen studies reviewed, in the practices classified as style C (program focus). Principals adopting this style, nevertheless, share a concern for ensuring effective programs, improving the overall competence of their staff, and developing procedures for carrying out tasks central to program success. Compared with style A, the orientation is to the task, and developing good interpersonal relations is viewed as a means to better task achievement. Compared with style B, there is a greater tendency to view the adoption and implementation of apparently effective procedures for improving student outcomes as a goal—rather than the student outcomes themselves.

> Leadership style D is characterized by almost exclusive attention to what is often labelled "administrivia"—the nuts and bolts of daily school organization and maintenance. Principals

adopting this style, according to all four studies, are preoccupied with budgets, timetables, personnel administration, and requests for information from others. They appear to have little time for instructional and curriculum decision making in their schools, and tend to become involved only in response to a crisis or a request. (pp. 12–13)

There is considerable evidence to warrant the claim that styles B and C make the greatest contribution to school improvement—especially style B (e.g., Leithwood and Montgomery, 1982; Heck, Larsen, and Marcoulides, 1990). Indeed, these four patterns appear to represent a hierarchy in terms of their contribution to school improvement with the student growth focus (B) making the greatest contribution followed in diminishing order by the program focus (C), the interpersonal relationships focus (A), and the building manager focus (D) (Leithwood and Montgomery, 1986; Hall et al., 1984; Stevens and Marsh, 1987; Trider and Leithwood, 1988). Such differences in effectiveness are partly explained by the increased inclusivity of patterns closer to the student growth focus; this focus, for example, also includes attention to building management, school climate, and school programs but as means to the student-growth end, not as ends themselves. In the present study, we inquired about whether the initiatives principals took toward school improvement corresponded to one or more of these four styles or patterns. We considered these patterns as variations in the degree of instructional leadership offered by principals.

Problem-Solving Processes

This study conceptualized principals' problem solving in terms of the multicomponent model described in varying detail in Chapters 3 through 6 (those who have not read those chapters may wish to review, for example, the Framework section of Chapter 6). Suffice to say here that this model reflects an information-processing orientation to problem solving and focuses attention on the processes used by administrators for considering: their interpretation of problems; the nature of goals and goal setting; the nature and role of their values; approaches to constraints; solution processes; and the mood or affective disposition which they bring to the problem.

In relation to each of the model's components, our previous research has described differences between the thinking of expert and nonexpert administrators. In Chapters 3 and 4, for example, we provide such description for principals and superintendents as they solve problems alone; In Chapters 5 and 6 we provide comparable description for problem solving in group situations. The collection of data about principals' problem solving in the present study was explicitly guided by the results of these previous studies.

The present study was intended to advance that previous research in three ways. First, principals included in our previous studies showed evidence of using primarily two of the four dominant forms of practice described above: "expert" principals were usually program managers (style C); those we labeled "typical" usually demonstrated a focus on interpersonal relations (style A). The present study offered the potential to learn more about the thinking of principals who used other styles or patterns of practice, as well. Second, women were grossly underrepresented in the samples of principals included in our previous studies; the present study provided an opportunity to redress this imbalance, in a modest way. Finally, our previous data was collected in response to a wide variety of administrative problems, many of which could be solved in a short period of time; the present study provided data about responses to a single type of problem, one requiring an extended or open-ended time frame for solution. As Mehan (1984) suggests, such a time frame is typical of many institutional problems and may stimulate different strategies for problem solving, about which little is known.

Method

Data Collection

Twelve schools in three districts (four schools per district) were selected for the study. Eight of these schools had volunteered to be pilot schools ("Lead Schools") for implementing the new Primary Program policy. Four were chosen from the seven elementary schools in one district which were initiating activities related to the policy.

Data related to principals' thinking and problem solving were collected at two points in the year (fall and spring). At the beginning of the school year (about 2 1/2 months after the start of implementation) principals were asked how they were going about solving the current school improvement problem, that is, how they were implementing the Primary Program policy. Using a semistructured interview schedule, principals were asked to describe the problem and then discuss what they wanted to accomplish, the values that might be influencing them, constraints that might be impeding progress, and the specific steps taken to solve the problem; these interviews indicated the nature of principals' individual problem solving.

Toward the end of the school year principals were interviewed again. This time they were asked to reflect on their thinking during a previously taped staff meeting called to address a problem related to implementation of the school improvement policy. Instead of having principals rely on their memories of what occurred at the meeting, an audio tape was used to stimulate recall. Data for this set of interviews were collected on three occasions. Prior to the staff meeting, principals were interviewed about the nature of the problem they would be working on, what they expected and wanted to happen at the meeting, and what they were planning to do. Next, an audio tape recording was made of the portion of the staff meeting addressing the chosen problem. Finally, after some preliminary instructions, the principal and interviewer listened to the tape of the meeting together, stopping frequently to ask questions or offer information about intentions and thought processes. This discussion was recorded on a separate tape, which was subsequently transcribed carefully to eliminate all identifying characteristics. These transcripts provided the data to describe principals' group problem-solving processes.

Data Analysis

Based on the findings of our previous research on the individual and group problem solving of expert and typical principals, along with some additional insights, coding forms for analyzing both types of problem-solving data were developed. In the case of group problem solving, the coding form focused most heavily on the solution process steps used by principals, although key items related to the interpretation, goals, constraints, and mood components of our problem-solving model were also included. New components examined were principals' use of problem-relevant knowledge, the degree/quality of self-reflection, and staff development as a goal for staff meetings. In order to quantify the analysis of group problem-solving processes, responses were classified according to the coding form and rated on a five-point scale (expert = 5 points, typical = 1 point). To earn a rating of five, responses had to be explicit and/or appear three or more times. Results of individual problem solving were not quantified.

Each group problem-solving transcript was divided into relevant statements made by the principal which were then numbered sequentially. Two researchers worked together, using two training protocols, to classify and rate each statement. Once the raters felt comfortable with their degree of understanding, they coded and rated the ten remaining protocols independently. Interrater reliability was .73 (Pearson Product Correlation). Although this is an acceptable level of reliability, a check of the data indicated that it did not adequately reflect the extent of rater agreement. Except for a very few occasions, ratings never differed more than one point and a T-test failed to identify any significant differences between the raters (t = 0.99, p = 0.32). In addition, when mean scores given by each rater for each principal were compared, the correlation was .87. All differences in ratings were discussed, disputes were resolved, and principals were assigned a single score for each of the 18 items (see Table 10.2) on the coding form. A mean score was also computed for each principal.

Results

How do the practices used by principals to foster school improvement differ? What is the nature of the thinking or problem solving giving rise to differences in these practices?

Patterns of Practice

Evidence concerning patterns of practice came from interviews with the 12 principals which focused on their efforts to implement the Primary Program. Data from these interviews were examined initially by one researcher for similarities and differences in overall approaches to school improvement. This resulted in identification of four broad categories of approaches to school improvement. Two additional researchers then were provided with a description of these patterns and the interview transcripts. They were asked independently to assign principals to one of the four patterns. There were no discrepancies in the judgments of the three researchers.

Two of the four patterns of practice closely correspond to what was described earlier as leadership styles D (building manager focus) and A (interpersonal relationships focus). Two of the 12 principals demonstrated a building-centered management (BCM) focus. These principals headed schools in a district which had hired primary consultants to help schools implement the Primary Program. These principals were little involved in policy implementation. Although this district's decision to rely on primary consultants appears to reduce the leadership demands on principals, it is interesting to note that the other two principals in the same district did not behave like building managers, suggesting that there were many useful leadership functions to be performed in addition to those performed by the primary consultants.

One of these two principals and one principal from another district engaged in a pattern of practice focused on interpersonal relations or teacher-centered management (TCM). These principals were supportive of the school improvement effort and reasonably knowledgeable about the Primary Program. They were also intellectually engaged in the improvement process, interacting from time to time with teachers, but their involvement was neither intensive nor particularly direct.

The two other patterns of practice, evident in our data, were variants on, rather than direct reflections of, what was described above as student growth and program-focused patterns of leadership. Five principals engaged in a pattern of practice we labeled "indirect instructional leadership" (IIL); one of these principals was from the district which had primary consultants. Principals engaged in this pattern were very knowledgeable about and supportive of the implementation effort. In addition, however, they were intensely involved in creating conditions in the school (second order changes) which would give teachers the best chance of successfully implementing the Primary Program (e.g., group meeting time, greater involvement in decision making). They developed a positive school climate and ensured opportunities for teacher collaboration, for example. They also monitored implementation progress, staying on top of it and making sure that it occurred. However, they did not become involved in modeling classroom practices.

Three principals were much involved in the classroom practices associated with the Primary Program. We labeled this pattern "direct instructional leadership" (DIL). It involved the demonstration of new practices, in-class assistance to teachers, coaching, and the like. These principals also paid close attention to the need for second order changes in their school, as well.

In sum, there were substantial differences in the practices used by principals for school improvement. These differences appeared to be manifestations, in a school improvement context, of three of the four patterns of practice observed among principals in a variety of other contexts, as well. The results also suggest that instructional leadership patterns of practice may take either direct or indirect forms.

Further, although not directly relevant to the purposes of this chapter, it should be noted that the larger study from which these data are drawn supports the claim that variations in patterns of principal practices are consequential for school improvement. In particular, patterns of practice labeled direct and indirect instructional leadership were strongly associated with teachers' ratings of principals' helpfulness, development of collaborative school culture, and teacher development (Leithwood, Steinbach, and Dart, in press).

Patterns of Practice and Individual Problem-Solving Processes

The six components of our problem-solving model provide the structure for reporting results in this section; within each component, similarities and differences in the thinking of principals (by themselves) using each of the four patterns of practice are described. Our intent is to illustrate that there are substantial differences in the thinking of principals related to the pattern of practice which they used in their schools.

Problem Interpretation.

the focus on the learning rather than a lock-step kind of sequential program that we had been doing was much more exciting for students.   (DIL)

It's not too unlike sitting down to a very, very large meal [with] a whole variety of things for you to savour . . . and it's not a 15-minute lunch break and so you can really sit down and relax. (IIL)

First of all, I don't believe it's a new primary program; it's a primary program that has existed for a long time . . . that is more than obvious when you work with the teachers who have been teaching in that model and style for a good number of years . . .

So here we are developing brand new structures in our school system with no guidelines, with administrators who are in the growing process themselves so it's like the blind leading the blind at the present time.   (TCM)

They [the primary teachers] convinced me there really wasn't much difference to what we're already doing. (BCM)

These quotations illustrate, in some cases, dramatically different interpretations of the problem of implementing the Primary Program.

The three direct instructional leaders (DIL) interpreted the problem as "a wonderful answer to the needs of all children" and they highlighted the importance of "teaching to the child as opposed to having the child adjust to the curriculum." They saw the problem as complex but manageable and they believed that the new primary program was the best way to teach children. The aspects that are problematic for them involve some of the details such as educating parents, reporting, assessment, and organization.

The five indirect instructional leaders (IIL) also viewed the innovation as a very welcome thrust because of the benefits for children and because it finally sanctioned "all of the little things that we have been doing and believing all along." Again, it was seen as complex but manageable, with the major focus being on the professional development of teachers.

Both building- and teacher-centered managers interpreted the problem very differently than did the instructional leaders. The two teacher-centered managers (TCMs) themselves differed in their interpretations. One saw it as business as usual, whereas the other saw it as a "massive upheaval in the way we operate our school system." Still, they both viewed it primarily as the teachers' responsibility: the first because he felt he had exceptionally capable staff and the second because he felt he lacked enough knowledge to lead effectively. They both saw the need to proceed slowly.

The two building-centered managers (BCMs) interpreted the program as one that teachers were very much in favor of and for which they needed the freedom "to do what they think is a good idea." They were accepting of the initiative and primarily saw the problem in terms of budget and organization—keeping things running smoothly so the teachers can do what they need to do. The above quotation also indicates a low level of involvement in the program.

Goals.   Given such different interpretations of the school improvement problem, different goals for problem solving are to be expected. These are reflected in the following comments:

When I saw the six goals and objectives of the program, I thought, "right on; you've got it." (DIL)

[It's critical for the teachers to understand and believe in the underlying notions of the program] so that they might do a different activity but it's only the activity that's different.   (IIL)

my approach has been to try to slow people down, because they're rushing too fast into something that doesn't have clear guidelines

How do you slow down the initiative and the drive and the snowball effect of the dedication of the teachers?   (TCM)

[I want to] get off to a smooth start.   (BCM)

Goals set by the direct instructional leaders, together with their staffs, focused mainly on programs or instructional activities ("Implement all the stuff that's best for kids"). A second goal for all of them was to fully involve the parents. Other goals included building commitment and teamwork and encouraging their teachers in the school improvement process.

Indirect instructional leaders identified a wide range of goals. Along with a strong desire to see the six goals of the program achieved in their schools, these principals wanted their staffs to believe in and understand the program. They wanted to be well informed and they wanted their teachers to be well informed. Other goals included ensuring the support of parents and productive working relationships among primary teachers.

The goals of the instructional leaders were in stark contrast to those expressed by principals using the other two patterns of practice. Teacher-centered managers had in common the goal of slowing down their teachers: one because he believed they were not ready due to lack of guidelines and materials; he was also afraid his mostly traditional staff would feel insecure. The second principal worried that his teachers would "burn out." Other goals expressed by these two principals were to learn about the program, keep parents informed, and move toward better instruction in the school.

Building-centered managers did not espouse any goals related to children, although one knew that "the main goal of the program is that kids should progress at their own rate." He went on, "I don't know how to do it, but we've got this year to find out." Other goals were to keep parents informed, provide teachers with time to plan, and get teachers to go to workshops. An implicit goal of both of these principals seemed to be to keep teachers happy.

Values. Differences in the values guiding solutions to the school improvement problem on the part of the four groups of principals are reflected in these comments.

> It makes each kid smarter. It makes each kid feel really valued, important.   (DIL)

> the role of the teacher is the key role in this and I need to do whatever I can to make sure that I focus on that.   (IIL)

> [the teachers are working so hard that] the second part of my concern is the stress level and the fatigue.

> I want them to feel secure.   (TCM)

> I don't impose on them [teachers]. All I do is approve or I might make a suggestion here or there with class lists.   (BCM)

Not surprisingly, the values of the direct instructional leaders reflected their dominant concern for consequences for children. They also placed great importance on fully understanding the program (knowledge), being able to take risks (courage), and encouraging participation and sharing. Leadership responsibility was taken very seriously. As one principal said, "My role as enabling and empowering the teacher is very clear. That doesn't change."

There was ample evidence that consequences for children (e.g., "[the Primary Program allows you] to create an environment that enables kids to grow as opposed to an environment that tells them what they can't do") and consequences for parents (e.g., "we have to have the partnership of parents") were important to indirect instructional leaders. However, these values were overshadowed by a concern for the consequences for teachers (and subsequently children): "I try to have all the staff meetings with a little bit of professional development in it," is an example of the kind of thinking that guided the practices of these administrators. Knowledge, respect for others, participation, sharing, and commitment were also frequently mentioned.

Concern for teachers' comfort was a value frequently mentioned by the teacher-centered managers. This was manifested in their desire to proceed slowly and with caution. One principal saw one aspect of his role as "advising teachers not to throw out the "basals with the bath water" (carefulness). The other principal said of his role "I didn't have much to do except slow the ship down and steer it maybe once in a while." Responsibility as an educator and consequences for students were evident but not as ubiquitous as with the instructional leaders. Knowledge, respect for others, sharing, and commitment were other values mentioned.

Both building-centered managers espoused great respect for their staffs and claimed that their teachers know best. They valued order and serenity. "I have a great staff; I've been here ten years and I've never heard a voice raised in anger. They get along very well." Specific role responsibility was the most prevalent value, a value which manifested itself in handing responsibility to teachers.

Constraints. Principals demonstrating different patterns of practice identified quite different constraints to be overcome in solving the school improvement problem. These constraints, as the following quotations illustrate, vary in the degree to which they are under the control of the principals:

> Probably the most difficult part has been, and it hasn't been terribly difficult, has been the parents.   (DIL)

> Another problem is teachers of varying ability—to pull them all along at the same rate is difficult.   (IIL)

> Teachers are moving too fast.   (TCM)

> The difficulty is really the lack of finance, the uncertainty, the options, . . . the numbers, . . . time, . . . space.   (BCM)

For direct instructional leaders, there were few constraints and these were not seen to be impenetrable barriers to success. There was, above all, the need to deal carefully with the community because, as one principal said, "parents fear that we've moved back to the loosey goosey '70s business." Getting information to the parents effectively without wasting their time was a concern, but all three administrators had identified numerous ways to do this. While there were some differences in staff readiness identified, these principals perceived this mainly as a challenge to find the best way to have everyone be comfortable and confident.

Because indirect instructional leaders viewed teachers as the most critical factor in school improvement, teachers who were not as willing and able to proceed were viewed as the biggest constraints. As one principal put it, "I am worried about that weak link." Other challenges were lack of clarity about specific details, time to meet, how to educate the parents, and dealing with the teachers' union.

Teacher-centered managers were most concerned about teachers making changes too quickly. One such principal was also having trouble accepting the philosophy upon which the Primary Program was based, but he thought he would accept it in time. His inability to lead, in this unfamiliar environment, coupled with the belief that most of his teachers were too entrenched in traditional ways of teaching to accept the change easily, were severe constraints. Both these principals identified as an obstacle the fast pace of change: "there's not much chance to sit back and reflect."

There was a lengthy list of constraints affecting the solution processes in the minds of building-centered managers, and lack of money headed the list. Although all principals would have liked more money, these seemed to want the funds to appease their teachers' excessive (in the principal's mind) demands for substitute teachers and materials—not because they were considered essential for school improvement. Dipping into the operating budget was one way of easing the financial dilemma and one principal covered a class so the primary team could have time to plan.

Solution Processes.   Data provided by the interviews regarding solution processes provided insights less about principals' thinking than it did about the consequences of their thinking for action. Differences in these consequences are evident in these reflections:

> Usually I as principal do the strategy with the whole staff partly to let them know I'm willing to risk and partly to teach it.   (DIL)

> First of all we have to become familiar with the new primary program.

> We have done a lot of jigsawing of the introduction to Goodlad's book, the Year 2000 document, and the primary program binder.   (IIL)

> I have somebody else who has more expertise in the primary doing a lot of the things that I should be able to do but can't. (TCM)

And if there's a problem I'll tell them "Look, I'll solve the problem for you, but I'd rather you do it yourselves, and then tell me what the solution is, if that's okay, fine, that's the way it'll be." (BCM)

The solution processes step that distinguishes direct instructional leaders from the other three groups is the fact that they modeled instructional strategies either in the classroom or at staff meetings. These administrators were either already very knowledgeable about the methods or else they made sure that they learned them. Other steps included hiring teachers who were willing and able to implement, educating themselves and the parents, and meeting regularly with the teachers to encourage and support.

For indirect instructional leaders, the steps involved in solving the problem were centered on making sure teachers were as knowledgeable as possible. They were diligent about providing information for their staffs and they treated their staff meetings like seminars where relevant articles were discussed. Staff meetings were carefully planned in advance. In addition to providing opportunities and encouragement, these principals made the necessary arrangements for teachers to visit other schools and to attend conferences and workshops. They often accompanied the teachers. Collaborative planning was important to them and one principal spent considerable effort on altering the school building "to get it ready for more teacher interaction."

Both teacher-centered managers depended on their teachers to lead the school improvement effort. One of these principals believed that his entire staff was extremely capable and already implementing 90 percent of the Primary Program; the other felt that he had one exceptionally expert primary teacher whom he had selected to coordinate school improvement activity. About that decision he said, "I think that's one of the smartest moves I made all year."

Providing time for teachers to attend extra conferences and workshops and buying books were the most important steps these principals took: "[I want to] gain every resource possible that I can for those teachers." What made these administrators different from the Indirect Instructional Leadership group is their degree of involvement with staffs. The indirect instructional leaders personally made sure (e.g., by attending meetings with their staff) that teachers had the knowledge, skills, and materials they needed; the teacher-centered managers were more likely to provide encouragement and opportunity for teachers to attend meetings. Other steps taken by these principals included learning more about the

Primary Program and informing the parents about its implementation in the school.

The solution processes of the two building-centered managers are best characterized as laissez-faire. The staffs made the decision to become lead schools and the principals provided as much money and release time as they were able. Other steps included informing the parents, creating a new primary classroom to handle the large numbers of children, attending institutes, and talking to teachers.

Mood. The following remarks demonstrate the wide range of feelings displayed by principals regarding the Primary Program—from elation to resignation:

> I am so lucky to be here right now. All the things we've been fighting for for special needs kids are there for everyone. Isn't it wonderful?   (DIL)

> because [staff] were so positive, it enabled me to feel that we could go forward very confidently into this.   (IIL)

> I really do feel blessed. They [the staff] are a dynamic bunch.

> I feel there's no one out there to get me going and feeling good about things. I'm the one supposed to be doing it for the teachers and they're feeling even worse.   (TCM)

> It's my perception that every time I turn around there's another blooming meeting going on somewhere.   (BCM)

The prevailing mood among the three direct instructional leaders was unalloyed excitement and delight that the Ministry was spearheading this wonderful program for kids. Although there was minor uneasiness about how some of the details would work themselves out, they were confident that "the fog will lift."

Indirect instructional leaders also were pleased about the initiative. They felt comfortable with it and were confident that "the way I solve problems will work in this case." Still, there was some nervousness around the logistics of school improvement and one administrator was feeling a little unsure about how to provide direction to her staff, especially because of the "union stuff."

The two quotations (one from each principal) from the teacher-centered managers signal two obviously different emotional states.

The first principal was mainly pleased (e.g., "I am excited about the teacher who has found that this is exciting for her") but he also felt uneasy with the rapid pace; he was disappointed that his school was not selected to be a lead school (he was not aware of the proper procedures). The second principal mainly was feeling uncomfortable and insecure, primarily because of his lack of knowledge. In addition, he was uncertain about the worth of several aspects of the program. However, he, too, felt quite lucky to have such an exceptional primary lead teacher to help him.

The prevailing mood among the building-centered managers seemed to be resignation to the fact of Primary Program implementation. There was also some resentment about having to take money from the operating budget for this purpose and exasperation about what they consider to be exorbitant demands for release time. One of these principals was frightened at first because of the uncertainty associated with implementing the Primary Program.

Patterns of Practice and Group Problem-Solving Processes

Are different patterns of practice or approaches to school improvement by principals associated with or perhaps even partly explained by differences in the processes used to solve problems in groups, as they appear to be in the case of individual problem solving? To answer this question, we compared differences in the total mean ratings for the group problem-solving processes of principals engaged in each of the four patterns of practice. As we indicate in Table 10.1, DILs and IILs exhibited greater expertise than TCMs or BCMs. A one-way analysis of variance was followed by a Tukey post-hoc procedure to locate pairs of means which differed significantly. Differences in expertise between BCMs and each of the other patterns were significant [$f(3, 8) = 14.18$, $p<.05$]. Principals engaged in both instructional leadership patterns also demonstrated substantially greater problem-solving expertise than did teacher-centered managers, but that difference did not reach significance. In sum, then, differences in patterns of practice are associated with differences in group problem-solving processes.

In Table 10.2 we report the total mean ratings on each of the 18 aspects of group problem solving examined in this study for principals engaged in each of the four patterns of practice. It is clear from this table that the scores for the building-centered manager pattern are substantially lower than those for the other three patterns on nearly every item. A one-way analysis of variance showed that those

Table 10.1   Mean Ratings of Group Problem-Solving Expertise for Principals Engaged in Four Different Patterns of Practice

STYLE	N	MEAN	SD
		Scale (1 = typical; 5 = expert)	
Direct Instructional Leader (DIL)	3	4.02	.27
Indirect Instructional Leader (IIL)	5	4.08	.49
Teacher-Centered Manager (TCM)	2	3.53	.35
Building-Centered Manager (BCM)	2	2.03	.04

differences were significant ($p<.05$) for items 9, 13, 16, and 17. BCM scores were also significantly lower than DIL and IIL (but not TCM) scores on items 1, 4, 14, 15, and 18. BCM and IIL leaders differed significantly on item 3. And for item 18, TCM scores were significantly lower than those for IILs. The nature of these statistically significant differences falls into three main categories (goals, skills and knowledge, and disposition) which are described in more detail in the remainder of this section.

Goals

Goal setting is vitally important in the running of any meeting and shared understanding of goals is of particular importance in collaborative problem solving. In a prior study (Chapter 5) we suggested that expert and typical principals were equally adept at sharing their own goals with others involved in problem solving. Similarly, all principals in the present study at least mentioned the purposes for problem solving at the outset of their meetings with staff. However, three goal-related dimensions of group problem solving did show significant variation among principals; they are items 1, 17, and 18.

Item 1.   The impact of instructional leadership on students is indirect. Among the most powerful mechanisms for exercising this leadership is influencing what teachers focus on by ensuring that the school's mission is clearly defined (Leitner, in press; Hallinger, Bickman, and Davis, in press). Group problem solving provides school leaders with an opportunity to draw attention to the school's mission and to assist staff in finding meaning in that mission by showing its relevance in the solution of everyday problems. Given the importance of the school's mission, more expert principals would be expected to invest more effort in helping staff place the immediate problem being addressed in relation to the larger mission and problems of the school (item 1). Such was the case with principals in this study.

Each DIL and IIL received a rating of 4 or 5 on this aspect of their problem solving. To illustrate, one principal introduced the problem to be addressed by staff in this way:

> The topic of retention is a contentious one for primary grades or any grades . . . and it forces us, as teachers, to examine the reasonings behind recommending retention or promotion. So we need to think about whether a student's education career should be driven by competence, by readiness, by age, or group solidarity, or whatever. It makes us—pushes us really to think about why we do certain things.

The mean score for the TCMs was 3.5. This indicated that the problem was seen in a larger context, but that the context often was limited to staff opinions or feelings. The problem of class assignment might be viewed just from the perspective of personnel, for example:

> So, that was a factor that they had, which impinged on their decision making, because they were not only thinking of the classes, they were thinking of personnel as well. Little factors such as, Mrs. M.—her last year's coming, she's going to retire. She doesn't want to do any major changes in this time of her career . . .

Each BCM received a score of 2 for this item. This means that the immediate problem was viewed in isolation. For example, one principal who was dealing with complaints of limited resources kept the problem at that level.

> So a lot of money has gone into it; it's really disappointing to see boxes of the same stuff arriving for each classroom . . . that's just my personal opinion.

Item 17. Research on social cognition places individuals' internalized goals at the center of explanations of self-motivation (e.g., Showers and Cantor, 1985). As Bandura (1977) explains:

Table 10.2 Dimensions of Group Problem Solving: Mean Ratings for Each Pattern of Practice

ITEMS	MEANS (SCALE = 1–5)				
	DIL (n = 3)	IIL (n = 5)	TCM (n = 2)	BCM (n = 2)	
*1 Immediate problem viewed in relation to the larger mission and problems of school	4.3	4.8	3.5	2.0	
2 Less of a personal stake in preconceived solution; want best possible group solution	4.3	3.4	4.5	2.5	
*3 Anticipates obstacles, responds flexibly to unanticipated obstacles, deals with constraints	3.7	3.6	3.5	1.5	
*4 Has well-developed/prepared plan for meeting	4.7	4.8	3.5	2.0	
5 Provides clear, detailed introduction to problem and its background to collaborators	4.3	3.8	3.5	2.5	
6 Outlines clearly the problem-solving process	3.7	3.6	3.5	2.5	
7 Without intimidating or restraining others, clearly indicates own view of problem	3.7	3.0	3.5	2.5	
8 Remains open to new information (flexibility)	3.7	4.0	4.0	3.0	

*9	Assists collaborative problem solving by synthesizing, summarizing, and clarifying	3.7	4.6	4.5	2.0
10	Has strategies for keeping group focused and allowing discussion	3.7	4.2	3.5	3.0
11	Checks for consensus, agreement, understanding, commitment	3.7	4.0	3.5	2.0
12	Ensures that follow-up is planned	3.3	4.0	2.5	2.0
*13	Always appears to be calm and confident	4.0	4.2	3.5	1.5
*14	Respect and courtesy shown to staff during meeting and interview	4.7	4.2	4.0	1.5
*15	Use of problem-related knowledge	4.0	4.2	3.0	1.5
*16	Indication of self-reflection, self-evaluation	4.7	3.6	3.5	1.5
*17	Broad range of goals (includes program/student goals)	4.3	4.6	3.5	1.5
*18	Staff development is an explicit goal of meeting	4.0	4.8	2.5	1.5

* items which showed significant differences

[they] represent future consequences in thought. . . . Many of the things we do are designed to gain anticipated benefits and to avert future difficulties. When individuals commit themselves to explicit goals, perceived negative discrepancies between what they do and what they seek to achieve create dissatisfactions that serve as motivational inducements for change. (p. 161)

In order for a school to pursue a common mission, individual staff members' practices have to be motivated by at least a significant core of common goals related to that mission. Among the especially important aspects of school leadership expertise, then, is the effort devoted to and success in creating that common core of goals among staff. Expertise is a function of both the nature of the goals school leaders assist staff to adopt and the extent to which a common core of goals is actually internalized by staff.

Significant differences were found among principals in relation to the nature of the goals espoused for problem solving, particularly in their breadth and in the incidence of program and student goals (item 17). Such goals are one of the defining features of instructional leadership (Leithwood and Montgomery, 1982, 1986) and principal expertise (Leithwood and Stager, 1989). All DILs and IILs in the present study were rated either 5 (explicit mention) or 4 (implicit mention) on this item. Student growth and/or program goals were used as benchmarks to help guide problem solving. For example one principal set student needs as a goal by saying: "So I think what we have to look at is what makes the best sense for the kids at this school." And, to help reach consensus about how to evaluate students using the new reporting procedure another principal said: "What we have to do here is get really clear in our minds that the report has got to enhance the learning of the child."

TCMs were weaker on this dimension (mean = 3.5): One TCM had several goals but none were related either explicitly or implicitly to what was best for children. He received a score of 3. The second TCM did indicate that reporting procedures should be a fair assessment of the child's development or potential. This implicit goal gave him a score of 4.

The main goal of both BCMs was to comply with the researchers' request. As one BCM said to his staff: "I believe what the [research team] would like us to do is to hear us talking over the difficulties of implementation (score = 1)."

The second BCM's goal was to discuss what was good and bad in the past year so priorities could be set. There seemed to be no higher learning goals—only task goals. (score = 2).

Item 18. The extent to which staff development explicitly was considered to be a goal by principals in solving school improvement problems with their staff was an aspect of problem solving not examined in our previous research. It was included in this study for two reasons. First, we chose to focus on the domain of school improvement problems, in particular. Inferences about effective practice derived from recent research on school improvement (reviewed by Fullan, 1991) argue that it is more productive to focus broadly on capacity building within the school rather than more narrowly on the implementation of specific innovations. The second reason is inherent in the meaning of collaboration. Authentic collaboration depends on a belief in the value of the contributions that can be made by one's collaborators. Such a belief requires principals not only to view staff as possessing capacities critical to the solution of school improvement problems but to aim at improving those capacities, as well.

Most DILs and IILs received high scores (4 or 5) on this dimension (one received a 3). They seemed to see their roles as instructional leaders for teachers as well as for students. The three DILs had a mean score of 4. The five IILs had a mean score of 4.8. These principals are attempting to accomplish student goals through staff development and they use staff meetings as opportunities to do this. Four of these five principals stated very explicitly that staff development was a goal for the staff meeting (score = 5), the fifth was slightly less explicit. Comments such as the following illustrate how this goal was expressed:

> I wanted them to understand the process that one goes through when you start putting a class group together.

> So I wanted all of this [talk] so that they could know what each other is thinking, where they're coming from.

The mean score for TCMs on item 18 was 2.5. Although there was definitely concern for teacher feelings, teacher development was not so clearly a goal. One TCM received a score of 2. He wanted to understand the staffs' rationale for their choice of class configuration and he wanted to ensure that staff were satisfied with their choice. The second TCM received a score of 3. He turned the meeting over to the teacher who had initiated the topic and attempted to ensure everyone had an opportunity to speak. The tenor of the meeting was very "empowering." BCMs had a mean score of 1.5. One BCM received a score of 1 because his only real goal was to comply with the researchers' request for him to tape a meeting. The second principal received a score of 2. His goals were to comply with the researchers' request, to make sure class lists were in order, to make certain that staff were organized to advise the new principal, and to discuss what was good and bad in the past year so priorities could be set. The score of 2 was given because, at the end of the meeting, he said to the interviewer, "I just expected them to be able to have a free expression of views more than anything."

Skills and Knowledge

The limits on individual problem solving, which Simon (1957) described as "bounded rationality," are due to short-term (or working) memory capacity; individuals are able to process or think about only five to seven separate items of information at a time. For this reason, individuals may (a) consider only a small number of the actually available alternative solutions to a problem, (b) possess less than adequate information about these alternatives, (c) consider the problem from narrowly biased perspectives, and/or (d) overlook relevant criteria in decision making. Each of these limitations on individual problem solving can be overcome in a collaborative context—two (or more) heads are better than one, under the right circumstances.

In our prior research on group problem solving (Chapter 5), we described some of the specific skills used by expert administrators to ensure such circumstances during their meetings. Results of the present study point to many of the same skills with differences between patterns of practice reaching significance on four items: 3, 4, 9, and 15.

Item 3.   The ability to anticipate obstacles and deal with them if they arise unexpectedly is a component of individual problem-solving expertise. It is an important feature of collaborative problem solving as well.

DIL, IIL, and TCM mean scores were very similar: 3.7, 3.6, and 3.5, respectively. All of these principals either anticipated obstacles and prepared themselves for them ("And so I had to be prepared for reluctance initially") or else responded casually and flexibly to unanticipated constraints. Although there was some frustration, it was not apparent to the staff.

In contrast, building-centered managers received a 2 and a 1 for this item (Mean = 1.5). For these two principals, obstacles were seen as anything that impeded the desired smooth path of the meeting, and they reacted to these stumbling blocks with poorly disguised anger.

the [partner school] issue is a separate issue, J and I'd like to talk to you about it, because you may not be aware of the time that [your school] is getting. So, I'll talk to you later. (Interviewer: You sound a little bit annoyed.) I am.

Item 4. "A plan," as Shank and Abelson explain, "is a series of projected actions to realize a goal" (1977, p. 71). Prior research on both individual and group problem solving by administrators suggested that experts, as compared with nonexperts, verbalized more detailed plans for how to solve their problems. In some cases, they were able to anticipate a series of a dozen or more actions they would take. Often they considered alternative steps in response to different possible outcomes of a given action (Leithwood and Steinbach, 1991; Leithwood and Stager, 1989). In a group context, such detailed contingent planning has both instrumental and symbolic value. Instrumentally it increases the probability of reaching one's goals and makes for a well-run meeting. Such planning also signals to staff that the issue being addressed in the meeting is important and that the principal does not want to waste their time.

DILs and IILs scored very highly on this dimension (mean scores were 4.7 and 4.8, respectively). Each of these principals had spent considerable time preparing for the meeting either by gathering materials (e.g., unifix cubes or research articles), or by making extensive notes summarizing the results of a previous meeting. As one principal noted:

> What I've done since that last meeting was . . . to take all the items listed on the board that members raised and try to cluster them into some kind of logical grouping.

TCMs did plan, but their plans were less elaborate; the mean score for this group was 3.5. "Those are my plans on paper, which they have a copy of. . . . I gave each of them . . . the three scenarios [they had arrived at]."

BCMs appeared to value spontaneity (although they reacted with annoyance if things did not go according to their own internal agenda); planning was kept to a minimum. For example, as one BCM said to his staff: "Umm, I guess they [the researchers] want to know how I deal with problems so I'll just toss it open for discussion."

Item 9. This item, perhaps more than the others, captures the critical skills necessary to facilitate collaborative problem solving. Except for the two BCMs, scores were consistently high (DIL =

3.7; IIL = 4.6; TCM = 4.5; BCM = 2). Most principals frequently summarized, synthesized, and clarified what had been said. Differences between scores of 4 and 5 indicated the degree of frequency with which they carried out these functions. Leaders who diligently synthesize, summarize, and clarify are letting their staff know that what is happening is important, that they want to make sure all understand what is being said so the best possible solution can be developed.

One principal said of her role in the meeting: "I kind of clarified, I kind of restated, I kind of asked them to substantiate what they were saying if somebody else didn't."

During the staff meeting, another principal said, at various points:

What kind of stuff are you implying? (asking for clarification)

Okay, learning difficulties. (restates for clarification)

What do you mean by that? By the teacher's ability to handle the children?

Do you think those characteristics fit into different categories? You know, you have short attention span, you have lack of social skills, you [have] chronologically young . . . are all those things to do with maturation? (synthesizing)

In contrast the BCMs were more likely to prevent teachers from having the opportunity to vent their frustrations (even though this was part of what both meetings were set up to do) by cutting off discussions prematurely. For example:

I felt we were sort of beginning to drift from what was close to the [school]. I'm quite happy with what goes on in school and you can see I'm not happy with what's gone on provincially.

And this from the second building manager:

I'm saying we could sit around and chat about this ad infinitum and I want to close it off so I think they've talked about that particular thing enough.

Item 15.   Evidence from many domains stress the importance of problem-relevant knowledge in accounting for expertise (e.g., Chi,

Glaser, and Farr, 1988; Lesgold, 1984). Indeed, Johnson-Laird (1990) claims that, in the study of intellectual development, emphasis has shifted from changes in cognitive structures and processes" toward the view that what really changes is the content of knowledge" (p. 485). Our prior research has paid little attention to domain-specific knowledge, but its importance could not be overlooked in the present study, especially in the face of the instructional modeling practices of the DILs.

All but one of the eight direct and indirect instructional leaders exhibited considerable problem-relevant or domain-specific knowledge. The one who did not was working on a problem that did not call for much display of such knowledge. The knowledge used by these principals was mainly about a specific, short-term problem faced in the schools, but these principals were also knowledgeable about the Primary Program.

The scores of TCMs on this item showed wide variation. One received a 2 and one received a 4.5. The score of 2 could be explained by the nature of the problem-solving session which did not require the display of much knowledge.

Building-centered managers exhibited little problem-relevant knowledge. Teachers were responsible for program-relevant knowledge, as these comments by one of the principals suggest:

Well do we know how much money is being allocated to the books? To the school?

I said to them, when do you see a kindergarten becoming what is in fact a k-1?

Dispositions/Attitudes

Three personal characteristics were significantly linked with expertise in collaborative problem solving: appearing calm and confident (item 13), demonstrating genuine respect for staff (item 14), and exhibiting habits of self-reflection (item 16).

Item 13.   Along with one's goals and existing knowledge, research in the field of social cognition identifies mood as a variable directly influencing the flexibility of one's thinking (Showers and Cantor, 1985). Cognitive flexibility, in turn, is central to expert problem solving. Schwenk's (1988) review of research provides evidence of this claim in relation to senior managers in private corporations, for example.

In our prior research we found expert administrators remaining more calm and confident during problem solving than did non-experts (Stager and Leithwood, 1989). In the present study, although all IILs and DILs overtly appeared calm and confident (all received scores of 4 or 5), four of the eight admitted to feelings of anxiety or frustration. As one said after listening to the tape recording of their staff meeting:

> this may sound strange to you [but I'm] always so worried about talking too much in the meetings and I don't feel as badly as I thought I would.

Another said:

> I felt rather frustrated at this point in the conversation because they wanted to talk about specifics. . . . (The frustration was not apparent in the meeting.)

Both teacher-centered managers admitted to being a little uncomfortable at some points in the meeting. With one principal, it was not evident (score = 4); it was slightly more evident with the other because of the excessive amount he talked (score = 3).

> Okay now probably it's my personality but the fact that they aren't talking in this meeting bothered me. . . . they didn't feel comfortable to open up and talk. (This principal did not give the teachers much of a chance to talk).

One of the most obvious differences between the BCMs and those in the other patterns is in the degree of annoyance felt and shown; the building-centered managers were frequently perturbed and were not concerned about hiding their anger.

> I would think I sounded a bit peremptory [at this point in the staff meeting]. And, if that's how I sounded, that's how I meant to sound.

Item 14.   One of the best ways to empower teachers is for principals to directly demonstrate their respect. However, it is crucial that this respect be genuine; teachers will know the difference.

For the most part, DILs and IILs were genuine and consistent in the high regard they showed their staff members (five received scores of 5, one received a score of 4). They knew their teachers well, valued their contributions, and praised them during and after the meeting. Attention to this factor is crucial for creating an atmosphere of trust in which teachers feel free to express themselves honestly. The following quotes illustrate how this respect was expressed in interviews with the researchers:

> Time is really precious to them and that's something else that is really important for an administrator to remember—don't waste their time. (*Subject 10*)

> this is a very good staff, a very confident staff, and I think, for any misgivings they have about it, once they got into it, I think they would make it really work. (*Subject 11*)

> With the teachers, you can't expect them to read everything, but at least you have to have it in a form so it's available . . . and, of course, it keeps the interest up when you give them a chance to do [something] . . . they've all signed up for another summer institute . . . (*Subject 3*)

> Terrific teacher! She's really very very good and tremendously conscientious, so this is why there's a bit of hesitancy on her part all of a sudden. (*Subject 7*)

> and M. was the one, by the way, who had all negative responses and it wasn't her fault. This is her first year in the school and she has just a very powerful class and a very powerful set of parents. (*Subject 8*)

Two of the indirect instructional leaders, however, were less consistent and they each received a score of 3. To illustrate:

> Well . . . one thing that was striking me obviously because it's bugging me again, there are a couple of people in there who are always wanting, whining. . . . And I have a hard time valuing their opinions sometimes.

Item 16. A central difference between experts and nonexperts in "knowledge-rich" domains of problem solving is that experts possess substantially more problem-relevant knowledge. This often allows experts to solve problems readily, primarily by recognizing them as instances of familiar problem types; lack of problem-relevant knowledge requires an often-difficult search for a solution, in contrast. But what explains the knowledge possessed by the expert? As Van Lehn (1990) argues: "the ultimate explanation for the form and content of the human expert's knowledge is the learning processes that they went through in obtaining it. Thus the best theory of expert problem solving is a theory of learning" (p. 529). Self-reflection and evaluation (item 16) are habits of mind that allow one to learn from experience. In the case of principals, those with greater expertise would be expected to demonstrate, in their problem solving in groups, more self-reflection and evaluation and this would help explain their expertise. Our data conformed to this expectation.

The scores of DILs differed substantially from IILs (mean = 4.7 vs. 3.6) on this item. DILs were very quick to notice errors they might have made. Perhaps they are always vigilant for opportunities to improve their practice. This vigilance is illustrated in the following comments on their own problem solving as they listened to the taped staff meetings:

> I should have jumped in here. Part of it, I was feeling a little bit of tension . . . part of it is that I'm not sometimes as aggressive as I should be in certain situations.

And from another:

> Okay, that was my first mistake . . . if I had to do it over again, I would have deleted it completely.

> I'm coming out of this meeting feeling, you know, I really haven't handled this very well because, in the end, I didn't get them thinking, "Hooray, let's just go for this!" But that may be a stage . . .

And this, from an IIL:

> I don't think I handled it particularly well because I'm a bit ambiguous on the topic.

TCMs were similar to IILs. Their mean score of 3.5 indicates a medium amount of self-reflection. BCMs, with a mean score of 1.5, showed little reflection.

Demographic Characteristics

Information about four demographic variables is summarized in Table 10.3. This table shows that: all instructional leaders (but one) were female and had considerably less experience as principals than did noninstructional leaders; three of the four noninstructional leaders were from the same district, all but one of the indirect instructional leaders were from the same district, and all direct instructional leaders were from the same district; school size may be related to pattern of practice. What do these demographic characteristics mean? Although there are several possible interpretations, the most plausible, in our view, appears to be a strong interaction effect between gender and district-level socialization and selection processes.

In our sample, there were seven female and five male administrators. All instructional leaders but one (an IIL) were female; all teacher-centered and building-centered managers were male. This lends support to the finding that female administrators, on average, devote greater and more direct attention than do males to classroom instructional practices (e.g., Shakeshaft, 1987). Gender alone, however, is not a sufficient explanation for leadership style. In addition to being female, all three direct instructional leaders were also first-year administrators. Two related interpretations are possible.

First-year principals may be more inclined to model instructional strategies in the classroom not because they are women, but because they are very familiar with the strategies and feel confident to teach them. This may well be the situation here, since the

Table 10.3 Demographic Characteristics of Principals

PATTERN	(N)	GENDER F	M	MEAN YEARS EXP. AS PRINCIPAL	DISTRICT AFFILIATION	MEAN SCHOOL SIZE (STUDENTS)
DIL	(3)	3	0	1	3 = D3	200
IIL	(5)	4	1	9 (4.5)*	4 = D2/1 = D1	280
TCM	(2)	0	2	20	1 = D1/1 = D3	373
BCM	(2)	0	2	16	2 = D1	280

* Mean years of 9 includes one principal with 28 years experience. Removing this person reduces average years to 4.5.

primary program policy encourages instructional practices that are quite different from those considered effective a decade ago and, thus, would not be as familiar to principals who had been in the role for a long time.

A related explanation concerns the notion that new administrators may be in a transition year and are finding a way to bridge the gap between the teacher's classroom and the principal's office. Support for this notion is provided by the fact that Indirect Instructional Leaders were also relatively new to the role, in contrast with those adopting the two other styles.

Whether it is due to reluctance to break with the past, a love of teaching, a strong belief that he/she knows how to do it best, or an awareness that teachers learn best when new strategies are modeled for them, number of years in the role may provide some of the rationale for leadership style.

The two anomalies in the sample tend to confirm the above interpretation. The one male instructional leader was from a district where all of the principals in our sample were Indirect Instructional Leaders (possible district effect), however, he had also been a principal for a short time (7 years). One instructional leader was in a district that had no other instructional leaders and had been a principal for 28 years, but she was female.

Although these data are far from conclusive, they do indicate some interesting connections and perhaps point the way to future research.

Conclusion

Using evidence collected from a larger study of school improvement initiatives, in this chapter we explored three questions. First, can variations in patterns of practice be explained by differences in problem-solving processes? Such processes appear to account for much of this variation. Principals faced with the same "objective" problem— how to implement the Primary Program—interpreted the problem in widely different ways, from "a wonderful opportunity to better meet students' needs" to a blur of confusing, uncomfortable demands. Much of how principals thought about the school improvement problem flowed from this interpretation. And much of this interpretation seemed to depend on how knowledgeable the principal considered herself to be with respect to primary programming. This finding led us to attend, more explicitly, to the role of domain-specific knowledge in administrators' problem solving. Differences in problem-solving processes linked to each of the four patterns of practice support a hierarchial view of these patterns. For example, instructional leaders thought about children, program, and teachers, as well as about organization and management details. Building-centered managers focused almost exclusively on maintenance issues.

Second, what is the relationship between variations in patterns of leadership practices and expertise in group problem-solving processes? Results from the group problem-solving interviews showed that principals engaged in direct and indirect forms of instructional leadership demonstrated significantly higher levels of group problem-solving expertise than did building-centered managers and substantially higher levels than did teacher-centered managers. Teacher-centered managers also demonstrated significantly greater group problem-solving expertise than did building-centered managers. Clearly, the thinking that gives rise to instructional leadership practices is similar to the thinking that creates an expert group problem solver. These results may help explain some of the variation in impact of different patterns of leadership practice. They also add validity to our growing accumulation of evidence about the links between problem solving and administrative expertise. At a minimum, results offer a more complete understanding of what is involved in each pattern of leadership practice.

To add further depth to our understanding of leadership patterns, we asked, finally, about aspects or dimensions of group problem solving within which principals differed most. There were ten such dimensions. Differences among principals in these dimensions of group problem solving were most evident in the (a) purposes, (b) skills and knowledge, and (c) dispositions principals brought to the process. With respect to purposes, higher levels of expertise were associated with the pursuit of student, program, and staff development goals and the ability to help staff place immediate problems in the context of the school's broader mission. Higher levels of expertise were associated with a larger stock of domain-specific knowledge and more refined skills in planning for group problem solving and assisting staff in being as productive as possible during their deliberations; this was accomplished through clarifying, synthesizing, and summarizing activities during those deliberations. Finally, dispositions associated with greater group problem-solving expertise included at least the *overt* management or control of intense personal moods, a high regard for staffs' potential contribution to problem solving, and habits of self-reflection and evaluation of one's thinking and practices.

Implications for research and theory. Although limited to 12 elementary principals solving school improvement problems in a common provincial educational context, there are a series of relatively obvious implications for future research related to external validity. These implications raise such questions as: Would similar problem-solving processes be used by school administrators in a different educational context? Is there something about the secondary school leadership role that stimulates the use of processes unlike those used by elementary school leaders? Would variations in a particular problem domain (school improvement) result in the use of different processes than those observed in this study?

Several questions other than those concerned with external validity are also prompted by the results. First, this study informs us more fully about the nature of problem-solving expertise. Nevertheless, little is known about the development of those purposes, skills and knowledge, and dispositions around which administrators differed most. Much remains to be done to fill that gap.

Although problem-relevant knowledge is known to have an influence on problem-solving expertise, as yet there has been little attention devoted to discovering what are the important problem domains for school administrators (for one example, see Chapter 2). This question has radical implications for administrator preparation curricula. It suggests that the propositional knowledge offered by such curricula could be organized, more meaningfully, around a grounded (or more phenomenological) conception of the principal's world than is presently the case. This would go some distance toward avoiding the acquisition of inert knowledge by aspiring administrators—knowledge stored in memory but of little practical value since the appropriate occasions for its application usually are not recognized.

Finally, results of the study raise questions about the stability of problem-solving processes across different school contexts. Hallinger, Bickman, and Davis (in press) report, for example, that principal leadership practices are best understood through contingency models. Variations in student SES, as well as such variables as gender and parental involvement, change what principals do. But do such variables have a bearing on how principals think—the processes they use to solve problems in groups, for example? Perhaps the thought processes remain stable and the changed practices are only the result of such processes responding to different information. Were this the case, the value of contingency models of leadership would need to be reconsidered.

Chapter 11

Total Quality Leadership: Expert Thinking plus Transformational Practice

Recent school restructuring initiatives have stimulated questions about appropriate forms of leadership practices to foster such restructuring. Efforts to address these questions argue for subsuming "instructional leadership" practices within more broadly focused forms of practice termed "transformational." In this chapter, we argue that such leadership is necessary but not sufficient—that expert thinking is also required to accomplish school restructuring goals. Evidence collected from principals and teachers in nine secondary schools is used to support this argument.

This chapter was first presented at the 1993 annual meeting of the American Educational Research Association (Atlanta, April) by the text authors and was subsequently published as K. Leithwood and R. Steinbach, 1993. Total quality leadership: Expert thinking plus transformational practice. *Journal of Personnel Evaluation in Education,* 7(4), 311–337. Reprinted with permission.

"As organizational leaders struggle to lead their organizations to become higher performing, quality organizations, there is an increasing recognition that a new leadership paradigm is required to successfully develop and sustain a motivated and committed workforce"

(Horine and Bass, 1993, p. 1)

The new "paradigm" alluded to in the opening sentence of Horine and Bass' paper is transformational leadership. This form of leadership, they argue, is demanded by today's restructuring organizations, especially those organizations inspired by the goal of "total quality management" (TQM). Many such organizations are attempting to move, for example, from fixed standards to continuous improvement; from individual process systems to team process systems; from control and command to commitment and teamwork (e.g., Bradley, 1993). These are several among the many changes that need to be made if organizations are to develop cultures defined by constant attention to quality, to the improvement of customer satisfaction: "the focus on customer satisfaction through quality must be built into the management processes of the organization, . . . the very fabric of organizational life, the organization's culture, must define and support TQM" (Sashkin and Kiser, 1992, p. 25).

There is strong empirical evidence to suggest that transformational leadership fosters many of the changes apparently required to accomplish the purposes of a total quality organization. Such leadership has been shown, for example, to liberate the capacities of organizational members (Conger, 1989), to increase commitment to organizational goals (Leithwood, Jantzi, and Fernandez, in press), to stimulate extra effort on behalf of the organization's mission, and to provide greater job satisfaction (Seltzer and Bass, 1990). There is good reason to believe that the move toward total quality organizations would be well served by the adoption of transformational leadership practices, as Horine and Bass claim.

Total quality organizations and transformational leadership, while concepts developed in noneducational organizations, are of increasing interest to those attempting to restructure schools (e.g., Willis, 1993; Bonstingl, 1992; Leithwood, 1992; Sergiovanni, 1990). The client-oriented focus of TQM, for example, reflects the commitment most educational restructuring initiatives have made to create a role for parents as partners in their childrens' education and to redesign schools from a constructivist model of student learning (Murphy, 1991; Newmann, 1993). Self-managing teams empowered to improve the quality of services they provide to customers, a central feature of TQM, for example, reflect the importance that transformational leaders attach to developing consensus about group goals and providing support to groups and individuals in pursuit of those goals.

We do not have a quarrel with these developments; indeed, we think they offer substantial promise. But, we do have a worry. That worry is fueled by the well-known tendency for educational innovation to be faddish, often to be fatally simplistic in what is selected for implementation, and frequently to assume the existence of a "silver bullet"—one simple solution to a complex network of problems. With this in mind, it is important, in our view, to forcefully draw attention to a dilemma associated with applying the "new leadership paradigm" in the interests of a total quality agenda for schools.

The dilemma is this. Based on the available research evidence, transformational leadership practices appear to offer promise across many organizational contexts, in general, striving toward total quality goals. Total quality improvements do not occur in general contexts, however. They occur in specific and always partially unique contexts. Such contexts present leaders with unpredictable problems to solve, contexts in which productive leadership responses will be contingent upon circumstances unique to the context. So, for example, there will be some school contexts in which it will be very effective for a principal to work hard on developing, with the school community, a vision for the school—good transformational leadership practice. However, there also will be school contexts already imbued with a vision in which the school community strongly believes. It may be unproductive for new principals entering such school contexts to spend time vision building. More likely, the problem for these principals is to figure out what leadership initiatives will take the vision forward (likely within a broad framework of transformational practices).

This takes us to the argument discussed in the remainder of the chapter:

1. In order for school leaders to be most productive, they need to think expertly about their own school contexts and the consequences for the practices which they choose;

2. Total quality leadership combines such expert thinking with the capacities to act transformationally, when such actions are warranted;

3. School leaders may be highly expert thinkers and yet not act as transformationally as do their less-expert colleagues, in

some circumstances; furthermore, high levels of transformational practice are not uncontestable indicators of highly expert thinking.

Data from a recent study carried out in nine secondary schools in Ontario, Canada, are used to demonstrate the meaning and plausibility of each of the elements of this argument.

Framework

If "total quality leadership" depends on a combination of expert thinking and transformational leadership practices, we need to understand what each of these factors mean.

Expert Thinking

Our meaning of expert thinking has been outlined in considerable detail in previous chapters. For a good description of how we framed such thinking for purposes of this study, the reader may wish to review the "Framework" section of Chapter 6; in this study, however, expert thinking was limited to what we have learned about individual (as opposed to group) problem solving on the part of administrators. Suffice it to say, for this study we conceptualized expert thinking in terms of our multicomponent problem-solving model. This model focuses attention on how administrators interpret or define problems; the goals they set for problem solving; the nature and use of values in problem solving; their orientation to constraints; the nature of their solution processes; and their mood or affective disposition toward the problem-solving process.

Transformational Leadership

Our meaning of transformational leadership is generally consistent with its treatment in noneducational organizations. Hunt (1991), for example, traces this meaning, especially the idea of charisma, to the early work of Max Weber. Contemporary, mature forms of transformational leadership theory were proposed by Burns (1978) and then by Bass and his associates (e.g., Bass, 1985; Bass and Avolio, 1989; Bass et al., 1987), as well as others in noneducational contexts (e.g.,

Podsakoff et al., 1984; Podsakoff et al., 1990). Systematic attempts to explore the meaning and utility of such theory in educational organizations are quite recent. Linked closely to the idea of transformational leadership is the idea of transactional leadership. Transactional forms of leadership are premised on exchange theory. Various kinds of rewards from the organization are exchanged for the services of the teacher who is seen to be acting at least partly out of self-interest. Transactional leadership practices help teachers recognize what needs to be done in order to reach a desired outcome. This, it is claimed, (e.g., Leithwood, Jantz, and Fernandez, in press) increases teachers' confidence and enhances motivation as well.

The corpus of theory and research traveling under the transformational leadership banner is by no means unified. It offers alternative prescriptions for leader behavior, alternative predictions about the effects of such practices on "followers," and alternative explanations of how these leader behaviors and effects are mediated (see Shamir, 1991). The conception of transformational leadership which seems most suitable for school restructuring has its theoretical genesis in Bandura's (1977, 1986) social cognitive theory and Shamir's (1991) self-concept-based explanation of charisma. According to this view, transformational leaders increase their staffs' commitment by "recruiting" their self-concept, by increasing the salience of certain identities and values to an organizational vision or mission that reflects them. These transformational leadership effects can be explained as a product of conditions which enhance staff motivation and perceptions of self-efficacy.

Podsakoff et al. (1990), reporting on the results of a comprehensive review of relevant research, suggested that almost all conceptions of transformational and transactional leadership are encompassed within eight dimensions of leadership practice. These dimensions have served as points of departure for the conception of leadership used in our own recent research (e.g., Leithwood, Jantzi, and Fernandez, in press; Leithwood et al., in press; Silins, 1992). They can be defined and their effects briefly explained as follows:

- *Identifying and Articulating a Vision*: behavior on the part of the leader aimed at identifying new opportunities for his or her school, and developing, articulating, and inspiring others with his or her vision of the future. When visions are value laden, they will lead to unconditional commitment; they also provide compelling purposes for continual professional growth.

- *Fostering the Acceptance of Group Goals*: behavior on the part of the leader aimed at promoting cooperation among staff and assisting them to work together toward common goals. Group goals that are ideological in nature are especially helpful in developing group identity.

- *Providing Individualized Support*: behavior on the part of the leader that indicates respect for staff and concern about their personal feelings and needs (verbal persuasion). This dimension is likely to assure teachers that the problems they may encounter while changing their practices will be taken seriously by those in leadership roles and efforts will be made to help them through those problems.

- *Intellectual Stimulation*: behavior on the part of the leader that challenges staff to reexamine some of the assumptions about their work and rethink how it can be performed. Such stimulation seems likely to draw teachers' attention to discrepancies between current and desired practices and to understand the truly challenging nature of school restructuring goals.

- *Providing an Appropriate Model:* behavior on the part of the leader that sets an example for staff to follow which is consistent with the values the leader espouses. This behavior is aimed at enhancing teachers' beliefs about their own capacities, their sense of self-efficacy. Secondarily, such modeling may help create perceptions of a dynamic and changing job on the part of teachers.

- *High Performance Expectations:* behavior that demonstrates the leader's expectations for excellence, quality, and high performance on the part of staff. Expectations of this sort help teachers see the challenging nature of the goals being pursued in their school. They may also sharpen teachers' perceptions of the gap between what the school aspires to and what is presently being accomplished. Done well, expressions of high expectations should also result in perceptions among teachers that what is being expected is also feasible.

Expert thinking and transformational leadership, as described in this section, served as a framework for collecting data from teachers and principals. The next section outlines how these data were collected and analyzed.

Method

Sample

Nine secondary school principals (four female, five male) from one large urban school system participated in this study. They were nominated by at least two central office administrators as particularly effective school leaders who were actively engaged in significant school improvement efforts.

Data Collection

Interview. Evidence about the principals' thinking and problem-solving processes were collected through interviews about their efforts to deal with a current school improvement problem. Interviews, semistructured and approximately one and one-half hours long, asked principals to select a school change initiative ("problem") underway in their schools that was a high priority for them; they were then encouraged to talk spontaneously about how they were solving that problem. Prompts were limited mainly to questions of motive and intent. Other prompts included questions about the background of the problem, who initiated it, and how many people and who was involved. After this spontaneous talk, specific questions related to our problem-solving model were asked. Principals were asked about what they hoped to accomplish, what values might be influencing their problem solving, what constraints might be impeding progress, and what were the specific steps taken to solve the problem. Most of this information was evident in the spontaneous talk, but these questions ensured a response from everyone.

Because in all cases their initiatives were ongoing, the interview was not, strictly speaking, retrospective. As a result, it avoids some of the objections to this type of verbal reporting (Ericsson and Simon, 1984).

Survey. As part of the larger study, staff members in the nine schools were surveyed about their perceptions concerning a wide array of conditions affecting their school improvement efforts. Relevant to this narrower study were the 47 items asking respondents to indicate, on a five-point scale, their perceptions of behavior in relation to six dimensions of transformational leadership. A total of 295 teachers responded to the questionnaire. More details about our survey methods are described in Leithwood, Jantzi, and Fernandez (1993).

Data Analysis

Interviews. Interviews were tape recorded, subsequently transcribed, and content analyzed. Protocols, devoid of identifying information, were parsed into idea units (segments), numbered, and then coded according to a checklist of expert problem-solving subskills developed during prior research (Leithwood and Steinbach, 1992). On a rating sheet, the numbers of each segment were entered next to the appropriate code and a score of 0, 1, 2, or 3 was assigned to each code item. A score of 0 meant there was no use of that subskill; a score of 1 meant there was some indication of use; 2 showed the skill was present to some degree; and a score of 3 indicated either that the skill was present to a marked degree (frequently) or (more qualitatively) that it was a particularly fine example of the skill. Ratings for each item on the checklist were added to provide a total score. This score was considered to be a measure of the quality of the principal's problem-solving process, as defined by our model.

To ensure reliable coding, an analyst, unfamiliar with this work, was trained in its use. For the training, two randomly selected protocols were independently coded by the analyst and one of the authors. Differences were discussed until a high degree of convergence was reached. The rest of the protocols were then independently scored by both analyst and author. Agreement ranged from a low of 76 percent to a high of 92 percent, with a mean level of agreement of 81 percent. In all cases, initial differences of opinion were discussed until complete agreement was reached.

Survey. Following data entry and cleaning, a data file was compiled for responses to the survey. The statistical package, SPSSX, was then used to calculate means, standard deviations, percentages, and correlation coefficients. The reliabilities (Cronbach's alpha) of the scales were calculated. Related T-tests were calculated to compare the total mean scores of each transformational leadership characteristic.

Results

Evidence collected in the study was examined from both quantitative and qualitative perspectives. Results of applying these perspectives are reported separately.

A Quantitative Perspective

Transformational leadership. In Table 11.1 we report teachers' ratings (means and standard deviations) of the extent to which they perceived each dimension of transformational leadership being provided in their schools. Across all nine schools, teachers rated most in evidence those leadership practices intended to develop consensus among staff about school goals (m = 3.66); least evident to teachers were leadership practices conveying high expectations for their performance (m = 3.40). Differences among the ratings of the remaining four leadership dimensions, although small (from 3.50 to 3.60) were statistically significant in a number of cases, as Table 11.2 indicates.

Also provided by Table 11.1 are teacher ratings of leadership dimensions for each school. School 8 received the highest rating on all dimensions of leadership combined (m = 3.79) as well as on all individual leadership dimensions except the creation of high expectations. Lowest rated, overall, was school 11 (m = 3.35) which also rated lowest or very low all individual leadership dimensions except providing intellectual stimulation (m = 3.56). While lowest, the overall mean rating of 3.35 for school 11 is still well above the midpoint of the rating scale, evidence that all nine schools were perceived by their staffs as providing a substantial degree of transformational leadership. Indeed, differences among schools were not statistically significant.

Who is the source of this transformational leadership? This question is addressed in Table 11.3, which reports the percentage of teacher respondents in each school who identified each of eight possible sources of leadership. Across all schools, the principal, the administrative team, and department heads acting as a group are the most frequently cited sources (by 55, 59, and 51 percent of respondents, respectively). Vice principals and ad hoc committees were cited next most frequently (42 and 44 percent). Least frequently cited were teacher committees (27 percent), individual teachers (34 percent) and "other" sources (14 percent). This evidence suggests that leadership, while perceived to be widely distributed within the nine schools as a whole, also was perceived by the majority of teachers to be provided by those in formal leadership roles.

We were particularly interested in the principals' leadership. Schools varied widely in the percentage of respondents who identified the principal as a source of leadership. Eighty-seven percent of respondents in school 7 identified the principal as compared with only 38 percent in school 8, for example. The significance of such differences are explored further in our qualitative analysis.

Table 11.1 Teachers' Ratings of the Extent to Which Transformational Leadership Was Being Provided (N = 295)

CON-STRUCTS	SCHOOL #3		SCHOOL #4		SCHOOL #5		SCHOOL #6		SCHOOL #7		SCHOOL #8		SCHOOL #9		SCHOOL #10		SCHOOL #11		Mean
	M	sd	M	sd	M	sd	M	sd	M	sd	M	sd	M	sd	M	sd	M	sd	M
Vision	3.56	.78	3.43	.65	3.49	.66	3.55	.65	3.35	.82	3.72	.59	3.61	.74	3.50	.64	3.26	.65	3.50
Model	3.64	1.01	3.63	.88	3.73	.78	3.58	.75	3.54	.86	3.87	.77	3.84	.80	3.43	1.06	3.21	.83	3.60
Grp. Goals	3.68	.81	3.67	.66	3.66	.56	3.66	.66	3.36	.87	3.93	.69	3.76	.64	3.60	.68	3.62	.57	3.66
Ind. Support	3.63	.82	3.54	.73	3.63	.69	3.70	.70	3.24	.87	3.77	.66	3.72	.76	3.59	.68	3.30	.79	3.57
High Expect.	3.25	.87	3.57	.63	3.50	.62	3.36	.76	3.58	.66	3.49	.92	3.51	.66	3.24	.87	3.13	.66	3.40
Intell. Stim.	3.48	.79	3.59	.54	3.51	.63	3.49	.51	3.37	.71	3.79	.68	3.54	.71	3.31	.79	3.56	.69	3.52
MEAN	*3.54*	*.76*	*3.57*	*.58*	*3.59*	*.59*	*3.56*	*.55*	*3.41*	*.70*	*3.79*	*.63*	*3.66*	*.65*	*3.44*	*.69*	*3.35*	*.59*	
RANK	**6**		**4**		**3**		**5**		**8**		**1**		**2**		**7**		**9**		

Table 11.2 Differences in Teachers' Ratings of Transformational Leadership: Dimensions across All Schools

	VISION	MODELING	GROUP GOALS	SUPPORT	EXPECTATIONS	INTELLECTUAL STIMULATION
Vision		*	*	*	*	
Modeling	*				*	*
Group Goals	*			*	*	*
Support	*		*		*	
Expectations	*	*	*	*		*
Intellectual Stimulation		*	*		*	

*p = <.05 using a related T-test

Table 11.3 Sources of Leadership

Sch. #	PRINCIPAL %	Freq.	VICE PRINCIPAL %	Freq.	ADMIN. TEAM %	Freq.	COMMITTEES DH %	Freq.	COMMITTEES TS %	Freq.	AD HOC COMMITTEES %	Freq.	INDIVIDUAL TEACHERS %	Freq.	OTHERS %	Freq.	TOTAL RESP.
3	53	(20)	55	(21)	58	(22)	58	(22)	34	(13)	63	(24)	50	(19)	8	(3)	38
4	58	(25)	33	(14)	58	(25)	58	(25)	21	(9)	44	(19)	26	(11)	21	(9)	43
5	54	(21)	49	(19)	64	(25)	49	(19)	31	(12)	36	(14)	44	(17)	13	(5)	39
6	48	(14)	52	(15)	52	(15)	41	(12)	21	(6)	41	(12)	28	(8)	10	(3)	29
7	89	(16)	33	(6)	39	(7)	39	(7)	11	(2)	39	(7)	11	(2)	11	(2)	18
8	38	(10)	31	(8)	50	(13)	54	(14)	27	(7)	58	(15)	38	(10)	23	(6)	26
9	71	(27)	37	(14)	63	(24)	47	(18)	26	(10)	58	(22)	55	(21)	8	(3)	38
10	48	(11)	30	(7)	61	(14)	65	(15)	17	(4)	17	(4)	17	(4)	9	(2)	23
11	44	(18)	49	(20)	71	(29)	46	(19)	44	(18)	34	(14)	24	(10)	17	(7)	41
Mean	**55%**		**42%**		**59%**		**51%**		**27%**		**44%**		**34%**		**14%**		**295**

Expert Thinking.   In Table 11.4 we summarize the analysis of principals' verbal protocols. Our six-component model of expert administrative problem solving was used as the basis for the coding. For each principal and each component of problem solving, the table indicates the number of relevant segments of transcribed text, the number of elements of expertise for which there was evidence, and the researchers' scoring of level of expertise. Also provided in Table 11.4 are scores of overall expertise for each principal and those aspects of the problem-solving model most and least evident in the verbal protocols.

Our procedure for scoring problem-solving expertise allocated a maximum of 114 points to a protocol. The nine principals were awarded scores ranging from 48 (principal of school 5) to 70 points (school 6), a substantial range, but there were three distinct clusters of scores. Principals 6, 9, 11, 4, and 10 scored in the 64 to 70 range, principals 7 and 8 scored 58 and 57, respectively, and principals 3 and 5 scored 49 and 48, respectively. Whereas the problem solving of most of these principals compares favorably with expert samples studied in our previous research, there are differences within the sample of a magnitude we would expect to be consequential in their practices.

Expert thinking and transformational leadership practices compared.

At the beginning of this chapter, we argued for a conception of total quality leadership as a combination of expert thinking and transformational leadership practices. Although this combination seems defensible in theory, what about in practice? More precisely, is this combination commonly evident among school leaders reputed to be very good at what they do? Is there a direct, linear relationship between expert thinking and transformational leadership practices?

In Table 11.5 we summarize evidence reviewed in the two previous sections of the paper in a manner that helps answer these questions. The nine principals are ranked, in terms of the expertise of their thinking, in the second column of the table. In the third column, they are ranked on the basis of teachers' ratings of the extent to which transformational leadership was being provided in their schools (remember that teachers were not just rating principals, however). The fourth column ranks principals based on combined expert/leader ratings: we simply added the two ranks together to get a score (e.g., principal 9 ranked second on expertise and second on transformational leadership, thus receiving a score of 4, the best of the nine scores).

Table 11.4 Principals' Problem-Solving Scores

SCHOOL #	INTERPRETATION			GOALS			VALUES			CONSTRAINTS			SOLUTION PROCESSES			MOOD			TOTAL SCORE
	scr[1]	segs[2]	elems[3]	scr[1]	segs[2]	elems[3]	scr[1]	segs[2]	elems[3]	scr[1]	segs[2]	elems[3]	scr[1]	segs[2]	elems[3]	scr[1]	segs[2]	elems[3]	
6	13	20	5	10	16	5	19	29	7	7	17	3	20	35	9	1	1	1	70
9	14	13	7	13	14	5	20	21	8	7	13	3	13	32	7	2	1	1	69
11	16	19	7	10	7	4	16	27	8	8	16	3	16	26	8	1	1	1	67
4	14	25	5	9	9	5	18	28	8	7	33	3	16	25	7	3	5	1	67
10	11	15	5	7	7	4	18	46	8	9	20	3	16	20	8	3	4	1	64
7	13	19	6	8	6	3	17	24	8	5	8	3	13	30	7	2	4	1	58
8	10	19	5	10	11	4	20	53	8	4	8	2	12	25	6	1	1	1	57
3	11	15	7	7	10	4	15	26	7	6	16	2	7	15	4	3	3	1	49
5	9	17	5	4	6	2	14	24	6	6	17	3	14	20	7	1	1	1	48
Mean	**12.3**	**18**	**5.8**	**8.7**	**9.6**	**4**	**17.4**	**30.9**	**7.6**	**6.6**	**16.4**	**2.8**	**14.1**	**25.3**	**7**	**1.9**	**2.3**	**1**	**61**

[1]scr = score awarded by raters
[2]segs = number of idea units coded
[3]elems = number of subcomponents for which there was evidence

Table 11.5   A Comparison of Principals' Problem-Solving Expertise and Levels of Transformational Leadership

RANK HI → LO	PROBLEM-SOLVING EXPERTISE (RANK ORDER)	TRANSFORMATIONAL LEADERSHIP (RANK ORDER)	COMBINED PS RANK AND TL RANK = SCORE (RANK ORDER)
1	S6	S8	S9 = 4
2	S9	S9	S6 = 6
3	S11	S5	S8 = 8
4	S4	S4	S4 = 8
5	S10	S6	S5 = 12
6	S7	S3	S10 = 12
7	S8	S10	S11 = 12
8	S3	S7	S3 = 14
9	S5	S11	S7 = 14

What does this table say about our questions? First, and not surprisingly, at least very high levels of total quality leadership are not common even among these reputationally effective principals. Principal 9 appears to clearly "have it"—but she is the only one who so clearly does; so a high level of TQM is possible but may be relatively rare, as far as we can tell from this study. Having said that, it is important to remember that all nine members of our sample demonstrated relatively high levels of both expertise and (to the extent our data can be relied on) transformational leadership; our answer must be interpreted in these highly relative terms. Second, evidence in Table 11.5 suggests that principals may be able to behave in ways that teachers perceive as transformational (keeping in mind the previous caveat about these ratings) even though we did not rate their thinking as expert as some of their colleagues who are perceived to behave less transformationally. The relationship between expertise and transformational practices appears to be nonlinear. Principals 6 and 11 are ranked highly in terms of expertise (first and third) but much lower on transformational leadership (fifth and ninth). In contrast, principals 8 and 5 are ranked quite high on transformational leadership (first and third) but relatively low in expertise (seventh and ninth).

These quantitative results, then, raise at least two interesting questions: What does total quality leadership actually look like in practice? What seems to explain the discrepancies between levels of expertise and transformational leadership? To answer these questions, we turn to a qualitative analysis of our data.

A Qualitative Perspective

Total quality leadership in practice. As the results of our quantitative analysis indicated, one principal of the nine in the study demonstrated both high levels of expert thinking and transformational leadership—our conception of the total quality leader. In this section, data collected through the problem-solving interview with this principal are used to exemplify total quality leadership in practice. The six components of our problem-solving model provide the primary framework for this description, but transformational leadership practices mentioned by the principal are noted as they emerge.

Let's call the principal Sarah. At the time of data collection Sarah was 48 years of age, had been a vice principal for 3 years and a principal for 2 years after a 20-year career as teacher and department head. Sarah had been principal of her only and present large (97 staff, 1650 students) secondary school for 2 years at the time she was interviewed. Although many changes were underway in the school, Sarah chose to discuss with us her thinking and practices related to implementation of anti-racist education. This was, for Sarah, focal among the many initiatives resulting from a formal needs assessment and "about fifteen, twenty other ways of collecting data" to help in the development of a strategic school plan. Although such plans were mandated by the school system, Sarah's comments indicated that such a plan would have been developed with or without the mandate. She believed the five-year plan she had inherited as the new principal had run its course ("It was a five-year plan but I think it was really outdated").

What was noteworthy about the processes Sarah used primarily to understand the needs of her school and the priorities for school improvement—her interpretation and goal setting processes? With respect to problem interpretation, Sarah's understanding of what anti-racist education would mean in her school and its importance as a priority for the school was arrived at in a highly deliberative fashion; this is clear in her references to data collection and in the systematic way she involved others in interpreting these data. Staff, students, parents, principals of feeder schools, and others were all part of this interpretation process, even though she "personally gathered . . . all the information together [and spent] about three months, just in the evenings going over things to learn more about the school."

A second noteworthy aspect of Sarah's problem interpretation was the link she made between the need for anti-racist education and an even more encompassing purpose, "the whole equity issue we felt was important" (this link had the quite practical consequence of making her school eligible for additional resources). Third, Sarah's interpretation of the problem, as with other experts we have studied, was quite clear even though the plan for solving it was "a fluid process. We monitor what we are doing and evaluate it and make changes to our plan, but we do have a general direction that we are heading." And this general direction was conceived of by Sarah in both substantive and procedural terms. Substantively, the problem was, for example, to "have much greater racial harmony and understanding and appreciation for the various cultures that are represented among our students and staff than we currently do. . . . We're losing out on some opportunities that we could be taking advantage of if we had a greater understanding of our student body and staff." Procedurally, Sarah described this as a "change problem" and assumed that it would be solved by adapting and applying many of the same techniques she had learned from previous change efforts.

A final noteworthy aspect of Sarah's problem interpretation was its grounding in a broader vision she was helping to develop for the school. It was a vision which embraced larger community concerns for racial harmony ("people honoring each other's heritages and cultures"), but could be acted on quite directly, within the school, through such initiatives as program changes and staff supervisory practices, for example. Nor was it a static vision. As Sarah described it, she and the staff were involved in an ongoing process of "working toward our vision of what this school should be." Sarah understood, as well, the need for the vision to be widely shared and understood in order for it to provide real direction for the staff, just as the more specific problem of implementing anti-racist education had to be widely shared and understood. This aspect of Sarah's problem interpretation processes appears to account for the high ratings her staff gave her on the transformational leadership practice *building shared vision*.

So, Sarah developed a relatively clear interpretation of her problem, one firmly rooted in a shared and dynamic vision of her school. What was noteworthy about the goal-setting processes in which she engaged, processes also aimed primarily at understanding the problem? First, she arrived at a set of goals sufficiently detailed to reduce the complexity of the problem to something manageable. Until decomposed in this way, implementing anti-racist education seems an overwhelming challenge. But that was not the form of the problem on which Sarah acted. Instead, she and her staff identified such goals or "manageable bites" as, for example, finding and funding a project coordinator, raising staff awareness of racist practices, initiating curriculum changes, convincing parents of the importance of the problem, communicating with feeder schools about this as a priority, and the like.

Noteworthy, as well, was Sarah's ability to keep the interests of the students at the center of her purposes: "We want to get beyond that stage [raising awareness] to the nitty gritty of making a difference in the curriculum for the kids in the classroom." Like other expert school leaders we have studied in the past, Sarah had goals which acknowledged a role for all legitimate stakeholders in the school. Goals were identified not only for students, but also for parents and staff: "it's an issue school wide, so we wanted to make sure that we had representation from the other areas of the school on board too, because the secretaries meet the students at the counter, caretakers and A.V. [people] work with students."

Finally, with respect to goals, Sarah's thinking demonstrated her appreciation for the importance of building a broad understanding and consensus among all stakeholders for the nature of the problem and the goals that would need to be achieved to solve it. In order for the goals to actually be accomplished, Sarah noted, they "had to be in the department head objectives, had to be in our objectives, mine as a principal, my admin team's objectives . . . and also teachers had to have ownership." Such consensus building began at the point of interpreting needs assessment data and took the form of encouraging widespread participation in decision making. Sarah mentioned discussions aimed at building goal consensus at department head meetings, at staff meetings where each teacher had an opportunity to indicate their own priorities, as well as "with the caretakers and the secretarial staff and our school community executive." Indeed, Sarah pointed out that three meetings were held with this last group "because they weren't quite as close to the issue" as people in the building and "we wanted to make sure they understood where these [goals and priorities] came from and what they might involve." It is not hard to understand why Sarah's staff gave her high marks for the transformational leadership practice *developing consensus about group goals*.

Processes included in components of our problem solving called *values* and *mood* help in both understanding and solving problems.

What was Sarah's thinking like with respect to these components and how was it related to transformational leadership practices? Our answer to this question is based largely on the nature and role of Sarah's values. Results of our previous research suggest that such values and/or principles are a pervasive aspect of expert school leaders' problem solving. This was certainly the case in Sarah's approach to identifying as a priority, and then implementing anti-racist education in her school. Indeed, one of her long-term goals for solving this problem indicates just how much value she attached to values; ultimately, she explained, we hope to "make a difference in the value system of the students and how they are going to feel for life."

Being able to explicate and then consciously use one's values, sometimes as substitutes for knowledge, is characteristic of expertise. Sarah's thinking was shaped by at least five reasonably explicit values. The most influential of her values was consequences for students, a pragmatic value that we and others have argued ought to be at the apex of a principal's values hierarchy (Green, 1987; Begley and Leithwood, 1991; Leithwood, Begley, and Cousins, 1992). Sarah believes that schools have an opportunity to make a difference in students' lives because they are at an age when their values are still developing. "We have to prepare them for the world they are going to experience when they finish school and the world they are going to live in." Students' self-image is important and this belief helps guide her problem solving. "I think they [students] have to have a really good self-image if they are going to be successful no matter what they do in life." Racism, of course, can do much to erode a student's self image.

Sarah's problem solving was also influenced by values which we label knowledge, participation, and respect for staff. That knowledge was valued by Sarah is evident, for example, in her extensive collection of information for problem solving. She spent considerable time, before entering the school, meeting with department heads individually to learn about the school and its value system so she could "help them to do their jobs better." She believed that if everyone was more aware of the actual cultural diversity in the school, they would be more likely to take advantage of it to enhance the curriculum. Other evidence includes her meetings with the school community executive so they could understand the issues and be able to make informed decisions.

Sarah valued widespread participation in decision making in her school. "There's no point in me saying hey folks, this is what we are going to work on. Wrong." She believes that participation leads to commitment. "If people feel a part of the decision making process then I think you are halfway there in terms of doing something about it." But the participation should be voluntary; people should not be dragged in. Participation also means sharing of ideas through committee structures which have interconnected pathways.

Sarah valued her staff. She valued them because many had considerable professional expertise, in her view. As well, however, she respected their basic rights to be treated humanely and fairly. This was evident even when staff behaviors were at odds with Sarah's own beliefs and values. For example, sexist or racist comments by staff were confronted directly ("I can't condone this in my school") but in a way that clearly separated the behavior from the person ("it's not that you are a bad person, and I like you as a person. It's the behavior that I can't tolerate").

A final "professional" value strongly held by Sarah we call role responsibility. This value was evident in her reflections on her own responsibilities in solving the anti-racist education problem. She believed that she must demonstrate that equity is an important focus. One way she did that was to acquire additional resources so that a project director could be hired. "You need," as she pointed out, "someone to be accountable or nothing is going to happen." Sarah also believed that it was necessary for her own values to be congruent with the school's; you must be authentic. "You have to be working from your own set of values to do a good job . . . you can't fake it and do a good job." Her role included being an educator. "I'm a principal, but first I'm a teacher. That's part of what principals do. You are still teaching but you are working with your staff as opposed to students directly."

In sum, then, Sarah was quite clear about her own values, and demonstrated the use of five such values as explicit instruments in her problem solving. In what ways, then, does this aspect of Sarah's problem solving touch on transformational leadership? First, her vision is value-based and hence offers the potential to attract strong, even ideological commitment on the part of others (Shamir, 1991); the vision may help transform staffs' prevailing views about the importance of their work, a means through which *high performance expectations* can be expressed. Second, Sarah strives to eliminate sources of conflict with dominant school values, potentially adding to the sense of coherence and meaningfulness people feel about their work in the school (Bandura, 1986), a form of *individualized support*. And, because she attempts to behave in ways that are consistent with the values she considers important, she *models behavior* important in moving toward the school's vision. Fourth, Sarah respects her staff and values their participation in the school, thereby creating important conditions for further developing their sense of self-efficacy; eventually this may strengthen their attachment to the school, increase their willingness to persist in solving school problems (Ford, 1992; Bandura, 1986)—one meaning of *providing intellectual stimulation*.

Evidence concerning Sarah's mood was relatively sparse and so we offer little comment about it here. Suffice it to say that, even though a relative novice in the principals' role, she displayed considerable self-confidence, a characteristic of experts generally. Such self-confidence is likely a product, in part, of being clear about one's values and having considerable experience in solving similar problems. Although new to the role, Sarah seems to have had such experience in other roles. Such self-confidence may encourage staff to risk the changes in practice required for school improvement and is sometimes offered as a partial explanation for attributions of charisma, a quality often associated with transformational leadership.

Components of our problem-solving model called constraints and solution processes are aimed primarily at solving problems. To avoid redundancy, we describe here only Sarah's approach to constraints and its relationship to transformational leadership practice. First, like other experts, Sarah appeared especially adept at anticipating obstacles or constraints and planning for how they could be managed ahead of time. She identified, for example, the usual constraints of resources and money and helped to address those by hiring a project director. Anticipating less than overwhelming agreement for anti-racist education as a priority, she involved all stakeholders from the outset in interpreting needs assessment information. Such anticipation is likely to foster a belief on the part of stakeholders that the context within which they are being asked to change will be supportive of their efforts. Such beliefs increase commitment and are part of *building consensus about group goals*.

Second, while Sarah identified several constraints, she viewed none of them as impenetrable. In fact she believed that if you want something enough, "you persist and work to remove those barriers . . . and there are ways to do it." Displaying this attitude is one way of expressing *high expectations* for not only your own performance but the performance of others, as well. It also expresses confidence in one's ability to solve problems.

Finally, Sarah displayed a reflective quality in her approach to constraints. For example, an invited speaker proved to be disastrous but she made the most of what could be learned from the event and also inspected her role in the debacle. "So part of it I think we weren't clear enough in our expectations when we discussed with her what we wanted." Consciously working in this way, particularly with staff to learn from mistakes, is yet another way of *providing intellectual stimulation.*

Explaining "partial quality leadership."   Among the nine secondary principals in the study, four provide especially interesting cases of what, on the basis of our quantitative analysis, seems to be "partial quality leadership" (see Table 11.5). Two principals (6 and 11) demonstrated exceptionally high levels of problem-solving expertise (ranked first and third, respectively) but were ranked substantially lower in terms of transformational leadership practices (fifth and ninth, respectively). Two other principals (8 and 5) demonstrated the opposite pattern: relatively high rankings for transformational leadership (first and third, respectively) but relatively low rankings for problem-solving expertise (seventh and ninth, respectively). What accounts for this partial quality leadership? As we puzzle through this question, it will be important to remember that at least seven of these nine principals are unusually expert and all are quite transformational as compared with more representative samples of principals. The term "partial quality leadership" in reference to any of the nine only makes sense when, for example, Sarah is the standard of comparison.

Let's consider, first, principals 6 and 11 whose problem-solving expertise ranked very high but transformational leadership practices ranked much lower. Three reasons help explain the lower transformational leadership rankings:

- *Scope of leadership influence:* The changes being initiated by both of these principals were in the early stages and had not yet begun to involve a significant proportion of the school staffs. Principal 11, for example, was working primarily with members of the administrative team and, when examined separately, we found that they rated the principal's transformational leadership very highly. So, lower transformational leadership ratings may mean that the principal's leadership practices have been experienced by relatively few staff members;

- *Stage in change process:* The initial focus of the change effort for both principals was programmatic, centered on developing classroom-based initiatives to foster student growth. Not until the substance of these changes was more fully developed was attention likely to shift to concerns for building the staff commitment and capacity needed to fully implement the changes;

- *Ambiguous exercise of power:* One of these two principals appeared to be uncertain about giving autonomy to staff members (facilitative power) as opposed to maintaining personal control over decision making. Because transformational leadership is rooted firmly in the exercise of facilitative power, staff members' perceptions of this ambiguity would be likely to lower their ratings of this principal's transformational leadership.

Two of these three reasons suggest that the transformational leadership ratings received by principals 11 and 6 may have been depressed because of the particular context in which they were working. Furthermore, evidence provided by the problem-solving interviews with these principals suggested considerable likelihood that, in different circumstances, staff would be likely to rate these principals' transformational leadership practices significantly higher. For example, both principals:

- articulated the kind of broad and compelling vision for their schools likely to attract high levels of teacher commitment ("I think the basic premise that faced us was that there were questions of equity . . . in this community . . . [and] that our students were sold short in terms of success in school and therefore in life");
- demonstrated sensitivity to the importance of building a consensus about school goals across the school staff, as a whole ("There can be individual means and differences, but there has to be a 'degree of commonality' and that commonality has to be addressed in terms of the goals and objectives and that commonality would best be expressed in terms of student outcomes");
- appeared to understand the importance of treating individual staff members uniquely, when necessary, and providing the support each needed to contribute to the changes being undertaken in the school ("we can provide . . . the professional development to help them get over, in some cases, their own fears or apprehensions");
- had plans for significant staff development as part of the changes they were developing with staff and saw themselves at least encouraging staff to question their existing practices ("raise people's understanding, almost begin to sow the seeds of . . . cognitive dissonance that would create that intraper-

sonal jarring note that . . . causes or that allows people, hopefully, to step back and begin to question their own practices");

- interpreted a number of their own actions as modeling beliefs and values they considered to be an important part of their school's culture ("I have represented the school at both of those [community resource groups] because I see that very much as part of my role as principal. Don't delegate this . . . ").

In sum, then, our evidence explains the lower transformational leadership scores of principals 6 and 11 largely as a function of the point in time in which we inquired about their work. Their thought processes displayed a propensity toward the use of transformational practices likely to become more evident to their staffs, we speculate, as their work progresses.

How can the combination of high transformational leadership and lower problem solving expertise rankings of principals 8 and 5 be explained? The answer to this question is fairly straightforward. Both principals were working on problems that addressed staff working conditions quite directly, rather than more fundamental problems of, say, student growth. Their leadership practices, in response to those problems, were highly visible to most staff members, were aimed at redressing important but short-term dilemmas, and resulted in immediate payoffs for staff. In neither case, however, was there evidence to suggest that these principals interpreted their change initiative as part of a larger, more fundamental problem to be resolved by the school. Similarly, the goals set for problem solving were relatively narrow in scope and largely concerned with staff as distinct from such other school constituents as students. Within the framework established by such goals, however, their thinking was fairly expert.

In sum, these two principals were perceived as highly transformational, but in response to relatively narrow, short-term problems to be solved in their schools. Because their thinking showed few signs, for example, of a broader vision for the school, we speculate some difficulty in maintaining high levels of teacher commitment to the school once these short-term problems are resolved.

Conclusion

Evidence from a study of nine secondary school principals has been used in this chapter to demonstrate what it means to conceptualize "total quality leadership" as a combination of expert thinking and transformational practices. One principal in our study, Sarah, exemplified total quality leadership in practice. The capacity only to exhibit transformational practices is not sufficient for total quality leadership, we argued; sometimes at least widespread application of such practices will be premature, as principals 6 and 11 demonstrated; and sometimes they will be applied in the service of excessively narrow purposes, as principals 5 and 8 illustrated. Expert thinking is particularly crucial for total quality leadership. It provides the cognitive flexibility leaders need to act productively in their highly contingent contexts. Such thinking also appears to create a propensity to act transformationally, in the long run, and in the service of relatively fundamental and broadly conceived purposes.

These claims, of course, rest on a small and shaky empirical foundation at this point. Subsequent research to shore up this foundation would employ measures of transformational leadership unambiguously about the principal, as opposed to multiple sources of leadership in the school, for example. Such research might also measure expertise in alternative ways, perhaps adding batteries of well-tested psychological instruments to our qualitative, less well-tested measurement procedures. Samples of principals more widely distributed in their expertise and transformational practices might also sharpen some of the distinctions we found to be useful in our data.

If total quality leadership is to be compared with other "new leadership paradigms," it parallels most closely the cognitive-behavioral perspective on leadership described by Sims and Lorenzi (1992), but with a focus on leaders' rather than followers' cognitions and behaviors. Transformational leadership theory is not sufficient for total quality leadership because it awards too little explicit weight to the mind of the leader. Expert thinking is not sufficient either; although it may increase the probability of transformational practices being used when appropriate, it is no guarantee. As more sophisticated evidence accumulates about the effects of transformational practices, we may anticipate increasingly reliable and contextually sensitive advice about potentially useful leadership behaviors. These are likely to be behaviors that are helpful to leaders' colleagues in developing personally constructed but socially shared understandings of their work (Leithwood and Duke, in press) and how the quality of such work can be continuously improved.

Part 5

—◄o►—

From Answers to Questions

Chapter 12

Improving the Problem-Solving Expertise of School Administrators

In most chapters in this book we have described aspects of school administrator expertise. While this is of some theoretical interest in its own right, the most practical reason for it is instructional: that is, to serve as one resource for systematically improving administrative expertise. Answers to three key questions seem necessary, however, before such instruction can proceed with confidence: Can problem-solving expertise be improved through systematic instruction? Will an instructional focus on general problem-solving processes enhance administrators' expertise? and, if so, What are the most promising forms

This paper was originally published as follows: K. Leithwood, and R. Steinbach, 1992. Improving the problem-solving expertise of school administrators: Theory and practice. *Education and Urban Society,* 24(3), 317–345. Copyright © 1992 by Sage Publications, Inc. Reprinted by permission of Corwin Press, Inc.

of instruction? To answer these questions, a four-day experimental program was designed and implemented with 22 school administrators and changes in their problem-solving expertise were compared with changes in a control group with similar characteristics.

Results suggest that problem-solving expertise can be significantly improved through problem-based forms of instruction designed to develop useful strategic knowledge among administrators.

In the context of an experimental instructional program, we explored a number of questions regarding the improvement of administrators' problem-solving processes. Can such problem-solving expertise be improved through systematic instruction? Will an instructional focus on the general processes used by expert administrative problem solvers enhance the capacities of others? And, if so, what are the most promising educational strategies for accomplishing this purpose?

Our efforts to address these questions built directly upon much of the research program described in other chapters of this book. Results of this research form one part of the framework for the present study. The second part of the framework was concerned with how expertise develops and what can be done instructionally to foster such development.

Program Goals: The Nature of Problem-Solving Expertise

Expert processes identified in the research. Problem-solving processes which the experimental program aimed to develop emerged most directly from our own studies which, as the readers of previous chapters will know, examined administrators' problem classification and management processes; developed a grounded model of administrative problem solving alone and in groups; examined the flexibility of principals' cognitions; inquired about the role of values in problem solving; and described the nature, number, and distribution of problems encountered by principals over an annual school cycle. Differences in problem-solving processes due to differences in role or organizational context have been examined and initial efforts made to better understand the relationship between socialization experiences and administrative expertise (Leithwood, Steinbach, and Begley, 1992). In some of this research, we have attempted to look at differences in the problem-solving processes of "expert" and "typical" principals. As in the research of many others using expert versus novice designs (reviewed by Alexander and Judy, 1988) our long-term purpose has been to clarify those aspects of expertise which might become a productive focus for selection, evaluation, and professional development of principals.

Earlier chapters have described our general information-processing orientation to understanding problem solving, as well as our six-component model of administrative problem solving. For this reason we include Table 12.1 here to briefly remind the reader of the components of that model and to provide a sample of what has been learned about expertise in respect to these components.

As is evident in Table 12.1, values play an integral role in expert problem solving; so does the problem solver's moods or affective states through their influence on problem-solving flexibility. Whereas both of these components of problem solving merit instructional attention, the experimental program described in this chapter touched on them less completely than the others. This was because we were not confident in the instructional approaches available to us. Instruction was mainly limited to making participants aware of research results concerning the nature and role of values and mood in the problem solving of experts. The program also encouraged self-instruction and self- evaluation as a means of regulating mood, techniques which seem to be helpful for this purpose (Meichenbaum, 1977; Wine, 1971).

Justifying a focus on general processes. Greatest emphasis in the program was focused on the other components of the model, which are a set of general cognitive skills and problem-solving strategies (i.e., problem interpretation, goal setting, identifying constraints, and solution processes). This focus is important to acknowledge because of the long-standing, continuing debate about the relative contribution to expertise, in many fields, of domain-specific (or local) knowledge as compared with generalizable, content-independent skills and strategies (e.g., Ogilvie and Steinbach, 1988).

Evidence brought to bear on either side of this debate is reasonably compelling: on the domain-specific knowledge side, see Chi, Glaser, and Farr (1985) and Lesgold (1984), for example; examples of evidence on the general skills side include Brown and DeLoache (1978) and Nisbett and Ross (1980). As Nickerson (1988–89) points out, however, this controversy is primarily a question of emphasis with widespread acknowledgement, in recent research, that both general thinking skills and domain-specific knowledge are important. In the absence of domain-specific knowledge, one has nothing

Table 12.1 Solving Unstructured Problems: Differences between Expert and Typical Principals

COMPONENT	EXPERT	TYPICAL
Problem Interpretation: a principal's understanding of specifically what is the nature of the problem, often in situations where multiple problems may be identified.		
(a) Basis for Priority	—consequences for school and academic growth of large numbers of students	—more concerned about consequences for themselves
(b) Perceived difficulty	—difficult problems are manageable if one used careful thinking	—difficult problems are frightening and stressful
(c) Ways to understand	—collects information —provides clear, comprehensive interpretation of problems	—makes assumptions in lieu of collecting information — irrelevant issues tend to cloud interpretation
(d) Use of anecdotes	—directly relevant to problem	— recounts difficult experiences rather than highly successful ones
Goals: the relatively immediate purposes that the principal is attempting to achieve in response to his or her interpretation of the problem	—concerned with implications for students and program quality —concerned with providing parents with knowledge —more concerned with knowledge	—more often mentions staff-oriented goals —concerned with making sure that parents are happy —more concerned with feelings

Table 12.1 Continued

COMPONENT	EXPERT	TYPICAL
Principles/Values: the relatively long-term purposes, operating principles, fundamental laws, doctrines, values, and assumptions guiding the principal's thinking	—considers slightly more principles —used as basis for determining long-term goals	—not mentioned —not mentioned
Constraints: barriers or obstacles which must be overcome if an acceptable solution to the problem is to be found.	—indicates few, if any, constraints —finds ways to deal with constraints	—indicates more constraints —sees constraints as obstacles
Solution Processes: what the principle does to solve a problem in light of his or her interpretation of the problem, principles, and goals to be achieved and constraints to be accommodated.	—detailed prior planning —consultation used extensively to get specific information —identifies detailed steps in solution process —stresses importance of information collection —follow-up planned for	—little attention to planning —consults less frequently with fewer specific purposes
Affect: the feelings, mood, and sense of self-confidence the principal experiences when involved in problem solving.	—calm, confident	—fearful

to think about. In the absence of reasonably well-developed general thinking skills, one's knowledge may not be applied in circumstances where it has potential use. For instructional purposes, it seems reasonable to approach the matter in a conditional way. The probability that a person will successfully solve a problem is a function of both the availability of problem-relevant knowledge and general thinking skills or heuristics and so both were addressed in the course.

The primary focus of instruction was on general problem-solving strategies with domain-specific knowledge provided by colleagues in the context of solving real-life administrative problems. A general strategies focus was chosen for three reasons. First, expert practice in many professions is centrally concerned with solving ill-structured problems for which there is relatively little available content knowledge and no readily available solution. As Schön (1984) suggests, it is problems "in the swamp" that are of greatest interest to experienced practitioners in many professions and there is a corresponding need to learn how to respond to such problems in an effective manner. Recent evidence suggests that as many as one in five problems faced by school administrators are ill-structured from their point of view (Leithwood, Cousins, and Smith, 1990).

Second, we believe that experienced school administrators are likely to have more opportunity to acquire domain-specific knowledge than general problem-solving skills. Descriptions of the content of contemporary preparation programs provide one source of evidence in support of this belief (Leithwood, Rutherford, and Van der Vegt, 1987; Blum and Butler, 1989). Hence, improvements in educational administrators' practices seemed likely by improving their capacities to use their existing knowledge more effectively through increasing their problem-solving skills. Finally, since our research showed that expert practitioners could be differentiated from their less-expert colleagues on the basis of their problem-solving skills, it seemed appropriate to at least try to teach those expert processes.

We believe our choice of focus on general problem-solving skills for the experimental program is justified by the case outlined above. Nevertheless, the term "general thinking or problem-solving skills" conveys an incomplete impression of the knowledge we attempted to develop through the program. A more comprehensive impression is conveyed by the term "useful, strategic knowledge."

Interpreting "general processes" as useful, strategic knowledge.

In the case of the experimental program, useful strategic knowledge refers to the explicit strategies and heuristics associated in our research with expertise, as well as the (usually) tacit knowledge required for its actual use in real-life administrative contexts. Our meaning of useful strategic knowledge is essentially the same as Sternberg and Caruso's (1985) definition of practical knowledge: "procedural knowledge that is useful in one's everyday life" (p. 134). Such knowledge is strategic or procedural in the sense that it is knowledge concerned with *how to* solve problems, rather than knowledge *about* problem solving (declarative knowledge). This distinction is common to both epistemology (e.g., Ryle, 1949) and cognitive psychology (e.g., Shuell, 1986).

The strategic knowledge of concern to us also had to be useful in two senses. First, such knowledge had to be sufficiently detailed so as to be of direct use in the context of the administrator's practice. This meant that the explicit problem-solving strategies identified in our research had to be combined with an extensive body of "ordinary" (Lindblom and Cohen, 1979) knowledge, usually tacit, in the mind of the learner. The importance of this type of knowledge is often overlooked in discussions of expertise. This combination acknowledges both the limited cognitive guidance provided by explicitly described, general strategies and the conditional nature of practical knowledge. With respect to strategic knowledge, expert practice requires explicit general strategies, detailed knowledge about how to use them, and knowledge of the circumstances under which their application is appropriate.

For our purposes, "useful" also meant that the knowledge provided by the experimental program had to be relevant to solving a wide range of administrative problems, contribute significantly to administrators' success in solving problems, and be potentially teachable. Perkins and Salomon (1988) argue that four conditions must be met for knowledge to be useful in this sense. The research from which the program emerged (see previous section) indicates that the program does meet them. That is, the program's focal strategies appeared to be used by experts in solving problems, played an important role in problem solving, were transferable across many problems, and were commonly absent among nonexpert administrators.

Program Methods: Problem-Based Instruction

Initial acquisition of useful, strategic knowledge. Our conception of how useful strategic knowledge develops was partly informed by schema theory and such related conceptions of cognitive structures as scripts (Shank and Abelson, 1977) and production systems (Sternberg and Caruso, 1985). According to this perspective, learners commonly acquire an initial understanding of (or primitive schema explaining) how to carry out some practice like solving an ill-structured problem, by experiencing the practice, being carried out by others. This experience may take the form, for example, of a verbal description or the observation of modeled behavior. Following Sternberg and Caruso (1985), the learner's initial schema is pieced together by identifying those elements of experienced information considered relevant to carrying out the practice ("selective encoding"), and putting this information together as an integrated structure ("selective combination"). This new structure is then related to structures or information already stored in memory through a process of "selective comparison." The resulting primitive schema then serves as a cognitive guide for the learner's initial performance.

As a result of initial performances, the learner is provided with information potentially useful in refining the initial schema. This is information about discrepancies between the actual performances and learners' schema-dependent understandings of what ought to have happened. Such information may indicate to the learners that: (a) their guiding schema requires further refinement and elaboration, and/or (b) their ability to perform does not yet match their understanding of what performance entails.

Development of increasingly skilled performances, based on increasingly sophisticated cognitive schemata, depend on opportunities for repeated practice and the quality of the feedback provided as a result of practice. A skilled coach, for example, already possesses a sophisticated schema to guide performance and knowledge of how best to provide feedback. As a consequence, such a person is likely to facilitate improvement in the learner's guiding schema and actual performance much faster than if the learner has available only his own analysis of discrepancies.

Burton, Brown, and Fischer (1984), using the teaching of skiing as a model of instruction, conceptualize the conditions provided by a skilled coach in terms of "increasingly complex microworlds" (ICMs). The learner is exposed to a sequence of environments or microworlds in which the task demands become increasingly complex. By manipulating the physical setting, the equipment (where appropriate), and the task specifications, the coach maintains a gap between the learner's initial capabilities and the requirements for performance that is challenging but manageable. Such a gap nourishes optimal adaptation of guiding schemata. As Burton, Brown, and Fischer (1984) point out: "The goal of a sequence of microworlds is not to remove all chances for misconceptions but . . . to increase the possibility that a student will learn to recognize, learn from and correct her mistakes" (p. 148).

Based on this partial conception of how useful strategic knowledge develops, it is reasonable to infer that instruction in expert administrative problem solving will be productive to the extent that it provides:

- models of expert performance;

- multiple opportunities for practicing administrative problem solving;

- a sequence of increasingly complex task demands; and

- feedback about the adequacy of performance and the sophistication of learners' guiding cognitive schema.

Although schema theory contributes to an understanding of how strategic knowledge develops, it is not sufficient. Nor does such theory speak directly to the usefulness of such knowledge. We relied on research concerned with the context in which learning takes place to complete our conception. This research explores the effects on learning of both the social context in which learning takes place and the purposes such learning is intended to help achieve; treatment of this former dimension of context will clarify our interest in developing useful strategic knowledge.

Most problems perceived by school administrators to be ill-structured are defined as such as a consequence of their social rather than technical character (Leithwood, Cousins, and Smith, 1990). Further, most such problems have to be solved by administrators in some form of collaboration with others (Leithwood and Steinbach, 1991). It is particularly important, for these reasons, to better understand the significance of the social context for administrative problem solving. One defensible conception of the relationship between individual learning and social context accepts, as its point of departure, Berger and Luckmann's (1966) well-known thesis that knowledge is socially constructed. This means that what counts as knowledge is defined through interaction with others and that many of the most helpful processes used by individuals to acquire knowledge in practical settings involve considerable such interaction. As Rogoff (1984) explains:

Central to the everyday contexts in which cognitive activity occurs is interaction with other people and use of socially provided tools and schemas for solving problems. Cognitive activity is socially defined, interpreted, and supported. People, usually in conjunction with each other and always guided by social norms, set goals, negotiate appropriate means to reach the goals, and assist each other in implementing the means and re-setting the goals as activities evolve. (p. 4)

For purposes of the experimental course, it was most important to conceptualize the nature of the contributions that social interaction could make to individual problem-solving capacity, as well as the conditions under which those contributions seemed most likely. One potential contribution of directed social interaction is the improvement of individuals' problem-solving expertise. Conditions required for this potential to be realized are evident, for example, in Vygotsky's (1978) concept of a "zone of proximal development." This zone is the gap between the problem-solving capacity of the individual learner and the capacity demonstrated by those with whom the learner interacts—such as colleagues within a group. Sensitive instruction, as Rogoff (1984) explains, at the learner's cutting edge of understanding, encourages participation at a comfortable yet challenging level. It also provides a bridge for generalizing strategies from familiar to more novel situations. In this way, the problem-solving processes of the group are internalized by the individual.

Social interaction also has the potential for increasing the individual's capacity to contribute more effectively to joint problem solving. In Mehan's (1984) observations of committee deliberations, problem solving was socially distributed: "the information upon which decisions are made is in the collective memory of the group, not in any individual's memory" (p. 64). In the case of the individual learner being stimulated by the group to develop better processes for solving problems individually, the group models performance from which more sophisticated guiding schemata can be inferred and provides socially compelling feedback about adaptations of existing schemata. In the case of becoming a more skillful contributor to a group's problem-solving process, the individual is stimulated to acquire another, higher order set of schemata to guide her participation in the group.

As we pointed out in Chapter 5, conditions likely to foster development of such expertise include:

- provision of group problem-solving processes likely to be more sophisticated than processes used by the individual;

- opportunities for the individual to reflect on or recover the elements of the groups' problem-solving processes;

- stimulation for individuals to compare their own processes to those of the group; and

- opportunities for the group to critically reflect on the roles played by individual members and to provide feedback to individuals about how their contribution could be improved.

Social interaction, we have argued, is a crucial feature of the context in which problem-solving expertise is learned and practiced. A second crucial feature of the context is the nature of the problems used as vehicles for developing expertise. For purposes of developing practical or useful strategic knowledge, such problems must be approximately isomorphic with the problems of practice and perceived as authentic by the learners. There are several compelling reasons for this to be the case. The "situated" nature of useable knowledge is one reason for using authentic problems as vehicles for developing expertise. As Brown, Collins, and Duguid (1989) argue, for example, the activity in which knowledge is developed is neither separable from nor neutral with respect to what is learned; "situations" (or problems used as instructional vehicles, along with the social context for instruction) coproduce knowledge. Whereas the instructor is not uninfluential in the process, often mediating the learning, it is the learner, finally, who is doing the selecting. What the learner selects from the situation in which learning takes place as the basis for developing meaning is unpredictable, at best. Furthermore, there will be substantial variation among learners in their selections depending on the nature of those existing cognitive structures used in the creation of meaning. The situation (or activity) in which learning takes place, therefore, cannot be separated from the knowledge to be learned; it is part of the knowledge that is stored in memory by the learner. The most certain way of ensuring appropriate understanding of what is learned, therefore, is to create situations the learner will encounter in practice. This not only aids in the initial creation of meaning, it also helps ensure appropriate application of knowledge subsequently.

A second reason why instructional situations and problems should be authentic has to do with the large amounts of usually tacit and/or "ordinary" knowledge (Lindblom and Cohen, 1979) required to actually use a general problem-solving strategy in practice. Authentic situations increase the probability that learners will make connections with appropriate, existing tacit knowledge. Artificial situations decrease this probability. When learners take advantage of social interactions among peers (as when a group of five or six school administrators try to solve an authentic problem together), the opportunities are increased for tacit knowledge to become explicit and thereby examined. Further, it is then possible to acquire the formerly tacit knowledge of one's colleagues, developed through hard experience. This formerly tacit knowledge of one's colleagues may be easily as important a contribution to problem-solving expertise as the research-based knowledge more typically the exclusive focus of formal instruction.

Finally, authentic situations are simply more motivating for learners than are situations abstracted from the context in which knowledge is to be used (Sternberg and Caruso, 1985). Indeed, our experience suggests that the use of authentic problems under conditions discussed to this point also adds to the domain-specific knowledge of some participants, as well as to their strategic knowledge. This may be part of what is motivating about authentic situations. Conditions to be met by an instructional program based on these views include:

- providing instructional situations which authentically approximate the circumstances of actual administrative practice; and

- encouraging the recovery, sharing, and evaluation of relevant knowledge which would normally remain tacit.

Additional interventions to foster transfer. The transfer of knowledge from the instructional setting to the real-life administrative setting is assisted through some conditions already examined: in particular, the use of authentic problems and settings. More can be done, however, to ensure appropriate application of strategic knowledge by drawing on results of research on transfer of training.

For purposes of designing the experimental program, transfer refers to:

the impact of learning a behavior [broadly defined] on the same performance in another context or on a different performance not simply containing the first in the same or a different context. (Salomon and Perkins, n.d., p. 5)

In order to design the program for greatest transfer, we were guided by an orientation to transfer proposed in a series of papers by Perkins and Salomon (Perkins and Salomon, 1988, 1989; Salomon and Perkins, n.d.). Two types of transfer are distinguished in this formulation ("high road" and "low road"), each produced by different cognitive mechanisms and stimulated by different instructional approaches. Because each type of transfer produces valuable although different outcomes, Perkins and Salomon (1988) argue that instructional programs ought to attempt to foster both. In general, transfer of any sort depends on how one initiates a search through memory for already-stored clusters of knowledge that might usefully be applied to the task one faces and the extent to which such schemata are linked to other potentially relevant clusters of knowledge stored in memory.

Low road transfer is characterized by the ready application of well-learned knowledge and/or skills to the same performance in contexts very similar to ones in which the knowledge and skills were originally learned, or in performances only modestly different from the originally learned performances. Such transfer occurs as a consequence of extensive practice in varied contexts until the application of the learned knowledge and skill becomes automatic; that is, until the presence of a situation or condition elicits the application of relevant knowledge and skill with little or no conscious thought. Practice extends the application of what has been learned from its initial performance or context to other similar performances and contexts. Variation in the application contexts or performances during practice gradually stretches the boundaries of application as the learner adapts to partially new circumstances in minor and largely unconscious ways.

The advantage of low road transfer is smooth and reliable application of mastered performances with little expenditure of cognitive effort. This suggests that low road transfer is most appropriate for knowledge and skills subject to routine and frequent use. The automaticity associated with low road transfer, on the other hand, inhibits reflection on matters such as when the application of existing skills and knowledge are appropriate.

Whereas low road transfer is relatively "mindless," high road transfer is "mindful." It involves applying a set of rules or principles extracted from one or more contexts and/or performances to other quite novel contexts and/or performances. The greater the degree of abstraction, the larger the range of instances such rules and principles subsume and to which they can be applied. High road transfer depends on: "both the decontextualization and re-representation of the decontextualized information in a new, more general form subsuming other cases" (Salomon and Perkins, n.d., pp. 10–11). This is not critically fostered by practice, although evidence suggests that limited amounts of practice are helpful. Rather, such transfer depends on bringing considerable conscious effort to bear on determining the generalizable features of the information. Not only must these generalizable features be determined by the learner, they must also be genuinely understood, evoked in the transfer context, and effectively applied.

Salomon and Perkins (n.d.) also point out that, because of the relatively mindless automaticity that comes with practice and expertise, experts may have difficulty mindfully transferring well-mastered skills and knowledge to novel contexts. This suggests that, especially with people who have considerable expertise, guided abstraction from (or reflection on) well-rehearsed practices may be quite important in helping them make better use of what they already know in responding to novel problems.

This conception of the transfer process implies a number of conditions to be met for successful transfer of problem-solving skills. In the case of frequently and routinely used skills (e.g., information collection), most suitable for low road transfer, it will be important to:

- provide many opportunities for application or practice across a wide variety of problem types; and

- provide feedback about the adequacy of performance and opportunities for further guided practice.

For general principles and skills most suitable for high road transfer, it will be helpful to:

- provide assistance in decontextualizing and abstracting generalizable features of existing problem-solving practices; and

- provide direct instruction in the key components of effective problem-solving practices and coaching in the application of such components to specific cases.

Fostering metacognition. Administrative expertise is partly a function of applying useful, strategic knowledge to the solution of ill-structured problems. The nature of that knowledge and how it is initially developed have already been described. We have also described how to help ensure that useful strategic knowledge developed in a formal instructional setting, for example, will be applied in appropriate, real-life administrative settings.

The strategic components of administrative expertise are not limited to the use of problem-solving strategies alone, however. Argyris' conception of double and single loop learning helps to illustrate why this is the case (e.g., Argyris, Putnam, and Smith, 1985; Argyris, 1982). The term "single loop learning" is applied by Argyris to a process in which the learner responds to a problem by initiating a chain of actions intended to resolve the problem. If that chain of actions proves less effective than desired, the learner chooses another chain of actions in a further attempt to resolve the problem, as the problem was originally conceived. So, whereas the solutions change as part of single loop learning, the variables governing the learner's understanding of the problem and the setting remain the same. In instances of double loop learning, the governing variables are themselves objects of conscious scrutiny and, as a consequence, the nature of the problem and the setting may be significantly redefined.

Individuals engaged in double loop learning are thinking about their own thinking; they are involved in managing their own cognitive resources and monitoring and evaluating their own intellectual performance. This is metacognition (Nickerson, 1988–89). Some would also refer to this process as a form of reflection in which experience is reconstructed in such a way as to enable one to transform one's own practice (Grimmett, 1989). Such reflection is dialectical since the learner engages in a "conversation" with the setting in an effort to better understand it and the meaning that the setting has for the assumptions underlying the problem-solving activity.

Conditions which seem likely to foster the development of metacognition include:

- the provision of cues to the learner which are likely to stimulate self-questioning;

- the modeling of metacognitive thinking by others; and

- direct instruction about the value of metacognition (since metacognitive activity is unlikely in the absence of a belief in its value) and the kinds of questions one might use as aids to self-reflection.

Instructional strategies used in the program.   In Table 12.2 we summarize the instructional strategies used in the experimental program to address those conditions we have identified as contributing to the development of useful strategic knowledge. As a whole, these strategies constitute our version of "problem-based instruction" (Bridges, 1992; Boud, 1985; Bransford et al., 1989). Currently used with promising results in a small number of institutions but across a wide range of professions (e.g., medicine, management, agriculture, architecture), problem-based instruction acknowledges especially

Table 12.2 Instructional Strategies Used to Meet Conditions for Developing Useful Strategic Knowledge

CONDITIONS	INSTRUCTIONAL STRATEGIES
1. provide models of expert problem solving	• audiotaped examples of expert administrators describe the process they use to solve a case problem • "live" administrators tell how they solved a real problem they faced
2. provide practice opportunities across wide variety of problem types	• ask individuals to write solution to own selected problem; colleague critiques • ask individuals to solve colleagues' problems; colleague critiques • groups of 5-6 participants solve problems together
3. sequence increasingly complex task demands	• problem-solving tasks for individuals and groups manipulated in terms of: evaluate other's solution vs. solve oneself; number of problem-solving components to consider; complexity of case problems
4. provide performance feedback on individual problem solving	• response by individual colleague, group, instructor to processes described in writing and described verbally
5. ensure participation in sophisticated group problem-solving processes	• careful instruction to groups prior to engagement in problem-solving task
6. encourage individual reflection on own and group problem solving	• individual participants required to think aloud about their own solving of problems or to write solutions to problems. Peers and instructors discuss their processes with individuals
7. provide performance feedback on contribution of individual to group problem-solving processes	• not done in this program
8. provide authentic instructional settings and problems	• instructional problems identified through research on problems encountered by principals and by having case problems written (or orally presented) by administrators as they encountered them

Table 12.2 Continued

CONDITIONS	INSTRUCTIONAL STRATEGIES
9. assist in recovering, sharing, and evaluating tacit knowledge	• work with a peer or group of peers to collaboratively solve problems, discussing alternative proposals based on experience and the thinking leading to such proposals
10. assist individuals in decontextualizing and abstracting general features of existing problem-solving practices	• most case problem solving by individuals or groups followed by "debriefing" in which the components of the problem-solving model were used as the framework for discussion • use of checklists of general strategies to be considered
11. provide direct instruction in effective strategies and coaching in their application	• brief presentations by instructors on characteristics of effective problem solving as identified in research; readings provided to students describing effective problem solving • coaching provided by both peers and instructors
12. provide cues to stimulate self-questioning	• instructors continuously monitor group problem-solving processes and intervene as warranted to provide cues or orienting questions • check lists
13. model metacognition and provide reasons for metacognition	• 15 percent of program devoted to looking at same problem from four different perspectives (legal, political, financial, educational) • each perspective presented by a person with special training or experience in the perspective (lawyer, trustee, business administrator, principal) • different, justified approaches to problem solving and solutions evident through observation of different perspectives • daily evaluation of program

well the situated nature of cognition and dilemmas associated with inert knowledge and lack of transfer. It does this by centering instruction around key problems of practice. Students acquire both domain-specific and useful strategic knowledge in the context of working through such problems. The contribution of problem-based instruction can be explained in terms of the readier accessibility of knowledge acquired through such instruction for application in practice. Such accessibility is a function of the way knowledge is organized and stored in memory initially, around problems of practice.

The experimental program required participants to work on parts or all of a total of nine problems. These problems varied in their degree of structure, although all were perceived to be relatively unstructured. In addition to degree of structure, two other variables were manipulated in order to provide Increasingly Complex Micro-worlds. One variable was the number of components in our problem-solving model (i.e., Interpretation, Goals, Principles, etc.). Participants were asked to address from one to all six of these components in relation to a given problem. A second variable was the function participants were asked to perform in relation to the components. These functions included: (a) describing how a model of problem solving (e.g., a principal talking about how he solved a problem) addressed the component(s), the simplest function; (b) evaluating the model's performance; and (c) addressing the component(s) oneself, the most complex function.

Other variables manipulated through the program were the social context for problem solving (individually, in pairs, in groups) and the form in which thinking was communicated (orally, in writing, or audio taped). Participants were required to evaluate the program at the end of each instructional day and a summary of their opinions was reported to them at the beginning of the next day, along with an indication of adjustments made to the program in response to these opinions. This was intended, in part, to stimulate thinking about the types of experiences most helpful in stimulating thinking.

Method

All principals and vice principals from one area of a large school board north of Toronto were invited to participate in the program; 38 volunteered. Fourteen principals and eight first-year vice principals constituted the experimental group. The principals were considered to be experienced administrators and the vice principals were new to the role. Ten principals and six first-year vice principals from the same board agreed to act as the control group. Efforts were made to match these groups as closely as possible for size of school, years of experience, gender, and type of school community. Members of the control group were promised the opportunity to have the intervention the following year. Both groups took the pre and post tests, but only the experimental group took part in the practicum.

The four-day program was evenly spaced over a period of four months and instruction was based on the model of administrative problem solving described earlier. Each component of the model was broken down into subskills which were explicitly taught.

Each session was organized around a theme—usually one or two components of the model—and the basic format was to have participants:

1. Identify the problem-solving strategy used by others;
2. Analyze and evaluate the processes used by the problem solver;
3. Practice the strategies themselves using a new problem; and
4. Reflect on their strategy use.

Table 12.2 details the instructional techniques used to help students improve their problem-solving processes. The effectiveness of the practicum was assessed using two kinds of measures: subjective appraisals by the participants and written solutions to four case problems.

Results

Subjective Appraisal

Daily evaluation questionnaires were administered which asked participants for their anonymous, subjective impressions of the program: in particular, (a) their overall impression of the day, (b) what they liked most and (c) least, and (d) what suggestions they had for improving the program. In addition, they were asked to rate, on a scale from 1 to 5, the extent to which the knowledge was new to them (1 = highly familiar, 5 = very unique), how intellectually engaging the day's program had been (1 = very boring, 5 = highly stimulating), and potentially how useful they thought the information might be (1 = not at all useful, 5 = extremely useful).

Overall assessments for each day ranged from excellent to good. People were also consistent in their choices of the instructional activity they liked best and least. For days one and two, the group interaction and sharing of ideas around problem solving were mentioned most frequently. On day 3, this activity was topped by the "live" modeling of problem solving. For day four, 17 out of 20 respondents said they liked the presentations of the various perspectives on problem solving best—again "live" modeling from practicing administrators. The facilities, length of day, and being away from school were the least-liked factors. Suggestions for improving the program were related to these least liked factors.

Ratings also indicated that 50 percent of the participants found the knowledge unique, 79 percent found the instructional activities highly stimulating, and 84 percent found what they learned extremely useful to their jobs as administrators.

On the last day of the program, participants were also asked, anonymously, to estimate the extent to which their problem-solving skills had been influenced by the whole program (choices were: not at all, slightly, moderately, substantially, and significantly). Out of 19 respondents, 15 said that there was substantial impact, one said there was significant impact, and three said their problem-solving skills were moderately influenced by the program.

Written Solutions

This measure was meant to test the objectives of the program directly. Experimental and control administrators were asked to provide written solutions for four hypothetical case problems—two for the pre test and two for the post test. Half of the administrators were randomly assigned set A for the pre test and half set B. They received the opposite set for the post test. This was done so that effects obtained could not be attributed to problem type.

Written protocols were analyzed holistically for the quality of both the problem-solving process used and the product or solution arrived at. They were also analyzed segment-by-segment for evidence of the strategies that were explicitly taught in the program.

Holistic analysis.   In their discussion of what is a good solution to an ill-structured problem, Voss and Post (1988) assert, pragmatically, that:

> a solution is regarded as good if other solvers find little wrong with it and think it will work. . . . [This] puts the burden of evaluation upon solvers with expertise similar to that of the solver proposing the solution. (p. 281)

Based on such reasoning, two expert practitioners[1], blind to both condition (pre or post test) and group (experimental or control), rated the solution to the first problem written for the pre and post tests in two ways. Rating 1 assessed the thoroughness of the *process*, or the quality of the thinking. Rating 2 assessed the quality of the solution, or the *product*. Both ratings were done on a scale from 0 to 3 with 0 being very poor and 3 being very good.

Expert one's ratings provide evidence that the experimental group improved substantially more than the control group in terms of both process and product. Although the differences between the groups are not statistically significant, they come very close. [Difference between groups for rating 1 = .77, $t(34) = 2.01$, $p = .052$; Difference between groups for rating 2 = .81, $t(33) = 1.92$, $p = .063$.] Expert two also found larger gains for the experimental group than for the control group in terms of both process and product but not as large as those reported by expert one.

Detailed analysis. In order to determine precisely what was learned, a detailed analysis was conducted of all the protocols (four for each subject). Data were coded according to the specific subskills taught within each component of the problem-solving model.

Protocols, devoid of condition or group identifiers, were first parsed into idea units (segments), numbered, and then coded to indicate the item on the subskill checklist of which it was an example. On a rating sheet, the numbers of each segment were entered next to the appropriate code and a score of 0, 1, 2, or 3 was assigned to each code item. A score of zero meant there was no use of that subskill; a score of one meant there was some indication of use; two showed the skill was present to some degree; and a score of three indicated either that the skill was present to a marked degree or that it was a particularly fine example of the skill. Ratings for each item on the checklist were added to provide a total score. This score was considered to be a measure of the quality of the process used, as defined by our model.

To ensure reliable coding, an analyst unfamiliar with this work was trained in its use. For the training, nine randomly selected protocols were independently coded by the analyst and one of the authors. Differences were discussed and disputes resolved until a high degree of convergence was reached. An additional set of ten protocols then were randomly selected and independently scored by both analyst and researcher. Agreement ranged from a low of 71 percent to a high of 95 percent with a mean level of agreement of 85 percent. One researcher subsequently parsed, coded, and rated the remaining 152 protocols.

Three indicators of growth were considered first; we were interested in determining if the program had an effect on the quality of the solution process as measured by the changes in total score obtained, the number of components dealt with, and the number of subskills addressed. A change score was calculated for each administrator for each of the three indicators. Ratings for both pre-test solutions were added together and divided by two and the same was done for both post-test solutions. In this way each administrator received a single rating for each indicator for the pre test and a single rating for each indicator for the post test. Finally, change scores were obtained by subtracting the pre-test scores from the post-test scores.

In Table 12.3 we display the mean change scores for the three indicators mentioned above. For all indicators, the experimental group improved more than the control group and two of those gains (total score and number of components) were statistically significant.

Finally, we were interested in learning which aspects of problem solving changed and where most (and least) growth occurred. Accordingly, for each component in our model, three change scores (total score received for each component, number of segments coded for each component, and number of subskills identified in each component) were calculated in the same way as discussed earlier. In Table 12.4 we display the mean change scores for each dimension within each component.

Table 12.3　Mean Differences between Pre and Post Test Written Solutions (Detailed Analysis)

	TOTAL SCORE		NUMBER OF COMPONENTS		NUMBER OF SUBSKILLS	
	Mean	S.D.	Mean	S.D.	Mean	S.D.
Experimental	+3.41	5.04	+.73	1.18	+0.84	3.09
Control	−0.91	5.31	−.25	0.86	−0.34	2.72
Difference Between Groups	4.32*		0.98**		1.18	

  * p < .02
** p < .01

Table 12.4 Mean Change Scores

	SCORE		# OF SEGMENTS		# OF SUBSKILLS	
	Mean	S.D.	Mean	S.D.	Mean	S.D.
Interpretation						
Experimental	+.95	2.02	+.43	1.57	+.20	1.23
Control	−.66	1.83	−.28	1.43	−.16	1.12
Difference Between Groups	1.61*		.71		.36	
Goals						
Experimental	+1.11	1.12	+.77	1.07	+.59	.78
Control	−0.19	0.79	−.44	.91	−.28	.61
Difference Between Groups	1.30**		1.21**		.87**	
Values						
Experimental	+.27	2.48	−.57	1.81	−.16	1.36
Control	−.75	2.29	−.59	2.11	−.16	1.56
Difference Between Groups	1.02		.02		0	
Constraints						
Experimental	+1.98	2.57	+.43	1.54	+.18	.76
Control	0	.98	0	.89	0	.71
Difference Between Groups	1.98*		.43		.18	
Solution Processes						
Experimental	+.14	2.56	−.93	3.08	−.27	1.42
Control	+.66	3.16	+1.16	3.94	+.22	1.28
Difference Between Groups	.52		.23		.49	
Mood						
Experimental	+.09	.33	+.09	.33	+.09	.33
Control	+.03	.13	+.03	.13	+.03	.13
Difference Between Groups	.06		.06		.06	

* p < .05   ** p < .01

For nearly every measure, the experimental group made substantially greater gains than did the control group, with five of the gains being statistically significant. The few exceptions are found in the Values and Solution Processes components. In the values component, both the experimental and control groups had fewer segments coded as values and used fewer subskills within that component in their post-test solutions. However, there was virtually no difference between the groups for those two measures.

A much more striking exception occurred in the solution processes component. Although the differences between groups are not statistically significant, the control group showed greater improvement than did the experimental group in all three measures in this component. In fact, for two of the measures, the experimental group's scores declined while the control group's scores increased, an anomaly discussed later.

The measure that showed the most consistently significant growth was the score received for each component. We feel that this measure most reflects the strength of expertise exhibited by an administrator and the quality of the response. Whereas the other measures also reflect degree of expertise, they rely more heavily on the quantity of information generated rather than on the quality of that information.

With respect to the components of our problem-solving model, the experimental group showed significantly greater expertise in their thinking related to the interpretation of the problem, the goals set for solving the problem, and their understanding of the importance of anticipating and planning for the handling of possible constraints. The most striking example of growth occurred in the goals component; every measure showed significant gains for the experimental group.

Discussion and Conclusions

We began this study with three questions: Can administrative problem solving be improved through systematic instruction? Will an instructional focus on the general processes used by experts enhance the capacities of others? and, What are the most promising strategies for improving problem-solving expertise? In this section of the chapter we summarize the answers provided by the study to these questions and examine several implications for research.

Can Problem Solving Be Improved?

Most of the data from the study affirm that problem solving can indeed be improved. Participants gave high daily ratings to the program's on-the-job usefulness. At the end of the program, most rated its overall impact on their problem-solving skills as very high. These subjective perceptions of participants were supported by two more independent (objective) assessments. Although not quite reaching statistical significance, the differences in holistic gain scores awarded by the two expert raters for both problem-solving processes and products unequivocally favored the experimental group's written responses to case problems.

The most rigorous assessment of problem solving used in the study was a detailed content analysis by the researchers of these same case problems. Gain scores computed for the process as a whole, number of components used, and number of subskills used all favored the experimental group. Greatest gains from the program were made in relation to problem interpretation, goal setting and anticipating constraints. Little impact from the program was evident with respect to the values and affect components. Although this is not surprising, since they did not receive systematic instructional attention, some additional exploration of this lack of impact is important.

Experiences with subsequent refinements to the experimental program provide us with optimism about having greater impact on the values component than was evident in this study. From such experiences, we have come to believe that it is possible to help administrators clarify their values, become more sensitive to the values of problem context and develop more defensible justifications for their value positions. It also seems possible to assist administrators in finding more productive ways to solve problems which entail serious value conflicts or ethical dilemmas. The work of Strike, Haller, and Soltis (1988) has been especially useful for these purposes. As in instruction about other components of problem solving, case problems provide a central focus of attention for participants. Such problems are especially useful when they turn on major value alternatives (e.g., representative democracy vs. professionalism). The instructor needs to play an especially active coaching role, in our experience, as participants struggle to identify these alternatives, articulate the basic arguments justifying these alternatives, and examine the facts of the case problem in light of such arguments.[2]

On the surface, the experimental program did not appear to have much impact on the solution processes component of problem solving either. A more detailed analysis of the evidence provided an acceptable explanation for this apparent deficiency in the program. Because participants in the experimental group devoted much more cognitive energy to other components of problem solving, than did those in the control group, participants had less need for the sub-skills associated with the solution process component. Experts in other fields, evidence suggests, devote considerable effort at the beginning of a problem-solving episode attempting to qualitatively understand the problem (Glaser and Chi, 1988); this is in contrast to novices who plunge into the solution process immediately. Such qualitative understanding is especially useful for ill-structured problems. It consists of building mental representations of the variables in the situation and their relationships leading to problem interpretation. Experts, Glaser and Chi (1988) also note, add constraints to their interpretation of the problem. Our data suggest, as well, that in the field of school administration, experts clarify goals and values, and these processes together greatly simplify the demands placed on solution processes.

The study lends support, in sum, to the claims made about the teachability of problem solving that have emerged from research in many domains (Nickerson, 1988–1989).

Do Better General Problem-Solving Processes Help?

On the face of it, this question appears to have been answered already. Administrators, having acquired many of the processes taught through the experimental program, seemed better able to solve swampy administrative problems than they could before the program. The program, however, provided more than general processes, as they are usually understood. This is evident in our conception of useful, strategic knowledge as the goal of the program and the resulting opportunities created for participants to explicitly share, with one another, the typically tacit, "ordinary knowledge" (Lindblom and Cohen, 1979) so crucial in everyday problem solving. In addition, although never a sustained focus of the program, a great deal of domain- or problem-specific knowledge was available to participants through the treatment of important types of case problems (e.g., teacher evaluation, school improvement, and labor relations problems). Often this involved someone with special, problem-relevant knowledge sharing that knowledge with participants in the context of modeling the solution to a case problem. Whereas the problems used for pre test and post test purposes were obviously different than the case problems used for instruction, some transfer of domain-specific knowledge cannot be ruled out. Furthermore, domain-specific knowledge acquired in this problem-based, situated fashion was likely to be organized in a more useful way and therefore more accessible for application to other relevant problems. Chi, Glaser, and Rees (1982) have pointed to differences in knowledge organization as an important explanation for differences in the problem solving of novices and experts.

What Instructional Strategies?

The study did not compare different approaches to problem-solving instruction. Rather, it assessed the impact of one theoretically promising approach in comparison with the non-instructional (or on-the-job) experiences of a control group. Evidence from the study supports two claims, both modest but important. First, the general approach to teaching problem solving, resembling to a significant degree what has been termed "problem-based" instruction (Bridges, 1992; Bransford et al., 1989; Boud, 1985), seems promising. Our data were not sufficiently detailed to confidently pinpoint the relative power of specific elements within this general approach to instruction. There is tentative support, however, for the special value of using authentic problems, small group, collaborative work on such problems, modeling effective processes, feedback to students, and a framework of components and subskills to cue the use of processes and to serve as a scaffold for problem solving. Given the theoretical elaboration for problem-based instruction provided early in this chapter, the power of these elements seems likely to depend on their being embedded within the broader context provided by many of the other less obviously powerful components that formed the whole problem-based approach to instruction used in the experimental program. The results extend the conditions for effectively teaching problem-solving strategies summarized by Nickerson (1988–1989, p. 18).

A second claim supported by the study is that on-the-job experience is a slow and unreliable way to improve one's problem-solving expertise, as compared with a well-designed program. This claim departs from the conventional view of administrators who usually rank on-the-job experience as the most helpful contribution to their expertise (Leithwood, Steinbach, and Begley, 1992). We think there are two related reasons for the conventional view: little or no personal experience with instructional programs which have improved their everyday problem solving; and, more specifically, little access through instructional programs to the enormously valuable and extensive "ordinary knowledge" of expert administrators that is required to replicate their successful everyday problem solving.

Implications for Research

To our knowledge, this was the first study to empirically address the three questions discussed above, in the context of the problem solving of educational administrators. As in the case of virtually any single study, limitations in the design of the study permit only cautious confidence to be placed in the answers it has provided. These limitations include, for example, small sample sizes, lack of an alternative program of instruction for comparative purposes, only limited and unsystematic introduction of domain-specific knowledge, instructional time extending over only a four-day period, little formal indication of how to address values, and the use of key measures of problem solving which have not been validated through previous research. We believe the three questions explored in this study remain the most important to be addressed in subsequent research concerned with improving administrators' problem-solving processes. Indeed, based on an historical review, Glaser and Chi (1988) recommend these as among the most critical questions for the next stage of problem-solving research in other domains, as well. Such research should also test for more distant forms of transfer than was the case in this study: transfer of problem-solving capacities to on-the-job problem situations and the use of problem-solving capacities after an extended period of time—perhaps a year after completing the program.

Finally, it would be helpful to know, through subsequent research, whether the extent of improvement in administrative problem-solving capacities was influenced by either levels of experience or levels of expertise upon entry to a program. Tentative evidence from this study, for example, suggested that less-experienced administrators (vice principals) tended to learn more than did their more experienced colleagues (usually principals). If this is the case, what are the explanations? Is there a ceiling effect on the acquisition of problem-solving capacity? Do less-experienced administrators have greater cognitive flexibility or greater motivation to learn than their more-experienced colleagues? Does domain-specific knowledge which accumulates with experience have a "downside," particularly in a practice where such knowledge is sometimes of questionable value? Or, as Ross (personal communication, 1990) suggested to us, was the zone of proximal development created during our program more appropriate for the needs of novices than it was for experienced administrators?

Regardless of these uncertainties, the prospects for improving the problem-solving expertise of school administrators appear to be promising.

Chapter 13

Concluding Thoughts

Like the development of expertise itself, learning about expertise is a long-term proposition. The chapters in the text reflect, we estimate, roughly ten person-years of effort and obviously there is a great deal remaining to be learned. At least by this point we understand much better the roots of Jack's practice—the principal we claimed in Chapter 1 to be the Wayne Gretsky of school administrators, but for reasons that puzzled us greatly in 1985.

Summary

We now know that expert educational administrators, like Jack, think about their professional problems in ways that are substantially different from their nonexpert colleagues. They find and define problems to spend their time on that have greater potential to be productive for their organizations. Furthermore, the goals they work toward in their problem solving are more inclusive, likely reflecting a broader interpretation of their problems to begin with, and are embedded in a vision for the school or school district in its community and larger social contexts. To the extent that experts' goals for problem solving are derived from such a larger, compelling sense of purpose, they stand an increased chance, in Shamir's terms (1991), of "recruiting the self-concepts" of their colleagues in support of organizational purposes. This is a central function of transformational leaders.

Expert educational administrators almost always aim to learn something personally from their problem-solving activities. This goal is consistent with a fluid or dynamic rather than a crystallized or static view of expertise—expertise as working at the edge of one's competence (Bereiter and Scardamalia, 1993). We know from the studies in this text that expert administrators are willing to risk defining quite fundamental problems in their schools, although they take few risks in the processes they use to solve them.

Values are pervasive in the problem solving of educational administrators, explicitly so in the case of experts; this was among the most significant results of the research, in terms of our own learning. A clear sense of their own personal and professional values provides expert administrators with the means to productively engage in solving problems about which they may have relatively little domain-specific knowledge. Or, it may be that a defining characteristic of a significant portion of educational administrators' ill-structured problems is that they are centrally about value choices and tradeoffs. In such cases, a clear understanding of one's own values, the values of others with a stake in the problem, and how to resolve value conflicts productively is the domain-specific knowledge required for expert problem solving. Such a position is generally consistent with the arguments offered by the field's philosophers (e.g., Hodgkinson, 1978; Greenfield, 1993), but it lends a more pragmatic cast to their arguments, as does the work of Strike, Haller, and Soltis (1988). This, we think, is crucial if administrators are to become engaged in seriously thinking about the role of values in their own practices.

Expert administrators also view constraints to problem solving differently than do nonexperts. They anticipate constraints more successfully and so, it would seem, are less frequently confronted with "crises"; they also view constraints as subproblems rather than as insurmountable hurdles. Since problem-solving energies are significantly consumed in overcoming constraints, the selection of good constraints to work on seems important to an explanation of expertise (Bereiter and Scardamalia, 1993).

Expert administrators are relatively planful and information sensitive in the solution processes which they generate. They also seem capable of fairly extended "if-then" thinking, thinking which allows them to plan forward, imagining possible contingencies should their initial solutions not work. Such thinking, however, quickly presses the limits of a single person's cognitive processing abilities and expert administrators are inclined to share most aspects of nonroutine problem solving with their colleagues, apparently in recognition of these limits. Unlike nonexperts, experts believe several heads are better than one and act accordingly. In group problem-solving contexts, this means investing one's energies heavily into processes for getting at the best ideas of the group and keeping one's own preferences from interfering.

As a general description, the thinking of expert administrators is flexible and reasonably error-free. This flexibility is probably accounted for, in part, by the normally calm affective states of experts in the face of ill-structured problems. And such mood states, themselves, may be a function of the sense of self-efficacy that expert administrators have acquired from successful experiences and by learning from their failures.

Does such expert thinking reflect itself in effective leadership practice? Yes. We saw this to be the case when effective practice was defined as "instructional leadership," as in Chapter 10, as well as when it was defined as "transformational leadership," as in Chapter 11. Can administrative expertise be taught? Evidence from the study reported in Chapter 12 suggests that it can. Would it be worthwhile to offer such instruction? If the evidence in Chapter 2 is to be believed, then school administrators face a high proportion of ill-structured problems, which experience alone provides little preparation for solving. Specific instruction seems like a good idea. Does organizational context shape the nature of administrators' problem solving? Apparently so, organizational size being the element of context about which our studies provide most evidence.

Three Big Problems for Subsequent Research

Empirical studies of expertise among educational administrators are relatively rare. In addition to those included in this text, at the time of this writing such studies were limited to chapters in an edited, soon-to-be published book (Hallinger, Leithwood, and Murphy, 1993), a special issue of the *Educational Administration Quarterly* (to be published in the summer of 1993), and no more than a handful of other sources. Indeed, among the sources cited above, a very small proportion of the studies focused directly on the nature of expertise itself.

Not surprisingly, then, we believe that the first item on the research agenda for the immediate future ought to be considerably more empirical work about the nature of educational administration expertise. The field's current interest in cognitive perspectives is being translated much more quickly into implications for instruction than it is into solid research about the nature of expertise itself. We think this puts the cart before the horse, and, whereas it may lead to more powerful forms of instruction, the question remains, instruction for what? Indeed, the tendency to become preoccupied with cognitive perspectives exclusively from an instructional point of view seems to implicitly discount the value of conceptualizing effective administration as the exercise of expertise. This is a compelling conceptualization and one that goes some distance toward addressing the limitations of other more behavior-based ways of describing effective leadership, as we have argued throughout the text.

As a closely related but distinct second item on our agenda for research, we include more attention to the nature of problems encountered by educational administrators. These problems form the bridge between concerns for the nature of expertise on the one hand and the development of effective forms of instruction using cognitive perspectives on the other. This is the case since such problems define the domain-specific knowledge upon which experts depend. In Chapter 2, we made a first pass at plotting the problematic territory trod by school administrators. This effort is a precursor to what we see as needed to meet this second research agenda: a fairly substantial body of evidence that indicates the nature of the ill-structured problems encountered by administrators in many different contexts.

Third, there is within this prior item on the research agenda the roots of a radical transformation of the content of the curriculum for preparing educational administrators. Whether or not the current content of such preparation in any way has the potential for increasing expertise is open to serious question. For example, does the content of organizational theory taught in conventional graduate courses or the content of courses on teacher supervision provide even the propositional knowledge to serve as a guide, when proceduralized, for informing expert practice? Our third problem for research, therefore, is to investigate the nature of domain-specific knowledge useful to administrators in solving their problems. Identification of such knowledge would inform the kinds of curriculum development work that might precede reformed educational administration education programs.

Current interests in cognitive perspectives, for the purposes of reforming instructional practice, tend to give short shrift to the value of propositional knowledge. This is an error. There is a great deal of propositional knowledge, we expect, underlying and informing expert problem solving in educational administration. True, much needs to be done to ensure that such knowledge, once acquired by administrators, does not remain inert but rather becomes proceduralized and conditionalized through use in authentic settings. Nonetheless, the importance of the knowledge itself should not be underestimated.

The three big problems we have recommended for future research offer a significant challenge. They demand, from those doing research in educational administration, much of the expertise of those in the cognitive sciences, along with knowledge and skills more conventionally associated with the field of educational administration. Such a cross-pollination of demands is the stuff of which progress is made, requiring us to work, in Bereiter and Scardamalia's (1993) terms, on the edge of our competence—a defining attribute of expertise.

NOTES

Chapter 3 Principals' Individual Problem-Solving Processes

1. Schön appears to view information-processing theory as a tool of technical rationality; see, for example, *Educating the Reflective Practitioner* (1987, p. 314). Although this may be the case with extreme forms of such theory, as in models of artificial intelligence, we have found nonmathematical, generic forms of information-processing theory (see Schuell, 1986, for example) to be highly compatible with Schön's description of the reflective process. Indeed, explicit use of such theory would increase the clarity and elegance of Schön's description of the reflective process. Indeed, explicit use of such theory would increase the clarity and elegance of Schön's explanation of the reflective process as found, for example, in *The Reflective Practitioner* (1983, chaps. 2, 3).

2. For discussion of the aspirations of the New Movement, see Halpin (1966) and Campbell and Lipham (1960).

3. Prior to initiating direct research on problem solving, our own explorations of school administration combined "technical action" and "decision-making" perspectives. The most visible product of this work was a multidimensional description of growth in principal effectiveness, *The Principal Profile* (Leithwood and Montgomery, 1986).

4. It is clear from Simon's work on problem solving over the past twenty years that he held a very broad conception of "decision making"; see, for example, Newell and Simon (1972), Simon (1973, 1975).

5. This article is concerned with expertise generally, as distinct from only problem-solving expertise.

6. A reviewer of this article raised a concern about a potential tautology in defining effectiveness using *The Principal Profile* because one dimension of the profile concerns principals' decision making (a form of problem solving). Our response to this problem is this; (a) The ways in which principals make decisions is an explicit dimension of most theories of leadership or descriptions of effective practice. In those few instances in which decision making is not explicitly defined, it is less explicitly embedded in those dimensions that are used to describe practice. The nature of a principal's decision making is typically considered important by practitioners, as well. For this reason, it is hard to image any formal or professional basis for selecting a sample of expert principals that is not, in some way, colored by an interest in decision making. (b) Decision making, as we claim in this chapter, is one form of problem solving and not one of central interest in our study. Our study focused on types of problems that required substantial amounts of interpretation, problem formulation, and solution generation. This is, of course, a distinction in emphasis rather than in kind, because one could conceptually decompose solution-generation into a long series of minute, discrete choices. To do so, however, would appear to do about as much injustice to the nature of the problem solving as Skinnerian psychology does to meaningful, conceptual learning. (c) *The Principal Profile* is multidimensional (goals, factors, strategies, and decision making). Judgments of a principal's overall effectiveness based on the profile weight each dimension equally. The "expert" principals designated in our study were rated as very effective in all four dimensions. Had the decision-making dimension not been considered, they would still have been rated as very effective. Indeed, if one dimension is more central to the profile than any other, it is the goals dimension: the labels on the four patterns of practice described in the profile reflect principals' goals.

7. The extended operational definitions used as the basis for coding data are available from the authors.

Chapter 6. Processes Used by Expert Superintendents to Solve Problems in Groups

1. Elements of the definition can be found in the work of Hodgkinson (1978), Rokeach (1975), Kluckhon (1951), and Williams (1968).

Chapter 12. Improving the Problem-Solving Expertise of School Administrators

1. One of those "experts" was a former secondary school principal and senior board/district administrator. This person had participated in previous research on administrator effectiveness, had designed professional development programs for school administrators, and had been involved for many years in the selection and evaluation of school administrators. He was widely respected within his district and through the Provinces for his administrative insights and for his personal problem-solving skills.

The second expert was an elementary school administrator regarded by senior administrators in her own district to be quite effective. She had also participated in the past in research on administrator effectiveness.

2. We invited Kenneth Strike to provide such coaching to members of the control group during the program subsequent to this study. Based on his model, we have subsequently done similar coaching in yet another program.

REFERENCES

Chapter 1. Introduction

Anderson, J. R. 1983. *The architecture of cognition*. Cambridge, MA: Harvard University Press.

Argyris, C. 1982. *Reasoning, learning and action*. San Francisco: Jossey-Bass.

Baird, L. L. 1983, March. *Review of problem solving skills* (Research report). Princeton, NJ: Educational Testing Service.

Bereiter, C., and M. Scardamalia. 1982. From conversation to composition: The role of instruction in a developmental process. In R. Glaser (ed.), *Advances in instructional psychology* (vol. 2) (pp.1–64). Hillsdale, NJ: Lawrence Erlbaum.

Berger, P. L., and T. Luckmann. 1966. *The social construction of reality*. Garden City, NJ: Doubleday.

Berliner, D. 1988. *The development of expertise in pedagogy*. Washington, D.C.: American Association of Colleges for Teacher Education.

Blumberg, A., and W. Greenfield. 1980. *The effective principal: Perspectives on school leadership*. Boston: Allyn and Bacon.

321

Boud, D. ed. 1985. *Problem-based learning in education for the professions.* Sydney: Herdsa.

Bridges, E. 1992. *Problem based learning for administrators.* Eugene, Oregon: ERIC Clearinghouse on Educational Management.

Brown, J. S., A. Collins, and P. Duguid. 1989. Situated cognition and the culture of learning. *Educational Researcher* 18(1), 32–42.

Burton, R. R., J. S. Brown, and G. Fischer. 1984. Skiing as a model of instruction. In B. Rogoff and J. Lave (eds.), *Everyday cognition: Its development in social context* (pp. 139–150). Cambridge, MA: Harvard University Press.

Chi, M. T. H., R. Glaser, and E. Rees. 1982. Expertise in problem solving. In R. A. Sternberg (ed.), *Advances in the psychology of human intelligence* (pp. 7–75). Hillsdale, NJ: Lawrence Erlbaum.

Clark, C., and P. Peterson. 1986. Teachers' thought processes. In M. Wittrock (ed.), *Handbook of Research on Teaching* (pp. 255–296). New York: Macmillan.

Clark, C., and R. Yinger. 1978. *Research on teacher thinking.* East Lansing, MI: University of Michigan (mimeo).

Cowan, D. A. 1990. Developing a classification structure of organizational problems: An empirical investigation. *Academy of Management Journal* 33(2), 366–390.

Cowan, D. A. 1991. The effect of decision-making styles and contextual experience on executives' descriptions of organizational problem formulation. *Journal of Management Studies* 28(5), 465–483.

Doyle, W. 1983. Academic work. *Review of Educational Research* 53(2), 159–199.

Duke, D. 1992. The rhetoric and the reality of reform in educational administration, *Phi Delta Kappan,* June, 764–770.

Dwyer, D., G. Lee, B. Rowan, and S. Bossert. 1983. *Five principals in action: Perspectives on instructional leadership.* San Francisco: Far West Laboratory for Educational Research and Development.

Ericsson, K. A. & H. A. Simon, 1984. *Protocol analysis:* Verbal reports as data. Cambridge, MA: The MIT Press.

Frederiksen, N. 1984. Implications of cognitive theory for instruction in problem solving. *Review of Educational Research* 54(3), 363–407.

Fullan, M., B. Bennett, and B. Rolheiser-Bennett. 1990. Linking classroom and school improvement, *Educational Leadership* 47(8), 13–19.

Gagné, E. D. 1985. *The cognitive psychology of school learning*. Boston: Little, Brown and Co.

Hallinger, P. 1992. School leadership development: An introduction, *Education and Urban Society* 24(3), 300–316.

Hallinger, P., L. Bickman, and K. Davis. In press. What makes a difference? School context, principal leadership and student achievement. *School Effectiveness and School Improvement*.

Hambrick, D., and G. Brandon. 1988. Executive values. In D. Hambrick (ed.), *The executive effect: Concepts and methods for studying top executives* (pp. 3–34). London: JAI Press.

Hayes, J. 1981. *The complete problem solver*. Philadelphia: The Franklin Institute Press.

Heck, R., T. Larsen, and G. Marcoulides. 1990, April. *Principal leadership and school achievement: Validation of a causal model*. Paper presented at the annual meeting of the American Educational Research Association, Boston.

Hogarth, R. 1980. *Judgement and choice: The psychology of decision*. Chichester: Wiley.

Johnson, G. 1992. *In the palaces of memory*. New York: Vintage Books.

Kennedy, M. 1987. Inexact sciences: Professional education and the development of expertise. In E. Rothkopf (ed.), *Review of research in education, 14*. Washington, D.C.: American Educational Research Association.

Lampert, M., and C. Clark. 1990. Expert knowledge and expert thinking in teaching: A response to Floden and Klinzing. *Educational Researcher*. 19(5), 21–23.

Leinhardt, G. 1992. What research on learning tells us about teaching. *Educational Researcher,* 49(7), 20–25.

Leithwood, K., and D. Montgomery. 1986. *Improving principal effectiveness: The principal profile*. Toronto: OISE Press.

Morris, V., R. Crowson, C. Porter-Gehrie, and E. Hurwitz. 1984. *Principals in action: The reality of managing schools*. Columbus: Charles E. Merrill.

Mortimore, P., P. Sammons, L. Stoll, D. Lewis, and R. Ecob, 1988. *School matters: The junior years*. Somerset, England: Open Books.

Murphy, J. 1991. *Restructuring schools: Capturing and assessing the phenomena*. New York: Teachers College Press.

Newell, A., and H. A. Simon. 1972. *Human problem solving*. Englewood Cliffs, NJ: Prentice-Hall.

Newell, A., P. Rosenbloom, and J. Laird. 1990. Symbolic architectures for cognition. In M. Posner (ed.), *Foundations of cognitive science* (pp. 133–160). Cambridge, MA: The MIT Press.

Nisbett, R., and T. D. Wilson. 1977. Telling more than we can know: Verbal reports on mental processes. *Psychological Review* 84, 231–259.

Perkins, D. N., and G. Salomon. 1988. Teaching for transfer. *Educational Leadership* 46(1), 22–32.

Posner, M. I. 1988. Introduction: What is it to be an expert? In. M. T. H. Chi, R. Glaser, and M. J. Farr (eds.), *The nature of expertise* (pp. xxix–xxxvi). Hillsdale, NJ: Lawrence Erlbaum.

Rogoff, B. 1984. Introduction: Thinking and learning in context. In B. Rogoff and J. Lave (eds.), *Everyday cognition: Its development in social context* (pp. 1–8). Cambridge, Mass.: Harvard University Press.

Schoenfeld, A. H. 1985. *Mathematical problem solving*. Orlando, FL: Academic Press.

Schön, D. 1983. *The reflective practitioner*. San Francisco: Jossey-Bass.

Schwenk, A. 1988. The cognitive perspective on strategic decision-making, *Journal of Management Studies* 25(1), 41–56.

Shulman, L. 1986. Paradigms and research programs in the study of teaching: A contemporary perspective. In M. Wittrock (ed.), *Handbook of Research on Teaching* (pp. 3–36). New York: Macmillan.

Simon, H., and C. Kaplan, 1990. Foundations of cognitive science. In M. Posner (ed.), *Foundations of cognitive science* (pp. 1–47). Cambridge, MA: The MIT Press.

Sternberg, R. J., and O. R. Caruso. 1985. Practical modes of knowing. In E. Eisner (ed.), *Learning and teaching the ways of knowing* (pp. 133–158). Chicago: University of Chicago Press.

Toulmin, S. 1972. *Human understanding: The collective use and evolution of concepts*. Princeton, NJ: Princeton University Press.

VanLehn, K. 1990. Problem solving and cognitive skill acquisition. In M. Posner (ed.), *Foundations of cognitive science* (pp. 527–579). Cambridge, MA: The MIT Press.

Vygotsky, L. S. 1978. *Mind in society*. Cambridge, MA: Harvard University Press.

Wagner, R., and R. Sternberg. 1986. Tacit knowledge and intelligence in the everyday world. In R. Sternberg and R. Wagner (eds.), *Practical intelligence: Nature and origins of competence in the everyday world* (pp. 51–83). Cambridge, MA: Cambridge University Press.

Webster's seventh new collegiate dictionary. (1971). Springfield, MA: Merriam-Webster.

Yukl, G. 1989. *Leadership in organizations* (2d ed.). Englewood Cliffs, NJ: Prentice-Hall.

Chapter 2. The School Administrators' World from a Problem-Solving Perspective

Boyd, W. L., and R. L. Crowson. 1981. The changing conception and practice of public school administration. In D. C. BeMiner (ed.), *Review of research in education: 9*. Washington: American Educational Research Association.

Crowson, R. L., and V. C. Morris. 1985. Administrative control in large-city school systems: An investigation in Chicago. *Educational Administration Quarterly*. 4(21), 51–70.

Duke, D. L. 1988. Why principals consider quitting. *Phi Delta Kappan,* December, 308–312.

Franklin, H., J. Nickens, and S. Appleby. 1981. What activities keep principals the busiest? *NASSP Bulletin.*

Gerston, R., D. Carnine, and S. Green. 1982. The principal as instructional leader: A second look. *Educational Leadership* 40, 47–50.

Gousha. R. P. 1986. *The Indiana school principalship: The role of the Indiana principal as defined by the principal*. Bloomington, Indiana: Indiana University.

Greeno, J. G. 1976. Indefinite goals in well-structured problems. *Psychological Review* 83(6), 479–491.

Johnson, J. M. 1983. *The myths and realities of principals' classroom supervisor*. Saskatoon: University of Saskatchewan, mimeo.

Kotkamp, R. B., and A. L. Travlos. 1986. Selected job stressors, emotional exhaustion, job satisfaction and thrust behavior of the high school principal. *Alberta Journal of Educational Research* 32(3), 234–248.

Leithwood, K. 1986. *The role of the secondary school principal in policy implementation and school improvement*. Toronto: Queen's Printer for Ontario.

Leithwood, K., and D. J. Montgomery. 1984. Obstacles preventing principals from becoming more effective. *Education and Urban Society* 17(1), 73–88.

Martin, W. J., and D. J. Willower. 1981. The managerial behavior of high school principals. *Educational Administration Quarterly* 17(1), 69–90.

Morris, V. C., R. L. Crowson, C. Porter-Gehrie, and E. Hurwitz, Jr. 1984. *Principals in action: The reality of managing schools.* Columbus: Charles E. Merrill.

Murphy, J. 1991. *Restructuring schools: Capturing and assessing the phenomena.* New York: Teachers College Press.

Schön, D. 1983. *The reflective practitioner: How professionals think in action.* New York: Basic Books.

Simon, H. A. 1973. The structure of ill-structured problems. *Artificial Intelligence,* 4(2), 181–201.

Willower, D. J., and J. T. Kmetz. 1982. *The managerial behavior of elementary school principals.* Paper presented at the annual meeting of the American Educational Research Association, New York.

Wolcott, H. F. 1978. *The man in the principal's office.* New York: Holt, Rinehart and Winston, Inc.

Chapter 3. Principals' Individual Problem-Solving Processes

Baird, L. L. 1983, March. *Review of problem-solving skills* (Research Report). Princeton, NJ: Educational Testing Service.

Bereiter, C., and M. Scardamalia. 1986. Educational relevance of the study of expertise. *Interchange* 17, 10–19.

Berliner, D. C. 1986. In pursuit of the expert pedagogue. *Educational Researcher* 15(7), 5–13.

Blumberg, A., and W. Greenfield. 1980. *The effective principal: Perspectives on school leadership.* Boston: Allyn & Bacon.

Campbell, R. F., and J. M. Lipham, eds. 1960. *Administrative theory as a guide to action.* Chicago: Midwest Centre, University of Chicago.

Chi, M. T. H., P. J. Feltovich, and R. Glaser. 1981. Categorization and representation of physics problems by experts and novices. *Cognitive Science* 5, 121–152.

Dwyer, D. C., G. V. Lee, B. G. Barnett, N. N. Filby, and B. Rowan. 1984. *Grace Lancaster and Emerson Junior High School: Instructional leadership in an urban setting.* San Francisco: Far West Laboratory for Educational Research and Development.

Frederiksen, N. 1984. Implications of cognitive theory for instruction in problem solving. *Review of Educational Research* 54(3), 363–407.

Glaser, B. G., and A. L. Strauss. 1967. *The discovery of grounded theory.* Chicago: Aldine, Atherton.

Glaser, R. 1984. Education and thinking: The role of knowledge. *American Psychologist* 39, 93–104.

Greenfield, T. B. 1986. The decline and fall of science in educational administration. *Interchange* 17, 57–80.

Greeno, J. G. 1976. Indefinite goals in well-structured problems. *Psychological Review* 83, 479–491.

Hall, G., W. L. Rutherford, S. M. Hord, and L. L. Huling. 1984. Effects of three principal styles on school improvement. *Educational Leadership* 41(5), 22–31.

Halpin, A. W., ed. 1966. *Theory and research in administration.* New York: Macmillan.

Hayes-Roth, B., and F. Hayes-Roth. 1979. A cognitive model of planning. *Cognitive Science* 3, 275–310.

Leithwood, K., and D. Montgomery. 1982a. The role of the elementary school principal in program improvement. *Review of Educational Research* 52, 309–339.

Leithwood, K., and D. Montgomery. 1982b. The role of the principal in school improvement. In G. R. Austin and H. Garber (eds.), *Research on exemplary schools* (pp. 155–177). New York: Academic Press.

Leithwood, K., and D. Montgomery. 1984. Obstacles preventing principals from becoming more effective. *Education & Urban Society* 17(1), 73–88.

Leithwood, K., and D. Montgomery. 1986. *Improving principal effectiveness: The principal profile.* Toronto: OISE Press.

Leithwood, K., and M. Stager. 1986, April. *Differences in problem-solving processes used by moderately and highly effective principals.* Paper presented at the annual meeting of the American Educational Research Association, San Franciso.

Leithwood, K., and M. Stager. 1989. Expertise in principals' problem solving. *Educational Administration Quarterly* 25(2), 126–161.

Martin, W. J., and D. J. Willower. 1981. The managerial behavior of high school principals. *Educational Administration Quarterly* 17(1), 69–90.

Miles, M. B., and A. M. Huberman. 1984. *Qualitative data analysis: A sourcebook of new methods.* Beverly Hills: Sage.

Newell, A., and H. A. Simon. 1972. *Human problem solving.* Englewood Cliffs, NJ: Prentice-Hall.

Norris, S. P. 1985. Synthesis of research on critical thinking. *Educational Leadership* 42(8), 40–46.

Schön, D. A. 1983. *The reflective practitioner: How professionals think in action.* New York: Basic Books.

Schön, D. A. 1987. *Educating the reflective practitioner.* San Francisco: Jossey-Bass.

Scriven, M. 1980. Prescriptive and descriptive approaches to problem solving. In D. T. Tuma and F. Reif (eds.), *Problem solving and education: Issues in teaching and research* (pp. 127–139). Hillsdale, NJ: Lawrence Erlbaum.

Shuell, T. J. 1986. Cognitive conceptions of learning. *Review of Educational Research* 56, 411–436.

Simon, H. 1957. *Administrative behavior: A study of decision-making process in administrative organization* (2d ed.). New York: Free Press.

Simon, H. 1973. The structure of ill-structured problems. *Artificial Intelligence* 4, 181–201.

Simon, H. 1975. The functional equivalence of problem solving skills. *Cognitive Psychology* 7, 268–288.

Trider, D., and K. Leithwood. 1988. Exploring the influences on principals' behavior. *Curriculum Inquiry* 18(3), 289–312.

Voss, J. F., T. R. Greene, T. A. Post, and B. C. Penner. 1983. Problem-solving skill in the social sciences. In G. H. Bower (ed.), *The psychology of learning and motivation* (pp. 165–213). New York: Academic Press.

Chapter 4. Superintendents' Individual Problem-Solving Processes

Begley, P. 1987, April. *The influence of values on principals' problem-solving processes.* Paper presented at the annual meeting of the American Educational Research Association, New Orleans, April.

Begley, P., and K. Leithwood. 1989. *The nature and influence of values on principals' problem solving.* Toronto: OISE, mimeo.

Bridges, E. M. 1982. Research on the school administrator: The state of art, 1967–1980. *Educational Administration Quarterly* 18, 12–33.

Campbell, G. 1988. *The relationship between principals' values and their decision making processes.* Unpublished doctoral dissertation, The Ontario Institute for Studies in Education, Toronto.

Clark, C. M., and P. L. Peterson. 1986. Teacher thought processes. In M. C. Wittrock (ed.), *Handbook of research on teaching* (3d ed.) (pp. 255–296). New York: Macmillan.

Coleman, P., and L. LaRocque. 1987. *Reaching out: Instructional leadership in school districts.* Vancouver, Simon Fraser University, mimeo.

Crowson, R. L. 1987. The local school district superintendency: A puzzling administrative role. *Educational Administration Quarterly* 23(3), 49–69.

Ericsson, K. A., and H. A. Simon. 1984. *Protocol analyses: Verbal reports as data.* Cambridge, MA: MIT Press.

Hambrick, D. C., and G. L. Brandon. 1988. Executive values. In D. Hambrick (ed.), *The executive effect: Concepts and methods for studying top managers* (pp. 3–34). London: JAI Press.

Hayes, J. R. 1981. *The complete problem solver.* Philadelphia: The Franklin Institute Press.

Hemphill, J. K. 1958. Administration as problem solving. In A. W. Halpin (ed.), *Administrative theory in education.* New York: Macmillan.

Isenberg, D. J. 1987. Inside the mind of the senior manager. In D. N. Perkins, J. Lochhead, and J. C. Bishop (eds.), *Thinking.* Hillsdale, NJ: Lawrence Erlbaum.

Klemp, G. O., and D. C. McClelland. 1986. What characterizes as intelligent functioning among senior managers? In R. J. Sternberg and R. K. Wagner (eds.), *Practical intelligence* (pp. 31–50). Cambridge: Cambridge University Press.

Leithwood, K. 1988. *How chief school officers classify and manage their problems.* Toronto: OISE, mimeo.

Leithwood, K., P. Begley, and B. Cousins. 1990. The nature, causes, and consequences of principals' practices: An agenda for future research. *Journal of Educational Administration* 28(4), 5–31.

Leithwood, K., and D. Montgomery. 1986. *Improving principal effectiveness: The principal profile.* Toronto: OISE Press.

Leithwood, K., and M. Stager. 1986, April. *Differences in problem solving processes used by moderately and highly effective principals.* Paper presented at the annual meeting of the American Educational Research Association, San Francisco.

Leithwood, K., and M. Stager. 1989. Expertise in principals' problem solving. *Educational Administration Quarterly* 25(2), 126–161.

Louis, K. 1987. *The role of school districts in school innovations.* Paper prepared for conference on Organizational Policy for School Improvement. The Ontario Institute for Studies in Education, Toronto.

March, J. G. 1974. Analytic skills and the university training of educational administrators. *Journal of Educational Administration* 12(1), 17–43.

Peterson, K. D., J. Murphy, and P. Halliday. 1987. Superintendents' perceptions of the control and coordination of the technical care in effective school districts. *Educational Administration Quarterly* 23(1), 79–95.

Rosenholtz, S. 1989. *Teachers' workplace*. New York: Longman.

Schwenk, C. R. 1988. The cognitive perspective on strategic decision-making. *Journal of Management Studies* 25(1), 41–56.

Shulman, L. S., and N. B. Carey. 1984. Psychology and the limitations of individual rationality: Implication for the study of reasoning and civility. *Review of Educational Research* 54(4), 501–524.

Simon, H. 1957. *Administrative behavior: A study of decision-making process in administrative organization*(2d ed.). New York: The Free Press.

Stevens, W. 1987. *The role of vision in the life of elementary school principals*. Unpublished doctoral dissertation. University of Southern California, Los Angeles.

Chapter 5. Processes Used by Expert and Typical Principals to Solve Problems in Groups

Alexander, P. A., and J. E. Judy. 1989. The interaction of domain-specific and strategic knowledge in academic performance. *Review of Educational Research,* 58(4), 375–404.

Bandura, A. 1977. *Social learning theory*. Englewood Cliffs, NJ: Prentice Hall.

Baron, J. 1985. *Rationality and intelligence*. Cambridge: Cambridge University Press.

Begley, P. 1987, April. *The influence of values on principals' problem-solving processes*. Paper presented at the Annual Meeting of the American Educational Research Association, New Orleans.

Bennis, W., and B. Nanus. 1985. *Leaders: The strategies for taking charge*. New York: Harper and Row.

Berger, P. L., and T. Luckmann. 1967. *The social construction of reality*. Garden City, NJ: Doubleday.

Bolin, F. S. 1989. Empowering leadership. Teachers College Record, 91(1), 81–96.

Campbell, G. 1988. *The relationship between principals' values and their decision making processes.* Unpublished doctoral dissertation, The Ontario Institute for Studies in Education, Toronto.

Damon, W., and S. E. Phelps. 1989. Critical distinctions among three approaches to peer education. *International Journal of Educational Research,* 13(1), 9–18.

Ettling, J., and A. G. Jago. 1988. Participation under conditions of conflict: More on the validity of the Vroom-Yetton model. *Journal of Management Studies* 25(10), 73–84.

Fullan, M., and F. M. Connelly. 1987. *Teacher education in Ontario.* Toronto: Ministry of Colleges and Universities, Ontario.

Leithwood, K. 1988. *How chief school officers classify and manage their problems.* Unpublished manuscript, The Ontario Institute for Studies in Education, Toronto.

Leithwood, K. 1990. The principal's role in teacher development. In B. Joyce (ed.), *Changing school culture through staff development* (pp. 71–90). ASCO Yearbook.

Leithwood, K., B. Cousins, and P. Begley. 1990. The nature, causes, and consequences of principals' practices, *Journal of Educational Administration* 28(4), 5–31.

Leithwood, K., B. Cousins, and M. Smith. 1989, June. *A description of the principal's world from a problem-solving perspective.* Paper presented at the Annual Meeting of the Canadian Association for the Study of Educational Administration, Quebec City.

Leithwood, K., and D. Montgomery. 1986. *Improving principal effectiveness: The principal profile.* Toronto: OISE Press.

Leithwood, K., and M. Stager. 1986, April. *Differences in problem-solving processes used by moderately and highly effective principals.* Paper presented at the annual meeting of the American Educational Research Association, San Francisco.

Leithwood, K., and M. Stager. 1989. Expertise in principals problem solving. *Educational Administration Quarterly* 25(2), 126–161.

Leithwood, K., and R. Steinbach. 1990. Characteristics of effective secondary school principals' problem solving. *Educational Administration and Foundations* 5(1), 24–42.

Leithwood, K., and R. Steinbach. 1991. Components of chief education officers' problem solving. In K. Leithwood and D. Musella (eds.), *Understanding school system administration* (pp. 127–153). Toronto: OISE Press.

Little, J. W. 1988. Assessing the prospects for teacher leadership. In A. Lieberman (ed.), *Building a professional culture in schools*. New York: Teachers College Press.

Maeroff, G. I. 1988. A blueprint for empowering teachers. *Phi Delta Kappan*, March, 472–477.

Rosenholtz, S. J. 1989. *Teachers' workplace*. New York: Longman.

Schoenfeld, A. H. 1989. Ideas in the air: Speculations on small group learning, environmental and cultural influences on cognition, and epistemology. *International Journal of Educational Research,* 13(1), 71–88.

Schwab, J. J. 1983. The practical 4: Something for curriculum professors to do. *Curriculum Inquiry* 13(3), 239–265.

Shulman, L. S. 1984. The practical and the eclectic: A deliberation on teaching and educational research. *Curriculum Inquiry* 14(2), 183–200.

Shulman, L. S., and N. B. Carey. 1984. Psychology and the limitations of individual rationality: Implications for the study of reasoning and civility. *Review of Educational Research* 54(4), 501–524.

Simon, H. 1957. *Administrative behavior: A study of decision-making process in administrative organization* (2d ed.). New York: Free Press.

Stager, M., and K. A. Leithwood. (1989). Cognitive flexibility and inflexibility in principals' problem solving. *Alberta Journal of Educational Research* 35(3), 217–236.

Vygotsky, L. S. 1978. *Mind in society*. Cambridge: Harvard University Press.

Webb, N. W. 1989. Peer interaction and learning in small groups. *International Journal of Educational Research* 13(1), 21–40.

Chapter 6. Processes Used by Expert Superintendents to Solve Problems in Groups

Anderson, J. R. 1983. *The architecture of cognition*. Cambridge, MA: Harvard University Press.

Argyris, C. 1982. *Reasoning, Learning and Action*. San Francisco: Jossey-Bass.

Beck, C. 1984. The nature of values and implications for values education. Unpublished manuscript, Toronto, OISE.

Begley, P., and K. Leithwood. 1989. The influence of values on school administrator practices. *Journal of Educational Administration and Foundations* 4(2), 26–39.

Bransford, J. In press. Who ya gonna call? Thoughts about teaching problem solving. In P. Hallinger, K. Leithwood, and J. Murphy (eds.). *Cognitive perspectives on educational leadership*. New York: Teachers College Press.

Brightman, H. J. 1988. Group problem solving: An improved managerial approach. Atlanta: Business Publishing Division, Georgia State University.

Chi, M. T. H., P. J. Feltovich, and R. Glaser. 1981. Categorization and representation of physics problems by experts and novices. *Cognitive Science* 5(2), 121–152.

Cowan, D. A. 1986. Developing a process model of problem recognition. *Academy of Management Review* 11(4), 763–776.

Cowan, D. A. 1988. Executives' knowledge of organizational problem types: Applying a contingency perspective. *Journal of Management* 14(4), 513–527.

Cowan, D. A. 1990. Developing a classification structure of organizational problems: An empirical investigation. *Academy of Management Journal* 33(2), 366–390.

Cowan, D. A. 1991. The effect of decision-making styles and contextual experience on executives' descriptions of organizational problem formulation. *Journal of Management Studies* 28(5), 465–483.

Daniels, W. R. 1990. *Group Power II: A manager's guide to conducting regular meetings*. San Diego, CA: University Associated Inc.

Day, D., and R. Lord. 1992. Expertise and problem categorization: The role of expert processing in organizational sense making. *Journal of Management Studies* 29(1), 35–48.

Gagné, E. D. 1985. *The cognitive psychology of school learning*. Boston: Little, Brown and Co.

Glaser, R., and M. Chi. 1988. Overview. In M. Chi, R. Glaser, and M. Farr (eds.), *The nature of expertise* (pp. xv–xxviii). Hillsdale, NJ: Lawrence Erlbaum.

Greeno, J. G. 1978. A study of problem solving. In R. Glaser (ed.), *Advances in Instructional Psychology*. Hillsdale, NJ: Lawrence Erlbaum.

Greeno, J. G. 1980. Trends in the theory of knowledge for problem solving. In D. Tuma and R. Fief (eds.), *Problem solving and education* (pp. 9–24). New York: John Wiley.

Hambrick, D. C. and G. L. Brandon. 1988. Executive values. In D. Hambrick (ed.), *The executive effect: Concepts and methods for studying top managers* (pp. 3–34). London: JAI Press.

Hayes, J. R. 1980. Teaching problem-solving mechanisms. In D. Tuma and R. Feif (eds.), *Problem solving and education* (pp. 141–150). New York: John Wiley.

Hayes, J. 1981. *The complete problem solver*. Philadelphia: The Franklin Institute Press.

Hodgkinson, C. 1978. *Towards a philosophy of administration*. Oxford: Basil Blackwell.

Hunter, J. E., F. L. Schmidt, and M. K. Judiesch. 1990. Individual differences in output variability as a function of job complexity. *Journal of Applied Psychology* 75, 28–42.

Jaques, E. 1986. The development of intellectual capability: A discussion of stratified systems theory. *The Journal of Applied Behavioral Science* 22(4), 361–383.

Kelsey, J. G. T. In press. Learning from teaching: Problems, problem formulation, and the enhancement of problem-solving capability. In P. Hallinger, K. Leithwood, and J. Murphy (eds.), *Cognitive perspectives on school leadership*. New York: Teachers College Press.

Kluckhon, C. 1951. Values and value orientations in the theory of action: An exploration in definition and classification. In T. Parsons and E. Shills (eds.), *Toward a general theory of action* (pp. 398–433). Cambridge, MA: Harvard University Press.

Leithwood, K., and R. Steinbach. 1990. Characteristics of effective secondary school principals' problem solving. *Educational Administration and Foundations* 5(1), 24–42.

Leithwood, K., and R. Steinbach. 1991a. Components of chief education officers' problem solving. In K. A. Leithwood and D. Musella (eds.), *Understanding school system administration* (pp. 127–153). New York: Falmer Press.

Leithwood, K., and R. Steinbach. 1991b. Indicators of transformational leadership in the everyday problem solving of school administrators, *Journal of Personnel Evaluation in Education* 4(3), 221–244.

Leithwood, K., and R. Steinbach. In press. The relationship between variations in patterns of school leadership and group problem-solving processes. In P. Hallinger, K. Leithwood, and J. Murphy (eds.), *Cognitive perspectives on educational leadership*. New York: Teachers College Press.

Mumford, M. D., and M. S. Connelly. 1991. Leaders as creators: Leader performance and problem solving in ill-defined domains. *Leadership Quarterly* 2(4), 289–315.

Naisbitt, J., and P. Aburdene. 1987. *Re-inventing the corporation*. New York: Warner Books.

Newell, A. 1975. Discussion of papers by Robert M. Gagné and John R. Hayes. In B. Kleinmuntz (ed.), *Problem solving: Research, method and theory* (pp. 171–182). Huntington, NY: Robert E. Kreiger.

Newell, A., P. Rosenblum, and J. Laird. 1990. Symbolic architectures for cognition. In M. Posner (ed.), *Foundations of cognitive science* (pp. 133–160). Cambridge, MA: The MIT Press.

Newell, A., and H. Simon. 1972. *Human problem solving*. Englewood Cliffs, NJ: Prentice-Hall.

Nickerson, R. S. 1988–1989. On improving thinking. In E. Z. Rotherkopf (ed.), *Review of research in education, Volume 15* (pp. 3–57). Washington, DC: American Educational Research Association.

Raun, T., and K. A. Leithwood. In press. Pragmatism, participation and duty: Values used by chief education officers in their problem solving. In P. Hallinger, K. A. Leithwood, and J. Murphy (eds.), *Cognitive perspectives on educational leadership*. New York: Teachers College Press.

Reitman, W. 1965. *Cognition and thought*. New York: Wiley.

Reynolds, A. 1992. What is competent beginning teaching: A review of the literature. *Review of Educational Research* 62(1), 1–35.

Rokeach, M. 1975. *Beliefs, attitudes and values*. San Francisco: Jossey-Bass.

Rubinstein, M. F. 1975. *Patterns of problem solving*. Englewood Cliffs, NJ: Prentice-Hall.

Rumelhart, D. E. 1990. The architecture of mind: A connectionist approach. In M. Posner (ed.), *Foundations of cognitive science* (pp. 93–132). Cambridge, MA: The MIT Press.

Schön, D. 1983. *The reflective practitioner*. San Francisco: Jossey-Bass.

Schwenk, C. R. 1988. The cognitive perspective on strategic decision-making. *Journal of Management Studies* 25(1), 41–56.

Senge, P. 1990. *The fifth discipline*. New York: Doubleday.

Shank, R., and R. Abelson. 1977. *Scripts, plans, goals and understanding*. Hillsdale, NJ: Lawrence Erlbaum.

Showers, C., and N. Cantor. 1985. Social cognition: A look at motivated strategies. *Annual Review of Psychology* 36, 275–305.

Simon, H. In press. Decision making: Rational, nonrational and irrational. *Educational Administration Quarterly*.

Srivastva, S. ed.. 1983. *The executive mind*. San Francisco: Jossey-Bass.

Suchman, L. 1987. *Plans and situated actions: The problem of human / machine communication*. Cambridge: Cambridge University Press.

Toffler, A. 1990. *Powershift*. New York: Bantam Books.

Vaill, P. 1989. *Managing as a performing art*. San Francisco: Jossey-Bass.

Van Lehn, K. 1990. Problem solving and cognitive skill acquisition. In M. I. Posner (ed.), *Foundations of cognitive science* (pp. 527–579). Cambridge, MA: The MIT Press.

Voss, J. F., and T. A. Post. 1988. On the solving of ill-structured problems. In M. T. H. Chi, R. Glaser and M. J. Farr (eds.), *The nature of expertise* (pp. 261–285). Hillsdale, NJ: Lawrence Erlbaum.

Williams, R. M. (1968). Values. In *International encyclopedia of the social sciences*. New York: MacMillan.

Chapter 7. Problem Interpretation: How Administrators Classify and Manage Their Problems

Begley, P. 1988, April. *The influence of values on principals' problem-solving processes*. Paper presented at the annual meeting of the American Educational Research Association, New Orleans.

Begley, P., and K. Leithwood. 1989. The influence of values on school administrator practices. *Journal of Educational Administration and Foundations* 4(2), 26–39.

Berger, P. L., and T. Luckman. 1967. *The social construction of reality*. Garden City, New York: Doubleday.

Campbell-Evans, G. 1988. *The relationship between principals' values and their decision-making processes*. Unpublished doctoral dissertation, The Ontario Institute for Studies in Education, Toronto.

Clark, C. M., and P. L. Peterson. 1986. Teachers' thought processes. In M. C. Wittrock (ed.), *Handbook of research on teaching* (3d ed.) (pp. 255–296). New York: Macmillan.

Ettling, J. T., and A. G. Jago. 1988. Participation under conditions of conflict: More on the validity of the Vroom-Yetton model. *Journal of Management Studies* 25(1), 73–84.

Fredericksen, N. 1984. Implications of cognitive theory for instruction in problem solving. *Review of Educational Research* 54(3), 363–407.

Hambrick, D. C., and G. L. Brandon. 1988. Executive values. In D. Hambrick (ed.), *The executive effect: Concepts and methods for studying top managers* (pp. 3–34). London: JAI Press.

Hodgkinson, C. 1983. *The philosophy of leadership*. New York: St. Martin's Press.

Kanter, R. M. 1983. *The change masters.* New York: Simon and Schuster.

Kolb, D. A. 1984. Problem management: Learning from experience. In S. Srivastva (ed.), *The executive mind.* San Francisco: Jossey-Bass.

Leithwood, K. 1986. *The role of the secondary school principal in policy implementation and school improvement.* Toronto: Ontario Ministry of Education, Queen's Printer for Ontario.

Leithwood, K., and D. Montgomery. 1986. *Improving principal effectiveness: The principal profile.* Toronto: OISE Press.

Leithwood, K., and M. Stager. 1986, April. *Differences in problem-solving processes used by moderately and highly effective principals.* Paper presented at the annual meeting of the American Educational Research Association, San Francisco.

Leithwood, K., and M. Stager. 1989. Expertise in principals' problem solving. *Educational Administration Quarterly* 25(2), 126–161.

Leithwood, K., and R. Steinbach. 1989, April. *Components of chief executive officers' problem solving.* Paper presented at the annual meeting of the American Educational Research Association, San Francisco.

Leithwood, K., and R. Steinbach. 1991. Indicators of transformational leadership in the everyday problem solving of school administrators. *Journal of Personnel Evaluation in Education* 4, 221–244.

Quinn, R. E. 1988. *Beyond rational management.* San Francisco: Jossey-Bass.

Shulman, L. S., and N. B. Carey. 1984. Psychology and the limitations of individual rationality: Implication for the study of reasoning and civility. *Review of Educational Research* 54(4), 501–524.

Tobert, W. R. 1984. Cultivating timely executive action. In S. Srivastva and Associates (ed.), *The executive mind* (pp. 84–108). San Francisco: Jossey-Bass.

Tobert, W. R. 1987. *Managing the corporate dream: Restructuring for long term success.* Homewood, IL: Dow Jones-Irwin.

Walberg, H. J., and W. J. Fowler. 1987. Expenditure and size effectiveness of public school districts. *Educational Researcher* 16(7), 5–13.

Chapter 8. The Nature and Role of Values in Administrators' Problem-Solving Processes

Ashbaugh, C. R., and K. L. Kasten. 1984. A typology of operant values in school administration. *Planning and Changing* 15(4). 195–208.

Barnard, C. I. 1983. *The functions of the executive*. Cambridge, MA: Harvard University Press.

Bayles, M. D. 1981. *Professional ethics*. Belmont, CA: Wadsworth.

Beck, C. M. 1984a. *The nature of values and implications for values education*. Unpublished paper.

Beck, C. M. 1984b, July. *The nature of teaching of moral problem solving*. Paper presented at a meeting of the Institute for Logic and Cognitive Studies, University of Houston, Texas.

Beck, C. M. 1984c, November. *Our faith confronts differing life styles and value systems*. Paper presented to the Islington United Church School of Religion.

Begley, P. 1988, April. *The influence of values on principals' problem-solving processes*. Paper presented at the Annual Meeting of the American Educational Research Association, New Orleans.

Begley, P. T., and K. A. Leithwood. 1989. The influence of values on the practices of school administrators. *Journal of Educational Administration and Foundations* 4(1), 25–39.

Blumberg, A. 1984. The craft of school administration and some other rambling thoughts. *Educational Administration Quarterly* 20(4), 24–40.

Brown, J. S., A. Collins, and D. Duguid. 1989. Situated cognition and the culture of learning. *Educational Researcher* 18(1), 32–42.

Campbell-Evans, G. H. 1988. *Nature and influence of values in principal decision making*. Unpublished doctoral dissertation, University of Toronto, Toronto.

Corson, D. 1985. Quality of judgment and deciding rightness: Ethics and educational administration. *The Journal of Educational Administration* 23(2), 122–130.

DeBono, E. 1985. *Six thinking hats*. Boston: Little, Brown and Co.

England, G. W. 1967. Personal value systems of American managers. *Academy of Management Journal* 10, 53–68.

Farquhar, R. H. 1981. Preparing educational administrators for ethical practice. *The Alberta Journal of Educational Research* 27(2). 192–204.

Fox, W. M. 1987. *Effective group problem solving*. San Francisco: Jossey-Bass.

Frankena, W. K. 1973. *Ethics*. (2d ed.). Englewood Cliffs, NJ: Prentice-Hall, Inc.

Greenfield, T. B. 1986. The decline and fall of science in educational administration. *Interchange* 17(2), 57–80.

Greenfield, W. D. 1985. The moral socialization of school administrators: Informal role learning outcomes. *Educational Administration Quarterly* 21(4), 99–119.

Hambrick, D. C., and G. L. Brandon. 1988. Executive values. In D. C. Hambrick (ed.), *The executive effect: Concepts and methods for studying top managers*. (pp. 3–35). Greenwich, CT: JAI Press Inc.

Hodgkinson, C. 1978. *Towards a theory of administration*. New York: St. Martin's Press.

Hodgkinson, C. 1986. *Towards a philosophy of administration*. Oxford: Basil Blackwell.

Kepner, C. H., and B. B. Tregoe. 1981. *The new rational manager*. Princeton, NJ: Kepner-Tregoe Inc.

Kluckhon, C. 1951. Values and value-orientations in the theory of action: An exploration in definition and classification. In T. Parsons and E. A. Shils (eds.), *Toward a general theory of action* (pp. 388–433). Cambridge, MA: Harvard University Press.

Leithwood, K., P. Begley, and B. Cousins. 1992. *Developing expert leadership for future schools*. London, The Falmer Press.

Leithwood, K., and M. Stager. 1989. Expertise in principals' problem solving. *Educational Administration Quarterly* 25(2), 126–161.

Leithwood, K., and R. Steinbach. 1990. Characteristics of effective secondary school principals' problem solving. *Journal of Educational Administration and Foundations* 5(1), 24–42.

Leithwood, K., R. Steinbach, and P. Begley. 1992. Socialization experiences: Becoming a principal in Canada. In F. W. Parkay and G. E. Hall (eds.), *Becoming a principal: The challenges of beginning leadership* (pp. 284–307). Boston: Allyn and Bacon.

Martin, W. J., and D. Willower. 1981. The managerial behavior of high school principals. *Educational Administration Quarterly* 17(1), 69–90.

Miklos, E. 1988. Administrator selection, career patterns, succession, and socialization. In N. J. Boyan (ed.), *Handbook of research on educational administration* (pp. 53–76). New York: Longman.

Raun, T. *The nature and sources of CEOs' values*. Forthcoming doctoral dissertation, University of Toronto, Toronto.

Rogoff, B., and J. Lave., eds. 1984. *Everyday cognition: Its development in social context*. Cambridge, MA: Harvard University Press.

Rokeach, M. 1973. *The nature of human values*. New York: The Free Press.

Simon, H. A. 1976. *Administrative behaviour* (3d ed.). New York: The Free Press.

Strike, K., E. Soltis, and J. Haller. 1989. *The ethics of school administration.* NY: Teachers College Press.

Toffler, B. L. 1986. *Tough choices: Managers talk ethics.* New York: John Wiley.

Weber, M. 1949. *The methodology of the social sciences.* New York: The Free Press of Glencoe.

Williams, R. M. 1968. Values. In *International encyclopedia of the social sciences.* New York: MacMillan.

Chapter 9. Cognitive Flexibility and Inflexibility in Principals' Problem Solving

Begley, P. 1988, April. *The influence of values on principals' problem-solving processes.* Paper presented at the annual meeting of the American Educational Research Association, New Orleans.

Ericsson, K. A., and H. A. Simon. 1984. *Protocol analysis: Verbal reports as data.* Cambridge, MA: MIT Press.

Glasman, N. 1986. *Evaluation-based leadership.* New York: SUNY Press.

Hayes, J. R., and L. S. Flower. 1983. Uncovering cognitive processes in writing: An introduction to protocol analysis.In P. Mosenthal, L. Tamor, and S. A. Walmsley (eds.), *Research on writing: Principles and methods* (pp. 206–220). New York: Longman.

Hayes-Roth, B., and F. Hayes-Roth. 1979. A cognitive model of planning. *Cognitive Science* 3, 275–310.

Kahneman, D., P. Slovic, and A. Tversky, eds. 1982. *Judgement under uncertainty: Heuristics and biases.* Cambridge, MA: Cambridge University Press.

Klemp, G. O., and D. C. McClelland. 1986. What characterizes intelligent functioning among senior managers? In R. J. Sternberg and R. G. Wagner (eds.), *Practical intelligence: Nature and origins of competence in the everyday world* (pp. 31–50). Cambridge, MA: Cambridge University Press.

Leithwood, K., and D. Montgomery. 1986. *Improving principal effectiveness: The principal profile.* Toronto: OISE Press.

Leithwood, K., and M. Stager. 1989. Components of expertise in principals' problem solving. *Educational Administration Quarterly* 25(1), 121–161.

Morine-Dershimer, G. 1986, April. *What can we learn from thinking?* Paper presented at the annual meeting of the American Educational Research Association, San Francisco.

Neisser, U. 1976. General, academic, and artificial intelligence. In L. Resnick (ed.), *The nature of intelligence* (pp. 135–144). Hillsdale, NJ: Erlbaum.

Nisbett, R., and L. Ross. 1980. *Human inference: Strategies and shortcomings of social judgement.* Englewood Cliffs, NJ: Prentice-Hall.

Nisbett, R., and T. D. Wilson. 1977. Telling more than we can know: Verbal reports on mental processes. *Psychological Review* 84, 231–259.

Schön, D. A. 1983. *The reflective practitioner: How professionals think in action.* New York: Basic Books.

Schwenk, C. R. 1988. The cognitive perspectives on strategic decision-making. *Journal of Management Studies* 25(1), 41–56.

Scribner, S. 1986. Thinking in action: Some characteristics of practical thought. In R. J. Sternberg and R. K. Wagner (eds.), *Practical intelligence: Nature and origins of competence in the everyday world* (pp. 13–30). Cambridge, MA: Cambridge University Press.

Showers, C., and N. Cantor. 1985. Social cognition: A look at motivated strategies. *Annual Review of Psychology* 36, 275–305.

Stager, M., and K. Leithwood. 1989. Cognitive flexibility and inflexibility in principals' problem solving. *Alberta Journal of Educational Research* 35(3), 217–236.

Sternberg, R. J., and R. K. Wagner. 1986. Tacit knowledge and intelligence in the everyday world. In R. J. Sternberg and R. K. Wagner (eds.), *Practical intelligence: Nature and origins of competence in the everyday world* (pp. 51–83). Cambridge, MA: Cambridge University Press.

Chapter 10. Problem-Solving Expertise as an Explanation for Variations in Instructional Leadership

Bandura, A. 1977. *Social learning theory.* Englewood Cliffs, NJ: Prentice Hall.

Blase, J., C. Dedrick, and M. Strathe. 1986. Leadership behavior of school principals in relation to teacher stress, satisfaction and performance. *Journal of Humanistic Education and Development* 24(4), 159–171.

Blumberg, A., and W. Greenfield. 1980. *The effective principal: Perspectives on school leadership.* Boston: Allyn and Bacon.

Brady, L. 1985. The supportiveness of the principal in school-based curriculum development. *Journal of Curriculum Studies* 17(1), 95–97.

Chi, M. T. H., R. Glaser, and M. J. Farr. 1988. *The nature of expertise.* Hillsdale, NJ: Lawrence Erlbaum.

Fullan, M. 1991. *The new meaning of educational change.* New York: Teachers College Press.

Hall, G., W. L. Rutherford, S. M. Hord, and L. L. Huling. 1984. Effects of three principal styles on school improvement. *Educational Leadership* 41(5), 22–31.

Hallinger, P., L. Bickman, and K. Davis. In press. What makes a difference? School context, principal leadership, and student achievement. *School Effectiveness and School Improvement.*

Heck, R., T. Larsen, and G. Marcoulides. 1990, April. *Principal leadership and school achievement: Validation of a causal model.* Paper presented at the annual meeting of the American Educational Research Association, Boston.

Hoy, W. K., and B. L. Brown. 1986, April. *Leadership of principals, personal characteristics of teachers and the professional zone of acceptance of elementary teachers.* Paper presented at annual meeting of the American Education Research Association, San Francisco.

Johnson-Laird, P. N. 1990. Mental models. In M. I. Posner (ed.), *Foundations of cognitive science* (pp. 469–500). Cambridge, MA: The MIT Press.

Leithwood, K., P. Begley, and B. Cousins. 1990. The nature, causes, and consequences of principals' practices: An agenda for future research. *Journal of Educational Administration* 28(4), 5–31.

Leithwood, K., and D. Montgomery. 1982. The role of the elementary school principal in program improvement. *Review of Educational Research* 52(3), 309–339.

Leithwood, K., and D. Montgomery. 1986. *Improving principal effectiveness: The principal profile.* Toronto: OISE Press.

Leithwood, K., and M. Stager. 1989. Expertise in principals' problem solving. *Educational Administration Quarterly* 25(2), 126–161.

Leithwood, K., and R. Steinbach. 1991. Indicators of transformational leadership in the everyday problem solving of school administrators. *Journal of Personnel Evaluation in Education* 4(3), 221–244.

Leithwood, K., and R. Steinbach. In press. The relationship between variations in patterns of school leadership and group problem-solving processes. In K. Leithwood, P. Hallinger, and J. Murphy (eds.), *Cognitive perspectives on educational leadership.* New York: Teachers College Press.

Leithwood, K., R. Steinbach, and B. Dart. In press. The consequences for school improvement of differences in principals' problem-solving processes. *Education Research and Perspectives.*

Leitner, D. In press. Do principals effect student outcomes: An organizational perspective. *School Effectiveness and School Improvement.*

Lesgold, A. 1984. Acquiring expertise. In J. R. Anderson and S. M. Kosslyn (eds.), *Tutorials in learning and memory* (pp. 31–60). New York: Freeman.

Mehan, H. 1984. Institutional decision-making. In B. Rogoff and J. Lave (eds.). *Everyday cognition: Its development in social context* (pp. 41–66). Cambridge, MA: Harvard University Press.

Primary Program. 1990. *Foundation Document.* Victoria, B.C.: British Columbia Ministry of Education.

Salley, C., R. B. McPherson, and M. E. Baehr. 1978. What principals do: A preliminary occupational analysis. In D. A. Erickson and T. L. Reller (eds.). *The principal in metropolitan schools.* Berkeley: McCutchan.

Schwenk, C. R. 1988. The cognitive perspective on strategic decision-making. *Journal of Management Studies* 25(1), 41–56.

Shakeshaft, C. 1987. *Women in educational administration.* Beverly Hills: Sage.

Shank, R., and R. Abelson. 1977. *Scripts, plans, goals and understanding.* Hillsdale, NJ: Lawrence Erlbaum.

Simon, H. 1957. *Administrative behaviour: A study of decision-making processes in administrative organizations.* New York: Free Press.

Stager, M., and K. A. Leithwood. 1989. Cognitive flexibility and inflexibility in principals' problem solving. *The Alberta Journal of Educational Research* 35(3), 217–236.

Stevens, W., and L. D. D. Marsh. 1987, April. *The role of vision in the life of elementary school principals.* Paper presented at the annual meeting of the American Educational Research Association, Washington, D.C.

Trider, D., and K. Leithwood. 1988. Exploring the influences on principal behavior. *Curriculum Inquiry* 18(3), 289–312.

Van Lehn, K. 1990. Problem solving and cognitive skill acquisition. In M. I. Posner (ed.), *Foundations of cognitive science* (pp. 527–579). Cambridge MA: The MIT Press.

Watson, D. J. 1989. Defining and describing whole language. *The Elementary School Journal* 90(2), 129–141.

Year 2000. 1989. *A curriculum and assessment framework for the future*. Victoria, B.C.: British Columbia Ministry of Education.

Chapter 11. Total Quality Leadership: Expert Thinking plus Transformational Practice

Bandura, A., 1977. *Social learning theory*. Englewood Cliffs, NJ: Prentice-Hall.

Bandura, A. 1986. *Social foundations of thought and action*. Englewood Cliffs, NJ: Prentice-Hall.

Bass, B. M. 1985. *Leadership and performance beyond expectations*. New York: The Free Press.

Bass, B. M., and B. J. Avolio. 1989. Potential biases in leadership measures: How prototypes, lenience, and general satisfaction relate to ratings and rankings of transformational and transactional leadership constructs. *Educational and Psychological Measurement* 49, 509–527.

Bass, B. M., D. A. Waldman, B. J. Avolio, and M. Bebb. 1987. Transformational leadership and the falling dominoes effect. *Group and Organizational Studies* 12, 73–87.

Begley, P., and K. Leithwood. 1991. The influence of values on school administrators' practices. *Journal of Personnel Evaluation in Education* 3(4), 337–352.

Bonstingl, J. 1992. The quality revolution in education. *Educational Leadership* 50(3), 4–9.

Bradley, L. H. 1993. *Total quality management for schools*. Lancaster: Technomic Publishing Company.

Burns, J. M. 1978. *Leadership*. New York: Harper and Row.

Conger, J. 1989. *The charismatic leader*. San Francisco: Jossey-Bass.

Ericsson, K. A., and H. A. Simon. 1984. *Protocol analysis: Verbal reports as data*. Cambridge, MA: The MIT Press.

Ford, M. 1992. *Motivating humans: Goals, emotions and personal agency beliefs*. Newbury Park: Sage.

Green, T. F. 1987. The conscience of leadership. In L. Sheive and M. Schoenheit (eds.), *Leadership: Examining the elusive*. 1987 Yearbook of the Association of Supervision and Curriculum Development.

Horine, J., and B. Bass. 1993. *Transformational leadership: The cornerstone of quality*. CLS Report 92-3 (January).

Hunt, J. G. 1991. *Leadership: A new synthesis*. Newbury Park, CA: Sage.

Leithwood, K. 1992. The move toward transformational leadership. *Educational Leadership* 49(5), 8–12.

Leithwood, K., P. Begley, and B. Cousins. 1992. *Developing leaders for future schools*. London: Falmer Press.

Leithwood, K., and D. Duke. In press. Defining effective leadership for Connecticut's future schools. *Journal of Personnel Evaluation in Education*.

Leithwood, K., D. Jantzi, and A. Fernandez. In press. Transformational leadership and teachers' commitment to change. In J. Murphy and K. Louis (eds.), *Reshaping the principalship*. Newbury Park, CA: Corwin Press.

Leithwood, K., D. Jantzi, H. Silins, and B. Dart. In press. Using the appraisal of school leaders as an instrument for school restructuring. *Peabody Journal of Education*.

Leithwood, K., and R. Steinbach. 1992. Improving the problem-solving expertise of school administrators: Theory and practice. *Education and Urban Society* 24(3), 317–345.

Murphy, J. 1991. *Restructuring schools: Capturing and assessing the phenomena*. New York: Teachers College Press.

Newmann, F. 1993. Beyond common sense in educational restructuring. *Educational Researcher* 22(2), 4–13.

Podsakoff, P. M., S. B. MacKenzie, R. H. Moorman, and R. Fetter. 1990. Transformational leaders' behaviors and their effects on followers' trust in leader, satisfaction, and organizational citizenship behaviors. *Leadership Quarterly* 1(2), 107–142.

Podsakoff, P. M., W. D. Todor, R. A. Grover, and V. L. Huber. 1984. Situational moderators of leader reward and punishment behavior: Fact or fiction? *Organizational Behavior and Human Performance* 34, 21–63.

Sashkin, M., and K. Kiser. 1992. *Total quality management*. Seabrook, MD: Ducochon Press.

Seltzer, J., and B. Bass. 1990. Transformational leadership: Beyond initiation and consideration, *Journal of Management* 16(4), 693–703.

Sergiovanni, T. J. 1990. *Value-added leadership: How to get extraordinary performance in schools*. San Diego: Harcourt Brace Jovanovich.

Shamir, B. 1991. The charismatic relationship: Alternative explanations and predictions. *Leadership Quarterly* 2(2), 81–104.

Silins, H. C. 1992. Effective leadership for school reform. *The Alberta Journal of Educational Research* 38(4), 317–334.

Sims, H., and P. Lorenzi. 1992. *The new leadership paradigm*. Newbury Park: Sage.

Willis, S. 1993. Creating total quality schools. *ASCD Update* 35(2), 1–4.

Chapter 12. Improving the Problem-Solving Expertise of School Administrators

Alexander, P. A., and J. E. Judy. 1988. The interaction of domain-specific and strategic knowledge in academic performance. *Review of Educational Research* 58(4), 375–404.

Argyris, C. 1982. *Reasoning, learning and action*. San Francisco: Jossey-Bass.

Argyris, C., R. Putnam, and D. Smith. 1985. *Action science*. San Francisco: Jossey-Bass.

Berger, P. L., and T. Luckmann. 1966. *The social construction of reality*. Garden City, NJ: Doubleday.

Blum, R. E., and J. A. Butler. 1989. *School leader development for school improvement*. Leuven, Belgium: ACCO.

Boud, D. ed., 1985. *Problem-based learning in education for the professions*. Sydney: Herdsa.

Bransford, J. D., J. J. Franks, N. Vye, and R. Sherwood. 1989. New approaches to instruction: Because wisdom can't be told. In S. Vosniadom and A. Ortony (eds.), *Similarities and analogical reasoning* (pp. 470–497). Cambridge: Cambridge University Press.

Bridges, E. 1992. *Problem-based learning for administrators*. Eugene, OR: ERIC Clearinghouse on Educational Management.

Brown, A. L., and J. S. DeLoache. 1978. Skills, plans and self-regulation. In R. Siegler (ed.), *Children's thinking: What develops?* (pp. 3–35) Hillsdale, NJ: Lawrence Erlbaum.

Brown, J. S., A. Collins, and P. Duguid. 1989. Situated cognition and the culture of learning. *Educational Researcher* 18(1), 32–42.

Burton, R. R., J. S. Brown, and G. Fischer. 1984. Skiing as a model of instruction. In B. Rogoff and J. Lave (eds.), *Everyday cognition: Its development in social context* (pp. 139–150). Cambridge, MA: Harvard University Press.

Chi, M., R. Glaser, and M. Farr. 1985. *The nature of expertise*. Hillsdale, NJ: Lawrence Erlbaum.

Chi, M., R. Glaser, and E. Rees. 1982. Expertise in problem solving. In R. A. Sternberg (ed.), *Advances in the psychology of human intelligence* (pp. 7–75). Hillsdale, NJ: Lawrence Erlbaum.

Glaser, R., and M. T. H. Chi. 1988. Overview, In M. T. H. Chi, R. Glaser and M. J. Farr (eds.), *The nature of expertise* (pp. xv–xxviii). Hillsdale, NJ: Lawrence Erlbaum.

Grimmett, P. 1989. A commentary on Schön's view of reflection. *Journal of Curriculum & Supervision* 5(1). 19–28.

Leithwood, K., B. Cousins, and M. Smith. 1990. The principals' world from a problem solving perspective. *The Canadian School Executive.* January-February-March (3 installments).

Leithwood, K., W. Rutherford, and R. Van der Vegt. 1987. *Preparing school leaders for educational improvement.* London: Croom-Helm.

Leithwood, K., and R. Steinbach. 1991. Indicators of transformational leadership in the everyday problem solving of school principals. *Journal of Personnel Evaluation In Education* 4, 221–244.

Leithwood, K., R. Steinbach, and P. Begley. 1992. The nature and contribution of socialization experiences to becoming a principal in Canada. In F. W. Parkay and G. E. Hall (eds.), *Becoming a principal: The challenges of beginning leadership* (pp. 284–307). Boston: Allyn and Bacon.

Lesgold, A. 1984. Acquiring expertise. In J. R. Anderson and S. M. Kosslyn (eds.), *Tutorials in learning and memory* (pp. 31–60). New York: Freeman.

Lindblom, C. E., and D. K. Cohen. 1979. *Usable knowledge.* New Haven, CT: Yale University Press.

Mehan, H. 1984. Institutional decision making. In B. Rogoff and J. Lave (eds.), *Everyday cognition: Its development in social context* (pp. 41–66). Cambridge, MA: Harvard University Press.

Meichenbaum, D. 1977. *Cognitive behavior modification.* New York: Plenum.

Nickerson, R. S. 1988–1989. On improving thinking. In E. Z. Rotherkopf (ed.), *Review of research in education,* vol. 15 (pp. 3–57). Washington: American Educational Research Association.

Nisbett, R., and L. Ross. 1980. *Human inference: Strategies and shortcomings of social judgement.* Englewood Cliffs, NJ: Prentice-Hall.

Ogilvie, M., and R. Steinbach. 1988, April. *Learning across domains: The role of generalized strategies.* Paper presented at the Annual Meeting of the American Educational Research Association, New Orleans, LA.

Perkins, D. N., and G. Salomon. 1988. Teaching for transfer. *Educational Leadership* 46(1), 22–32.

Perkins, D. N., and G. Salomon. 1989. Are cognitive skills context-bound? *Educational Researcher* 18(1), 16–25.

Rogoff, B. 1984. Introduction: Thinking and learning in social context. In B. Rogoff and J. Lave (eds.), *Everyday cognition: Its development in social context* (pp. 1–8). Cambridge, MA: Harvard University Press.

Ryle, G. 1949. *The concept of mind*. London: Hutchinson.

Salomon, G., and D. N. Perkins. n.d. *Rocky roads to transfer: Rethinking mechanisms of a neglected phenomenon* [mimeo]. Tel Aviv: University of Tel Aviv.

Schön, D. 1984. *The reflective practitioner*. New York: Basic Books.

Shank, R., and R. Abelson. 1977. *Scripts, plans, goals and understanding*. Hillsdale, NJ: Lawrence Erlbaum.

Shuell, T. J. 1986. Cognitive conceptions of learning. *Review of Educational Research* 56, 411–436.

Sternberg, R. J., and O. R. Caruso. 1985. Practical modes of knowing. In E. Eisner (ed.), *Learning and teaching the ways of knowing* (pp. 133–158). Chicago: University of Chicago Press.

Strike, K. A., E. J. Haller, and J. F. Soltis. 1988. *The ethics of school administration*. New York: Teachers College Press.

Voss, J. F., and T. A. Post. 1988. On the solving of ill-structured problems, In M. T. H. Chi, R. Glaser, and M. J. Farr (eds.), *The Nature of Expertise* (pp. 261–285). Hillsdale, NJ: Lawrence Erlbaum.

Vygotsky, L. S. 1978. *Mind in society*. Cambridge, MA: Harvard University Press.

Wine, J. 1971. Test anxiety and the direction of attention, *Psychological Bulletin* 76, 92–104.

Chapter 13. Concluding Thoughts

Bereiter, C., and M. Scardamalia. 1993. *Surpassing ourselves; An inquiry into the nature and implications of expertise*. Chicago: Open Court.

Greenfield, T. B. 1993. *Greenfield on educational administration*. London: Routledge.

Hallinger, P., K. Leithwood, and J. Murphy. 1993. *Cognitive perspectives on educational leadership*. New York: Teachers College Press.

Hodgkinson, C. 1978. *Toward a philosophy of administration*. Oxford: Basil Blackwell.

Shamir, B. 1991. The charismatic relationship: Alternative explanations and predictions. *Leadership Quarterly* 2(2), 81–104.

Strike, K., E. Haller, and J. Soltis. 1988. *The ethics of school administration*. New York: Teachers College Press.

SUBJECT INDEX

Act theory. *See* Adaptive control of
  thought (Act) theory
Adaptive control of thought (Act)
  theory, 13;
  values and, 128
Administrative expertise.
  See Expertise
Administrivia, 221
Affect
  defined, 95
  group problem solving,
    105, 113
Analogies, 127, 209
Anecdotes in problem solving, 52,
  54, 77
Application of theory, 10, 11
Associative stage, cognitive skill,
  13, 14
Assumptions
  suspension of in group
    learning, 144
  use of in problem solving,
    53–54, 102

Attributional bias, 12
Authentic dialogue, 117
Authentic situations, 291–292
Autonomous stage, cognitive
  skill, 13–14
Availability heuristics, 199

Backward planning, 88
Behavior channeling, 174, 176
Behaviors, and problem-solving
  processes, 8
Bounded rationality, 70
  and group problem solving,
    96–97
  short-term memory and, 242
Brainstorming, 127

Causality, 14, 199
Charisma, 256, 257
Chemistry, 9
Classroom, task structure
  of, 10
Cognitive context, 18

351

increasingly complex microworlds (ICMs), 288
initial understanding, 287–288
knowledge transfer, 292–294
ordinary knowledge, 287, 291–292, 306, 308
useful strategic knowledge, 286–287
zone of proximal development, 290
Interpretation in problem solving, 46, 62, 63
defining the problem, 150
for direct vs. indirect instructional leaders, 227–228
in group problem solving, 102–106
influence of context on, 151, 168, 168–169
meaning and schema, 124
principals, 50–54, 102–106
structured problems, 52–54
by superintendents, 74–78
understanding processes, 123–125
unstructured problems, 50–52

Judgmental heuristics, 199

Knowledge
cognitive development, 13–15
conditionalizing of, 14
depth vs. breadth, 166–167
domain-specific, 14, 122, 196, 247–248, 250, 283, 286, 298, 307, 308
explicit values as substitutes for, 176
flexibility in problem solving, 198, 199, 207, 209
inert, 15
"lean," 40
ordinary vs. strategic, 287, 291–292, 306, 308
practical, 287
problem-relevant, 244, 252, 286
rationality and, 184

social construction of, 14
tacit, 287, 291, 292
transfer of, 292–294
types of in problem solving, 161
useful strategic, 286–287, 289, 296–297
Knowledge structures, 199–200
overuse/misuse of, 202

Leader(s)
attributional bias, 12
effective vs. expert, 12
Leadership
authentic dialogue as central to, 117
dimensions of practice, 257–258
direct instructional, 226
indirect instructional, 226–250
partial quality, 274–276
situational, 7
styles, 221–222
transactional, 257
transformational, 93, 95–96, 113–114, 116–117. See also Transformational leadership
Leadership opportunities, 33
Learning
artificial vs. authentic situations, 291–292
cognitive perspectives on, 8, 14–15
constructivist model of, 6, 220
double vs. single loop, 294–295
effect of social context on, 289
metacognition, 295
organizational or group, 142–145
problem-based, 8
problem-solving expertise, 287–292
schema theory and, 289
situated cognition and, 15, 298
social interaction in, 14, 289–290
Low road/high road transfer, 15

Managers, 167
Materialism, 83, 179

NAME INDEX